I'll Take the Sunny Side

By Gordon Forbes

A Handful of Summers (1978)
Too Soon to Panic (1995)

I'll Take the Sunny Side

A Memoir

Gordon Forbes

Best wishes
Gordon Forbes

BOOKSTORM

© Gordon Forbes, 2017

All rights reserved. No part of this book may be reproduced or transmitted in
any form or by any means, electronic or mechanical, including photocopying,
recording or any information storage or retrieval system,
without permission from the copyright holder.

Every effort has been made to trace the original source material contained in this book.
Where the attempt has been unsuccessful, please contact the publishers
to rectify any omissions.

ISBN: 978-1-928257-44-8
e-ISBN: 978-1-928257-45-5

First edition, first impression 2017

Published by Bookstorm (Pty) Ltd
PO Box 4532
Northcliff 2115
Johannesburg
South Africa

www.bookstorm.co.za

Edited by Pam Thornley
Proofread by Wesley Thompson
Photographs courtesy listed copyright holders
Cover design by publicide
Book design and typesetting by Triple M Design
Printed by ABC Press, Cape Town

No winners cheque, no instant fame
We play because the game's a game.
And win or lose it's all the same
I see the funny side.

To start our games and keep them fair
I spin my racket in the air.
And if you serve I don't much care
I'll take the sunny side.

GF, 2017

To my family; to the Table;
and to the men and women who played tennis with me
to share some of the happiest times of my life.

Contents

	Author's Note	xi
1	The Rainbow Room	1
2	The Two Yachts	9
3	The Need for Oysters	12
4	Our Game	16
5	Beauty or Skill?	25
6	Strawberries at Home	34
7	Harvey	42
8	An Urge to Write	49
9	What's in a Name?	52
10	Bird Calls	56
11	Intellect at Sea Level	61
12	The Specific Gravity of Lead	66
13	Reaching the Top	75
14	The Winding Road	82
15	The Forbes Family Band	89
16	The Beautiful Bay	93

17	The Game Plan	100
18	A Worthwhile Passion	105
19	A Wider World	112
20	The Competitors' Enclosure	123
21	Segal's Knack	128
22	The Players Who Live on My Shelves	132
23	Panting to Compete	147
24	Stout of Heart	152
25	The Next Signpost	157
26	The Excitement of the Chaste	164
27	Out of Ten	180
28	The Big Book	189
29	Luck or Skill?	196
30	Give and Take	201
31	Rounding the Horn	204
32	The Black Dog	211
33	The Prodigal Son	216
34	The Sea of Galilee	222
35	In Search of a Niche	231
36	People, Parties and Persuasion	236
37	In Patagonia	240
38	The Ball and the Tortoise	248
39	Segal versus Woodcock	251
40	The Man Behind the Man	255
41	The Small Folk	264
42	Old Lamps for New?	270
43	Pray Silence for …	281
44	The Finest Kind	288

45	The Writers	300
46	The Spoken Word	304
47	The Challenge	309
48	The Otter Trail	312
49	The Light at the End of the Day	319
50	All Things Begin and End	323
51	The Top of the Pass	330

Postscript   334
Acknowledgements   343

G F on the cover of British Lawn Tennis *magazine*

Author's Note

My first book, *A Handful of Summers*, emerged from a sheaf of notes that I made at the request of my sister Jean to remind her of events and adventures during the unique era when tennis changed from an amateur game to the grand spectacle it is today.

This book comes from a series of lunches I've been having with a group of literary types – men of learning and letters who not only love words, but also teach, read and write many of the finest kind. While my first book was inspired by the antics of fellow tennis players, this one is born out of the words and humour of my lunch companions. They're a watchful bunch who love life, have lived it and observed every part of it.

The lunches began about five years ago and soon developed a law allowing equal opportunity to listen or talk and I thus felt entitled to admire, listen, tease, be teased and relate the odd story. However, just when I was about to finish the book, both Abe and Tim let me down by unexpectedly dying. It was a terrible blow to us all, but after consulting the others and getting their blessing, I decided simply to leave everything as if they hadn't died. It seemed better that way.

Every friend's death diminishes you, but for every one of us there are those few who, when they die, take part of our own lives with them. Both were such friends. Abe died first, and in all our sixty years together, it was the first time he'd let me down. Tim I'd known for only the five years, but he had inside him something that made me feel I'd known him, too, all my life.

Fortunately for me, both Abe and Tim had good senses of humour, for I'm afraid that the book is somewhat harassed by whimsy. When I gave it to publishers to read, one of the first questions they asked was, 'Is it fiction or non-fiction?' and when I said I wasn't sure, they gave me a sideways look.

'Most of it is non-fiction,' I said hastily. 'But some of it may not be. It is more a semi-fictional book, where some of the things did happen, while others may only nearly have happened – like a history of England, only shorter.'

There was a long silence. You don't often find publishers reduced to silences, so I thought I should try to explain further.

'The book begins with eight older people having lunch. *They* are real people – that much I can vouch for, because I've seen them eating and drinking, and I've actually passed them the salt and pepper. In the book, I claim that they say and do certain things, and although they may not have, they would have if they'd thought of it.'

There was still silence.

'Another complication,' I said, 'is that most of them have memory loss, so even when they did exactly what I say they did, they may not have remembered doing it. We're all getting on, and while at times we have moments of great clarity, we also go through tracts of thick mist,

AUTHOR'S NOTE

and for most of us, mist is more frequent …'

'What we'll have to do,' said the publishers at last, 'is have a long meeting about your book, because at long meetings we seldom reach firm decisions, and this is an ideal book not to reach a firm decision about.'

'That's exactly how I felt when I wrote it,' I said, relieved. 'In fact, the whole book was written without a single firm decision being taken.'

Disclaimer

Neither author nor publisher is responsible for this book.

I

The Rainbow Room

'And these lunches too, are a part of our lives we should never forget,' I said, looking around the table. We were all there that Friday, and although it was some years ago now, I still recall the thoughtful looks. It was one of those days – November, if my memory serves me, summer breeze, massive cloudscapes, jacarandas in blossom, a pair of geese nibbling at the lawn outside. And Friday afternoons still had about them that certain lull that we remembered from our working days, although by then we'd all retired.

'To be on the safe side I'll make a memorandum,' said James, taking out his pen and notebook, the tip of his tongue appearing between his lips as he wrote, '*Lunches a part of life*.' After his full stop he looked up. 'Got it,' he said. 'Now, has Richard ordered some decent wine?'

I recall that particular lunch more vividly than some of the others, because it was then that the idea was born. Memories of the good old days were always rife – natural, I suppose, for we were all getting on – but that day they presented themselves in such vivid glimpses that for a few moments I relived every one of them; so when Richard mentioned another book, I couldn't help thinking that with a bit of luck it might just be possible …

※

The Johannesburg Country Club has one of the loveliest rooms in the city – in the country, some might say – an elegant, lofty semicircle, with light pouring through tall windows that give views of gardens and glimpses of the cricket field and its pavilion through the branches of old camphor trees. It has an English feel to it – Hurlingham on a summer's day, if you know the place – and such a strong aura of permanence and comfort that you can't help feeling everything's all right. The Rainbow Room, it's called, the name alone a happy sort of accident, suggesting sunlight in a shower of rain.

On Fridays they have a Seniors' Lunch, where the traditional Country Club buffet is served at a reduced price. It began as a Pensioners' Lunch, but there were rumblings from the members' lounge and the lunch was renamed to allow pensioners to be seniors. Nothing else changed – the buffet is the same and there are still a few crutches, walking sticks and a field of grey heads waiting in line, plates in hand, murmuring the phrases that go with such occasions.

'Oysters! By Jove!'

'Beetroot salad. Plenty of iron in it …'

'Damn good batsman, that De Villiers fellow …'

'Shrimps in avocado …'

'Oh, to putt like the Irish chappie!'

'I do hope they've de-pipped the olives – last week dear old Dermot struck one at full gallop and demolished one of his last molars …'

'Friday at last, rugby tomorrow …'

'Mustn't forget to feed the cat …'

Seniors making plans! A good thing about old age is that there's no longer need for grand plans. Simple ones will do – another cup of coffee, a rest after lunch, nine holes at four, a good book. Odd thing, getting old. *Getting* – already a misnomer. You wake one morning, the last ten years seem unaccounted for, and you're seventy-nine.

'Right. Now. Where are we? Tuesday, isn't it? Where's Marge with my tea? A look at the papers, a walk in the park. Better get a bottle of Bell's, old Charlie Gallagher's coming for a game of chess – Black & White, mind you, is perfectly drinkable, cheaper, and damn little difference, especially after the first one.'

It's harmless enough, old age, and it seems to have a built-in safeguard against itself. Oh, all right, I admit there are limitations. But if you're in good health – have good eyesight, hearing, teeth, working joints and so on, it comes with a mild sort of contentment, where such things as warm days, good coffee, and whiskies at six are happy presentiments.

※

The Rainbow Room is our established venue. There are usually eight round the table, seven of them learned fellows – writers, scholars, ex-editors, several cyclists – all with leanings towards decent food, wine, letters, general knowledge and philosophy. James, the born humourist; Mark, the headmaster; Tim and Charles, both historians; two Peters – one of them a guiding light of South Africa's most discerning newspaper, the other, an ex-editor, now a broad-spectrum fellow with an inner force-field suggesting a kind of perpetual motion. Then there's Richard, the thoughtful one – observer, realist, ex-editor of words, now editor of life, and, by mistake (he claims), a best-selling author! Their minds, normally in repose, are capable of intellectual surges that emit keen perceptions.

'Not always,' murmurs Charles, a born realist who adds to his broad understanding of life an ironical kind of modesty.

Quiet chaps, really, and except perhaps for the One Peter (who is still grappling with the working world), generally disciples of the old order, stoically regarding the new one as inevitable.

'Futile not to,' said Charles. 'Like living in a desert and complaining about sand.'

I began attending these lunches and making notes in my late seventies while still dreading eighty (I don't any more). You wouldn't think that you could find new friends at that age – good ones, I mean – but there they were, and a good mix too. Unusual formula – not the usual hail-fellow-well-met, have another beer, Bill's shanking his iron shots, what's the rugby score kind of thing. These chaps hide understanding, real knowledge, I mean, under layers of humour. They love academic excursions into the ways of life, dissecting them, adding their own views. Looking back at what this book has become, I haven't really done them justice, but they won't mind …

I am the only one of the land. Once a Karoo boy and very nearly a farmer, I am conscious of the weight of general knowledge around me, and have learned to find refuge by shutting up and listening. In a way I remind myself of the captain of our school cricket team who was also a wary country boy – Pietie Roux, his name was – the very best of fellows, a good bat and a good captain. When he left school to take over the family farm, he had a card printed with the inscription: 'Pietie Roux, FM-NAF', which he handed out at every opportunity with a proud explanation: 'Failed Matric – Now A Farmer'. I managed to pass matric and missed being a farmer by a narrow margin, so my card would read MP-NAF – Managed To Pass, Nearly A Farmer. (Pietie also passed his matric, so his card was in fact a fraud.)

James is captain. Apart from writing a column that has amused people for over thirty years, he is the author of innumerable books, loves birds, animals, people, literature, and is the one who organises bicycle rides all over Europe. It was he who once decided that his team should cycle along the Danube River from its source to the Black Sea, on the basis that if water could flow, the entire route must be downhill.

'I was right about the water, but wrong about the cycle path,' he wrote afterwards. 'Sometimes it eschewed the river and went uphill, so to follow it we had to pedal like mad causing friction that caused heat. Simple physics, really. To allow for cooling we had to stop at foreign pubs, and by my calculations we managed about fifteen kilometres to the litre.'

'We'd warned him,' said Richard. 'Not about pubs, about hills. Reminded him that as we wouldn't be riding on the surface of the water ...' and there, with a wave of his hand he stopped – a habit he has when he feels that more words are unnecessary.

'I didn't know cycle paths could eschew rivers,' said Tim.

⁘

But wait! someone may cry. Who are these eight people? The point is, it doesn't matter. There is nothing unique about our Table, it's simply that we all happen to love the written word. Look around the room and you see many tables, each with its own particular flairs and fancies – people looking back on life, wondering where it's gone, and making the most of what's left of it. They all have secrets, dreams, desires, stories to tell, even the grey-haired lady trying to get back to her table without spilling her custard. She will once have been the belle of some ball, smiling wide, hair done up, tripping the light fantastic toe and ready to be swept off her feet by the right man.

Our lunches have become tradition. We take our places, pullovers guarding against draughts, pills taken – some to prevent things happening, others to make things happen. We've all had modest beginnings, fought the good fight, had hopes, dreams, good line-calls and bad ones, always kept a best foot forward. But as James recently remarked, the older one gets, the more one's feet look alike so that if he could get one to go forward, either would do.

James has given us each what he calls 'bailiwicks' – areas in which we are supposed to know what we're talking about, and we've come to enjoy one another's yarns to the extent that everyone else listens, having agreed that we no longer like lunches where people all talk at once. As one of the chaps said, 'There is nothing as frustrating as being stuck next to a woman talking about her daughter's wedding dress while a rugby expert is explaining what South Africa needs to win the World Cup.'

Most of those at the Table have written a book, are writing one, or are about to write one. As of now, Tim has just completed *The Great Silence*, and Richard is on the last part of *Unafraid of Greatness*, the life of General Smuts. He's cagey about it ('it's nothing, really, just a thing I've always wanted to do') but he's a dark horse and even in its early stages one had the feeling that it would be a good book (it proved to be a best-seller). Charles is busy refurbishing the Jameson Raid (apparently the Americans had a finger in that pie), James is busy with animals, and Mark has just launched his second book on great South African schools, called *The Cross, the Sword and Mammon.*

'Why that title for a book on education?' Richard asks him. 'Now, had it been about crusades and pirates …' And again he gives his wave.

'Well,' explains Mark, pleased with such curiosity, 'the Cross emphasises the initial involvement of the Church. The Sword symbolises the military wanting to include such things as history, cadets, uniforms, obedience, and so on; and Mammon, because education has now become a commodity.' And he explains how business enterprises sell it as a product. 'To make mammon,' he says with a smile. 'I thought the word would make the title more arresting. *The Cross, the Sword and Money* wouldn't be the same, would it?'

'Mammon, money. Money, mammon,' murmurs James, testing the word. 'A pocketful of mammon. On the furtive side. One could hardly give a schoolboy pocket-mammon, or play tennis for prize mammon.' While murmuring he has been reading the label on the empty wine bottle. 'We'll be needing more of this …'

'Education a commodity, you said?' Tim has picked up another nuance. 'An interesting notion. Seems to suggest one could walk into a store and say, "I need two kilograms of mathematics, 500 grams of geography, and a dozen fresh adjectives for my new book."'

'And if the sword was put to use in our schools,' adds James reflectively, 'you'd get a higher pass rate.'

Laughter. There is often this whimsy. A lunch or two ago, there was also irony. In the foyer there is a signboard giving directions to various functions and venues. That day the top line said 'Rainbow Room – Seniors' Lunch' and, immediately below it, 'Terrace Room – Elimination of Fatalities Meeting' and although it had to do with safety in mines, Tim felt it was something we should get to know more about.

2

※

The Two Yachts

News and stories about politics, books and in particular, sport, are *de rigueur* at our Table. We generally review the past month, and give all players, coaches, referees, writers, politicians, amongst others, fair hearing. Opinions are encouraged, people air their views, and if reflections go on too long, we simply sit back with a drop more port or Irish coffee, content, meditative and, as Joseph Conrad put it, often fit for nothing but placid staring.

One subject leads to another. For example, at a recent lunch the One Peter remarked about how television has affected the antics of modern sportsmen. He cited the howls and grunting in tennis matches, feigned agony in soccer, the elaborate hair-dos, beards and tattoos, the slow-motion close-ups, graphically showing such things as Andy Murray's snarls or his mother's eye-teeth. We all agreed that modern sportsmen, well aware that for hours on end their every move is filmed in high definition, instinctively do heroic deeds – fielders dive to stop balls well out of reach, soccer stars invent injuries and agony, tennis players punch the air, remove their shirts, throw sweaty bits to people in the crowd, hug each other and kiss the ground – as if trying to win some kind of 'look at *me*!' contest.

'Undoubtedly,' concluded the One Peter, 'television has affected sportsmen and women nearly as much as mammon. They can't resist showing off. Never did so in the old days, simply got on with the game.'

Of us all, being the youngest (and most alert) he is seldom whimsical, often preoccupied with the astute columns he writes which, if they were understood by our president, would make him more popular and the country run better.

The remarks about television reminded me of a long-ago activity on Dunkeld, our old Karoo sheep farm near a town called Burgersdorp in the North-Eastern Cape (the region was called that in those days).

'Like the story of the two yachts,' I murmured, and was asked to elaborate – typical of how conversations could go from one thing to another.

'In the living room of our farmhouse was a Pilot radio that whistled and snarled when you turned its knobs,' I began.

('We too had one,' said James.)

On Sunday mornings, I continued, it was my brother Jack's job and mine to listen to the news and report to our parents, who indulged themselves with tea in bed.

Above the house was a shallow dam that filled with muddy water when the Stormberg River came down in flood. Although no more than about a metre and a half deep, it had a large surface area, several hectares, that softened the arid landscape. We loved that dam. The shallow end was a wetland of reeds and grasses where birds nested and where we could find such things as turtles, frogs, baby ducks and moorhens, and wade about on summer days searching for birds' eggs for our collection. In the deeper end we'd swim for hours, even though the bottom of the dam was silted up with chocolate-coloured mud that oozed between our toes and gave our skin a brown aspect.

One day, my father, an inveterate handyman, built us a boat with a wooden frame and sheet-iron body that at once became our prize possession. Although it was really a rowboat, when the south-easter blew we would haul it up to the shallow end, erect a makeshift mast, attach an old tarpaulin for a sail, hang on for dear life and scoot across the three hundred metres or so of water to make landfall at the deep end.

One Sunday morning, listening to news, we happened to hear the newsreader announce that some rich Greek mogul had damaged his yacht and put it out of action for some weeks. Jack and I looked at each other and smiled. We went to the bedroom and after relating the war headlines, told our parents that some rich Greek's yacht had been damaged and put out of action.

'But our yacht is fine,' Jack added, with pride, 'we're planning to sail it this afternoon!'

Now had we had television and been able to *see* the Greek yacht in all its splendour, we wouldn't have been so cocky, but with only the radio, we were actually able to pity the poor mogul.

'Same with tennis,' Richard agreed. 'If you only heard Murray's snarls, you'd pass them over, but when you see them in ultra-slow motion, you wonder that linesmen feel safe.'

This bit of intelligence precipitated an in-depth discussion concerning the effect of modern technologies on future generations, ending in unanimous agreement that we were quite happy with our share of the passage of Time.

3

The Need for Oysters

At a recent lunch Richard claimed it was his turn to choose the wine, and while he studied the list the Other Peter, who had assessed the starter buffet on his way to the table, arrived looking uncharacteristically solemn.

'They've stopped serving oysters,' he said bleakly. 'Apparently the Club feels that over a certain age, oysters no longer have effect. They're not getting away with it' – he glared around to see whether his words were striking home.

James, who had just returned from the hors d'oeuvres table with a modest plateful – smoked salmon, lemon, beetroot, Melba toast, three olives and an egg in a pool of mayonnaise, arrived in time to hear the Other Peter complaining.

'Did I hear oysters?' he asked, unfolding his napkin. 'Well, you're quite right, they are no longer. Do you really think there's something in what's said about them?'

'I read somewhere that Casanova used to have fifty oysters for breakfast every morning, if that throws any light,' offered Tim.

'Fifty. My God. That's a lot of oysters! If that's how many it takes, then what price the half-dozen one gets these days? It just goes to show …'

'Apparently they contain zinc and amino acids,' said Charles, 'both key ingredients. Of course there may not be enough in half a dozen …'

'On the other hand, fifty might be going *too* far …'

'Speak for yourself,' the Other Peter again. Being a man who likes instant information he has produced an elaborate smartphone and is summoning the Internet. Giving a grunt of satisfaction, he begins to read:

> *A team of American and Italian researchers analyzed bivalve molluscs – a group of shellfish that includes oysters – and found they were rich in rare trace elements that trigger increased levels of sex hormones in mammals.*

He gave a Richard-type wave. 'I suppose we're all mammals, and if Italians can be convinced, there must be something to it.'

'I have a friend, with Italian blood in him,' I submitted tentatively. 'Name of Paolo, also a mammal, just turned eighty, been a bachelor all his life, loves oysters, eats them by the dozen and swears by them. Claims they never fail to build up a decent head of steam.'

'Malt and cod-liver oil also cause internal combustion,' said Tim. 'Nothing like the old remedies. Molasses, wheatgerm, garlic, yeast, all give hope. Of course there comes a time when nothing helps. Take every vitamin known to man and all you get are distant memories' – and he mutters on about the ratio of age to output – dogs chasing buses, not knowing what to do when they catch them; old writers getting stuck in the first paragraph. His remarks may initiate brief discussion about unexpected heads of steam in older people, but I must say that this type of conversation is not typical.

They are thinkers, these chaps, what with the One Peter trying to save the country's people, the Other Peter its fauna, James writing two books at the same time, Charles researching Jameson, Richard resuscitating Smuts, Mark with his mammon. Tim's new book is about the gallantry of South African troops at Delville Wood. *The Great Silence*, it's called – inspired by a journey he made to the old battlefields with their rows of white crosses in fields of red poppies. James has written over thirty books, Tim about twelve, Mark two, and Charles a goodly number of really thick books. Only the Two Peters haven't written any, although the Other Peter says that as a younger man he would have written a best-seller if the urge to write hadn't left him at the last minute.

'Odd things, urges,' said Tim thoughtfully. 'The way they come and go.'

'What I *am* going to write is a strong letter about the oysters,' the Other Peter declared. 'We've paid our dues for forty years and we deserve oysters, no matter what the Committee thinks. Smoked salmon and beetroot don't do the trick.'

He sits down, gives the Table a collective nod, and goes on in the same no-nonsense way. 'Well, good day, everyone. What's on the agenda? Any breaking news?'

And when none is forthcoming he looks at me with a shrug and twirls a forefinger at the side of his head. 'Only to be expected, I suppose. They're all closing down.'

As odd man out, they tend to bounce their insults off me because as a near sheep farmer immune to oysters, I am non-aligned.

'And you, I suppose, will be off to Wimbledon one of these days?'

'No,' I said, emphatically. 'This year Frances and I have decided to stay home.'

Frances is my wife.

'But why?' he asked with a frown.

4

Our Game

Tennis. It's been with me from the day I got my first sawn-off racket to long after the day Abe Segal and I lost a doubles semi-final on the Wimbledon Centre Court – all my life, really. We'd played each other at singles in the Plate Event the day before (they don't have Plate Events any more) and Sod's Law required him to pull a groin muscle – the only muscle he ever pulled in his entire career. So in our doubles match he had to serve at half pace.

Funny how memories return. I still see him battling to serve, remember his rough, fearless optimism, and feel the pain of losing a place in the final to two young Mexican players who we felt we could beat. They won Wimbledon. We lost to them in four long sets, shook hands, tried to smile, bowed to the Royal Box, walked off the court, stood in the showers and shed a few tears. Another year past, another chance gone. I remember the pain – feel it again now, fifty-two years later. If only, I sometimes whisper …

'Never dwell on the past,' says my brother Jack, but I can't escape pangs of sadness when I see a player kissing a Wimbledon trophy.

My first Davis Cup Team, 1955. From left: G F, Ian Vermaak, Skip Duminy (Team Manager), Russell Seymour and Abe Segal.

Once, in a moment of self-pity, when I asked him why I never got to kiss one, the simplicity of his answer was strangely consoling.

'Probably because you weren't quite good enough. Be pleased you did the best you could.' Jack, now eighty-three, lives quietly in our hometown of Burgersdorp, near which our farm Dunkeld used to be, and he allows life to wash over him in gentle waves. 'I've allowed myself to stop pursuing things,' he said to me. 'Leave it to the kids.' Two of his children, now in their forties, run farms nearby. Sheep farms. That part of the country is made for them.

'Never mind sheep farming near Burgersdorp,' said Richard. 'You've made Abe Segal sound more interesting.'

'Oh good Lord, yes. Abe Segal!'

Even as I murmured the name, I sensed the flood of memories – some clear, others simply the strange feeling you get when some nudge from the past gives your soul a jolt.

'Abe Segal. We've driven each other mad ever since we met in 1955.'

Strangely, we were thrown together as doubles partners by some Davis Cup manager, and instead of bouncing off each other, we stuck together – cohesion, I think it's called – the force of attraction between atoms of a different kind, or so my science master said. Fundamentally, Abe is odd – not in the sense that he's hump-backed or has a crooked leg. It's simply that all his life he's been doing things normal people wouldn't do. I've spent the last sixty years telling him to gang warily … (*Gang warily* was the motto of the Drummond Clan, and often one of my father's instructions.) To no avail. You won't believe how many times I've said to him, 'Good Lord, Abie, now look what you've gone and done.'

'Can you validate that?' Richard doesn't like irresponsible utterings.

'All right. I'll tell you one thing he did. Only one, because one's all I need.'

It happened at Wimbledon, I continued, a long time ago in the eighties. During the second week it has senior invitational doubles challenges for over thirty-five and forty-five-year-old players who were previous winners or near winners. That year, both Abe and I had gone to Court 4 to watch Manuel Santana and Alex Olmedo (both previous singles champions) playing a veterans' doubles match against a younger pair, I forget who. They were out of shape and practice, and Santana missed an easy volley.

'Did you see that, Forbsey?' Abe asked. 'Neither of us would have missed that.'

This photo is just to show the kind of people Abe hobnobbed with. One wouldn't go as far as calling them rogues – they're all famous. The question that arises is, of course, what for? The chap far right in the back row, Denys Hayden, is my age and still a bachelor. Many of the older women in town will remember him – a fairly reliable sort of bloke who I thought would know the names of the others in this soccer team (they used to get these Walter Mitty-like moments when they felt they were masters of any given sport). Of course he knew Abe, back row, third from left; and Manny, fifth from left; Peter, bottom front; and Youngy (Brian Young) lying down with his sons behind him. Denys also picked out Hilly, Michael and Maurice, but then started saying things like 'that's the English guy who had an affair with the blonde girl we all dated', or 'he was bloody good at golf' or 'he owned a lot of horses that his girlfriends rode every Sunday. I know them all like the back of my hand – their names will come back to me after a Bell's'.

I tentatively agreed with him, and as we left to watch the Centre Court game we saw Chris Gorringe, the Wimbledon CEO, walking towards us. Now if ever there was a true gentleman, it was Chris – which is why Abe got away with stepping in front of him and barring his way.

'Listen, General,' Abe said, slapping him on the back. 'Santana and Olmedo are out there playin' badly, so why can't Forbsey and I have a go next year? We can play badly just as well as they can.'

Fortunately, Chris knew all about Abe so he didn't seem surprised, but instead of telling him that Wimbledon didn't invite players who'd become semi-fossilised, he came over all polite and told him that he'd see what could be arranged, and after a few more backslaps, we went our separate ways.

'Abie,' I said, as we watched Chris walk away, 'don't you think we should gang warily? We're both nearly sixty. My backhand is worse than it was, your serve has gone to the dogs, we never won Wimbledon, we haven't played a tough match for over twenty years, and we're completely out of shape. You don't think there's a message there? Food for thought, maybe?'

Abe hates it when I come with what he calls larney words. 'Food for thought!' he snorted. 'Forbsey, we've got a whole friggin' year to get in shape. We'll be competitors again, we can sit in the box, change in the locker room, go to the players' restaurant and eat ourselves stupid. And if we lose first round, what do you think they'll do? Arrest us? Jesus, buddy, get a grip! Food for thought? You haven't changed, have you?'

There wasn't much more to be said just then. I'd had to put up with these Segalesque impulses for over sixty years, and in any case I was quite sure that Chris Gorringe would soon come to his senses. I was wrong. A few months later, an All England Club letter arrived inviting Mr G L Forbes and Mr A A Segal to play in the senior doubles event for over forty-five competitors. Abe has only got one name, but ever since his first Wimbledon tournament, they've awarded him another A.

'That Chris Gorringe guy must have realised I was right,' were Abe's first words when he phoned me. 'We better get ourselves in shape.'

I must admit that we tried hard to build up suitable heads of steam, but from the start it was an uphill battle. We practised on the Wanderers courts, and tried to further hone our bodies by jogging round the cricket field.

'Hone?' said Abie. 'Is that what you call it? Jesus, Forbsey. Okay. Let's get ourselves honed before June.' But it was slow going.

One day Brian Lidgey, a previous champion, watched us from the side of the court, his most ironical smile in place. 'Younger, stronger, fitter, faster men would be better equipped,' he proclaimed. 'And luck is going to have to have to play its part …'

'Jesus, Lidge,' said Abie. 'Wimbledon courts are still grass and Forbsey and I are good on grass.'

'Wrong tense, Abe. You *were* good. Make sure you tell your opponents, in case they don't remember.'

'What the hell is a tense?' Abe wanted to know.

To apply even more pressure on us, Abe's friend Deborah began a publicity campaign, alerting everyone, getting Nike to sponsor us, even trying to get Super Sport to televise our match as a possible late-in-life classic. Here even Abe saw a red light flashing, and made what might be one of the great understatements of the age.

'Listen, Deborah. Relax! It's not impossible we lose in the first round!'

Fast forward to the next Wimbledon, second week. Abe was right. For a while it was like the old days – we could go virtually where we pleased, into the locker room, the competitors' stand, the players' cafeteria, practise on the grass courts at Aorangi Park, use the players' transport to take us wherever we wanted to go. The only slight problem was that being competitors, we eventually had to compete. We practised like mad on the grass, and Abe even arranged a trial match against Stan Smith and Bob Lutz, ex-Wimbledon doubles winners who both qualified for what my father would have called 'salt of the earth' status. It wasn't much help.

'You may need a few better shots up your sleeves,' said Stan in a kindly voice, after they won the first set 6-1, but our sleeves were empty and they beat us at a canter.

When I told that to Abe, he said, 'A canter, hey? Then we'll just have to figure out a way to gallop' – a bit grimly, because it was beginning to dawn on him that galloping at our age was asking a lot. Anyway, he said, we got two games in the second set, so we must be getting better.

'What you mean,' I said, 'is that the rate at which we're getting worse is slowing down,' but Abe overlooked the irony, and told me to pull myself together.

'Which, of course, gets more difficult as one gets older,' said James. 'I've had days when no matter how hard I pull …' and he gave Richard's wave.

When the draw was made, we found our opponents to be Alex Metreveli of Russia and Jan Kodes of Czechoslovakia.

'We're lucky,' said Abe. 'They've never had much grass behind the Iron Curtain, so Russians don't like it' – but when I mentioned that Kodes had won Wimbledon, and Metreveli had reached the final, and that they were both still in their forties, he got a thoughtful look on his face and said it was too soon to panic. I remember saying it was too *late* to panic, but by then it didn't matter a hoot whether we panicked or not.

Our match was to be played on Court 11 and, remote as it was, a whole lot of South African friends turned up to watch us – amongst others, Sol Kerzner, Tony and Gisela Bloom, the Ulphanes, the Wolpes, the Menells, Frances and Jamie, also Roy Emerson with an unruly group of Australians, sundry smaller folk and et ceteras, because bush telegraph had announced that something unusual was going to take place on Court 11.

There was nothing for it. We changed into our magnificent Nike gear, made our way to the court, I spun my racket, we won the toss, elected to serve, took up our positions, and the warm-up wasn't too bad. Throughout our partnership it had always been Abe who served first, but an odd kink had got into his swing, and we agreed that I should begin. Nonetheless, he retained his old habit of walking up to me and saying 'grip your racket and watch the ball, Forbsey', which he used to feel calmed me down. The umpire called 'Play!' An expectant hush fell over the crowd, I tossed the ball into the air above my head, and from that moment on the trouble started. It didn't take long for even Abe to realise that things were not going according to plan.

I stopped there and looked around the Table.

'Finish your story,' said the Other Peter. 'What happened?'

'Very little of note,' I said shortly. 'We got routed. Trounced would also do. It's no fun getting badly beaten, I can tell you. After the match, as I walked back to the locker room with my head hanging, I suddenly felt a powerful bear hug, and I heard Roy Emerson's voice, with a touch of pure glee in it. 'Forbsey, you and big Abe were *pitiful*.'

'Did you get any games?' asked the Other Peter.

'Three. The same number that Olmedo and Santana got,' Abe

pointed out. 'Relax, Forbsey. I told Chris Gorringe we could play badly just as well as them. And I'll tell you another thing. All those people had a better time watchin' us get killed than if we'd won. Weird, I know, but that's the way the bread crumbles.'

'The cookie,' I said, but he wasn't listening.

The interesting thing was that as first round losers, we each got prize money of 2500 pounds – much more than we'd earned in the whole ten years of our prime. I accepted my cheque feeling slightly shamefaced, but Abe said there was absolutely no need to feel shamefaced, because what was good for the goose was good for the gander – a bit mysterious, I thought, but at least he got the saying right.

5

Beauty or Skill?

The Other Peter said wearily, 'You still haven't answered my question. Why aren't you going to Wimbledon?'

If they have another thing in common, these old-timers, it is their love of sport, with tennis near the top of the list, and Wimbledon sacrosanct.

'The main reason,' I replied, 'is tennis itself. Or rather, I should say the way it now is, compared to what it used to be.' The questioning looks surrounding me confirmed that I was on dangerous ground.

'You mean that tennis is not as good as it was in your day?'

'No, I don't mean that. Not at all. Technically, it's much better. It's something else much more subtle. Obscure, you could say … It began when I was young, seven or eight, I guess, and I ran onto the court with my sawn-off racket while the adults had their tea. It was my game, and it stayed my game through all the years of soaring hopes and fading dreams.'

They hadn't expected quite such an outpouring, but having started I had to see it through.

A game played in white, if you get my meaning. Even as children, Mother made us wear the white shirts and pants she bought at the general dealers. It was a simple, noble game then, but a game, you follow me, and I've always loved it that way. Now it's a business. Yes, yes, silly I know, things change, I should accept the changes and in a way I do. It's impossible for me to dislike tennis, but I don't *love* it any more. Purple shoes, Mohican haircuts, blue courts; clenched fists; yelping and grunting; injuries to order; solemn faces; rich young people trying to get richer ... understandable, I suppose ...

I was groping for words. 'It's as if the game I knew has been polluted – become mass-produced, so to speak. Wrapped in plastic ...'

'Mammon!' said the One Peter. 'Tennis is not the only thing that has changed. Even newspapers are not what they were.'

'Every sport has changed,' I said, relieved. 'When Jimmy Connors made his famous remark, he didn't realise how right he was! You'll all remember some reporter asking him about his match, how he'd played and so on, and him saying it had been "a hard day at the office".'

A hard day at the office. Well, yes, I suppose it was! Just as it is these days when, say, Nadal plays Ferrer for four hours, and every point is a rally of ten shots or more, all hit the same way. Hit very well, but all identical.

There was a contemplative silence round the Table, so I went on.

If you studied the top fifty players of my era, you'd find that every one of them had a different style of play, so that in every match you'd have one style versus another – pace versus steadiness, power versus cunning, a bit of humour, hand-crafted rallies, brilliant moments, spectacular blunders ... Now, nearly all the top fifty players play identical tennis – poker faces, dead serious. Fundamentally, tennis has boiled

BEAUTY OR SKILL?

down to three things – forehands, backhands and services, with the odd drop-shot, volley or lob thrown in. Rallies all follow the same pattern – for every point won, a fist punching the air, a glance at a coach, a finger pointed at a ball-boy. Towel! And make it quick! Fake injuries, bandages, coaches looking wise with their beards and their shades and their caps on back to front. Mind you. The one thing that I can't deny is that tennis, one track as it is, is superb. No other word for it. But after a while I can't help finding the repetitiveness a bit tedious …'

'Steady on!' said the One Peter. 'Some people like long rallies …'

'Yes, yes, I know. But you did ask, and I did say it was my own opinion. An enigma, really. The tennis is better, but I swear I'd rather watch Rod Laver playing Ken Rosewall. (Laver and Rosewall were two of the best and most stylish players of all time.) There is of course this one big but. Maybe two …' and this, of course, raised eyebrows.

'And that is?'

'Every now and again I see magnificent matches – usually played by Federer in some or other Grand Slam final. He adds an elusive ingredient to any type of game he plays via some indefinable sort of magic. Magic. In the truest sense – effortless style, a one-handed backhand, a silky, lethal forehand, a smooth service action, all of which make tennis look ridiculously easy. I can't classify Federer. I've seen him make too many impossible tennis shots – I imagined myself trying them and realised just how impossible they are. And on top of it all, he makes it seem easy. *Never* seems to be having a hard day at the office. Bloody Federer! How come he's so good while the rest of us have to battle away …'

'Relax!' the One Peter. 'You mentioned there were two buts …'

'When two of the highly skilled labourers play each other – David

Ferrer versus the Japanese fellow, for instance, all you see are endless topspin forehands and two-handed backhands underlined by heroic grunts. Time passes at a much slower rate, and although you have to admit they're great athletes, you tend to doze off. Does that make any sense?'

'It all depends. Write about it, if you feel so strongly,' said Richard. 'Tennis as it was, and tennis as it is.'

'No sense in that,' I replied. 'I'd simply be asking for trouble.'

When I was about fifteen, I told the Table, I went to a music store in East London and asked the man to play me the latest music. He put on the Benny Goodman Quartet playing a tune called *After You've Gone*, and I liked it so much that I bought the record with my last bit of pocket-mammon. When I wound up our old farm gramophone and put it on, my father said, 'Gordon. Please stop that noise! Why can't they stick to the tune instead of trying to show how clever they are?' Same thing in a way. I liked Glenn Miller playing *In the Mood*. Father liked Gracie Fields singing *Roses of Picardy*. I liked Laver's artistry. People today like Nadal's power.

'So you think that Rod Laver and Benny Goodman had something in common?'

'Yes. They were both great artists.'

'And what is Nadal?'

'A great athlete. An efficient machine that mass produces the world's best topspin and sells it for vast sums of mammon!'

'A machine that doesn't play beautifully?'

I took refuge in another story. Only answer.

There was a Danish fellow I knew. Unusual chap. Name of Torben Ulrich. Canny tennis player. Intelligent, quirkish, eccentric – slightly

BEAUTY OR SKILL?

Torben Ulrich.

barmy, some said. Used to love music so much that he carried a record player around with him, and one day he spent an entire rainy afternoon talking to me about beauty and skill. Kept putting on pieces of music, then waiting for my reaction. Apparently it wasn't satisfactory, because after a while he leaned back and said, 'You know, Gordon,' – he had this slow, musical way of talking – 'there is beauty and there is skill, and you must see the difference.' And he stopped playing bits of jazz and put on the second movement of the Brahms Violin Concerto.

For about ten minutes, we listened, me in awe – I was young, you see, just twenty or so, and I wanted him to think I was into Brahms. To my surprise, I realised I was. When the last note ended, he stopped the player, sat quiet for a minute or so, then he said, even more slowly than usual, 'That music was beautiful and the violinist was skilful ...'

I left Ulrich's room a different person. Funny how one afternoon can touch your life! Ever since then I've been conscious of Torben's notion, and for me Laver's tennis is beautiful, and Nadal's is skilful – in a tedious sort of way if you watch it for too long. His game, I mean. Yet it has won him nine Roland Garros titles so far – and I gave a Richard-type wave to indicate a miracle.

Only a few weeks ago, I told the Table, my feelings were confirmed – to my own satisfaction, anyway – by a match I watched in the second round of the 2015 Wimbledon Championships. I put on the television and came upon a player called Dustin Brown playing Rafael Nadal – a foregone conclusion, you'd think – but I soon realised I was witnessing something extraordinary. There was this tall, dark, bearded man with beads and dreadlocks, a German, if you can believe it, the last thing you'd expect on the Wimbledon Centre Court. Dreadlocks, I mean. Most amazing of all, he was playing one of the most attacking tennis games I'd seen in years, dismantling Nadal's methodical perfection with all kinds of excursions and raids on the net. 'No way,' I said to myself, 'this can't be,' but there it was. And no flash in the pan, I tell you, but a masterful assault that continued for four sets – short, sharp rallies, net-rushing, angled volleys, all the old-fashioned methods, you understand, one of the most absorbing games I'd seen in years. And he beat Nadal, but unfortunately, like so many low-ranked players – in the eighties, I believe he was – he couldn't do it again and lost in the next round. Some columnist wrote: *A cheque for £77,000 will come in handy, allowing him to fund his travels in a more relaxed way than skipping around Europe in a camper van.* Never mind. In one astonishing match, the old way beat the new way with all the old intrigue – separate styles of play – exactly the reason the Borg/McEnroe games had so delighted us …

They seemed interested. One thing about that Table, it was always

BEAUTY OR SKILL?

interested in things strange and true, so I dared to expound another of my theories.

As in history there is a BC and an AD, so in tennis there ought to be a BB (before Borg) and an AB (after Borg) for it was he who first introduced the rock-solid safety of topspin and baseline tennis. At the time no one ever realised the effect of his methods – he was simply a player with great talent and a brand-new way of playing. The fact that he had as his opponents some of the most colourful players of all time merely underlined his patience, consistency and astonishing accuracy. Five times he won Wimbledon, beating Nastase, Connors (twice), Tanner and McEnroe. We never realised that much of the fascination lay in the different styles of play – that Borg playing McEnroe was magic, while two 'Borgs' playing each other would produce the long, repetitive rallies I find boring. Now, with huge sums of mammon at stake, both coaches and players have obviously decided that Borg's way is the best way. Only a theory, mind you, but Nadal versus Dustin Brown did seem to prove my point …

※

Meanwhile, deep inside me there is genuine regret for many of the changes in tennis have saddened me, and I've always been so certain that my love of tennis would last forever. But I watch it now with interest and the kind of admiration you might feel when you see an expert workman doing his job. I put on the television, come upon someone playing someone in Monte Carlo or Madrid or Hamburg, and it's the guy in the red shirt playing the guy in the yellow shirt in one of a succession of men's singles matches in which I don't care who wins – very

Abe had his own way of relaxing. On his left is the Dutch champion, Tom Okker.

important, that. You should care who wins. And, I ask you, where are the women? For me, the separation of men and women in nearly all events other than the Grand Slams, is a tragedy. Without the subtle contrasts of women's tennis, a succession of men's singles matches can become, well, boring. You get up and make tea …

'But the power?' asked the Other Peter. 'The sheer speed of play these days?'

'In 1957 Abe Segal and I had to play a Davis Cup match against the Italians in Florence,' I said. 'When we got there, we discovered that during the same week there was to be a Formula 1 motor race in the town with all the top drivers competing.'

BEAUTY OR SKILL?

Abe wanted to see a driver called Juan Manuel Fangio, claiming he was the best driver of all time. 'We've gotta see this Fangio, Forbsey. He's somethin' else!' For Abe, all the people he most admired got labelled *somethin' else* – Frank Sinatra, Lew Hoad, Arnold Palmer, Clint Eastwood. Roger Federer had lately become 'somethin' else'. Anyway, the Italian tennis players heard Abe's plea, and arranged for a little platform for us near a town track lined with bales of hay, banners, pennants, coffee stalls and excited aficionados. We all waited with glasses of Coca-Cola in our hands while a variety of machines flew past us, all looking much the same to me. Suddenly there was a great sigh of 'Fangio' and, sure enough, he came flying round the corner in a car that, if you stood it beside the cars of today, resembled a streamlined lawn-mower.

Anyway, although he was going at only about half the speed they go at nowadays, he managed to skid, bounce off a bale of hay, zoom down the straight and just miss a telephone booth before disappearing with a puff of smoke and an exultant backfire. Abe was happy, the crowd cheered like mad, and you couldn't help feeling that somehow those people believed that they were all a part of the race and that Fangio was simply their driver. Speed wasn't everything …

'Exactly what I find with my cycling,' said James. 'The other day, on a downhill straight I decided on a burst of speed, but it didn't materialise. Like Fangio, I managed a backfire, but only a gentle one without any smoke.'

6

Strawberries at Home

During the years when business made it impossible to travel, we celebrated the Wimbledon finals at home, brought in a supply of strawberries and champagne, invited a few special people, and listened to wise old commentators telling us about friends winning the title – Roy Emerson, Manuel Santana, John Newcombe and, in 1968, the first Open Wimbledon, Rod Laver again.

Abe Segal and I were invited to participate, so I took time off work to play again for the last time, and that year I was able, from the competitors' stand, to watch Laver win his third Wimbledon singles title. As it turned out, in the second round of the doubles, Abe and I played Alex Olmedo and Pancho Segura, and lost the first set 32-30, still the longest set of men's doubles in Wimbledon history. (We lost the match in four sets.)

In 1985, with our hearts in our throats, we watched Boris Becker defeat our own Kevin Curren, and in 1986, he (Becker again) beat Ivan Lendl in a tense match that produced one of Des Lindberg's classic remarks. In a dramatic Shakespearean voice, he murmured the words, 'Neither a Boris nor a Lendl be.'

STRAWBERRIES AT HOME

Left to right: Pancho Segura, Alex Olmedo, Abe and G F. We hold the Wimbledon record for the longest set of doubles: 32–30.

In 1986 the Last Eight Club came into being, and Frances and I travelled to Wimbledon every year until 2012, entranced by a succession of champions such as Andre Agassi, Pete Sampras, and the astonishing emergence of the young Roger Federer. In 2001, Goran Ivanisevic beat Pat Rafter in one of the most dramatic finals I have ever seen.

I have a game that I play with other sportsmen where we name sporting occasions that have most moved us – difficult, of course, but the ones I always mention are (a) when South Africa won the Rugby World Cup in 1995; (b) when Ernie Els won his first US Open; and (c) when Ivanisevic beat Rafter. (The worst was when Allan Donald and Lance Klusener ran each other out in the 1999 Cricket World Cup semi-final!)

The Last Eight Club is just inside Gate 5, a little lounge and bar, with wicker chairs and tables, and walls lined with TV screens and photos. To be a member, you have to reach the quarter-finals of the singles, or the semi-finals of the doubles, hence the name. It was founded in 1986 as a reward for players who had fought the good fight but never won it. Old friends meet there, get free tea, relive memories, pore over photos and murmur to themselves about players of their time in the hope of retrieving old feelings for a moment or two. You get special seats on the Centre Court, and at 7 pm there is a happy hour, with drinks and sandwiches, and old friends who say things like, 'Do you remember our doubles game on Court 11 that ended in the dark? I still think you and Abe were lucky to win, because none of us could see a bloody thing ...'

As my bailiwick is tennis, I am supposed to keep track of the current stars and answer questions about the modern game, in spite of the fact that I don't watch it as much as I should. Fortunately, the questions are not too technical. Things like:

> *Were players in my day as fit and strong as they are today?*
> *Do they play better tennis than you did?*
> *Does modern equipment really make such a difference?*
> *Is Federer the best player who ever lived?*
> *How can Sharapova look so good and sound so bad?*
> *Shouldn't Nadal wear bigger pants?*
> *If Andy Murray played at Wimbledon in a kilt, would it have to be white?*

One day, while complaining about the haughty antics of the young billionaires, I was asked whether I envied the large sums of mammon they made. (In our day, tennis was strictly amateur.) It was easy to say that I did not. 'We played tennis our way and loved every minute of it' – and we talked about how things had changed, how money has come into all sports and affected the spirit of them. It was one of those quiet moments, lunch was over, the Table cleared, the room half-empty, Irish coffee about to arrive – ideal for the telling of tales.

'Only a few months ago I got a phone call from Peter Waters,' I began, and of course they wanted to know who Peter Waters was.

I told them that Peter Waters was a tall, skinny young bloke who travelled the tennis circuits in my day. He was five years younger than me, not bad looking, at that time poor as a church-mouse, had a winning way, loved tennis – every part of it – playing, teaching, watching, dreaming about winning – *every* part, if you get what I mean. Decent serve, good volley, grinned as he played his groundies ... groundies ... what he called his ground-strokes, which, I can tell you, were pretty patchy. We used to meet up at many of the smaller tournaments, and in the Gstaad event he won his first round and in the glow of victory asked me to lend him a pound. He needed to eat that day, he said, and his money hadn't arrived from South Africa; should arrive any minute. 1962 it was ...

I looked around at the seven faces, noted complacency, and felt free to continue.

I lent him the pound, and somehow forgot about it, which, I can tell you, was unlike me, because a pound was money in those days. Anyway, just a few months ago (fifty-four years after the loan, in fact) he phoned me, out of the blue – I was in Plettenberg Bay – and said he wanted to give me back my pound and to take me to lunch at the best restaurant on the South Coast, a place called Zinzi, very upmarket. Well, as you can imagine, I was surprised. I went along, we had a damn good lunch, and he told me his life story. Still tall and skinny, he was no longer poor. He'd battled on with championship tennis for a few years, hadn't won much of note, had given up on being a tennis star and instead began coaching at Umhlanga Rocks (near Durban, KwaZulu-Natal) where he still coached. (Eight hours a day, sometimes ten, Forbsey, for over fifty years.) He'd saved money like mad, bought a small house, sold it, bought a bigger one, and so on, and by the bottle of wine he ordered, it was easy to see he'd got it right – he owned properties in Natal, a holiday house in Knysna, talked of dividends and so on.

'And I still coach,' he said proudly, 'but only for four hours a day.'

It was all quite moving, I might add. More memories. Val (my first wife) and I had won the mixed doubles that year in Gstaad and been presented with silver cups by Elizabeth Taylor, with Richard Burton standing next to her. She had violet eyes. Not blue, violet. Peter Waters also remembered her eyes. 'I got close enough to see them,' he said. He knows more than I do about tennis, and also thinks that the modern game is sometimes boring. 'If I watch it for more than ten minutes at a time I get restless …' Anyway, he bought me lunch …

'Interesting,' interrupted Charles, 'but it took you a long time to make the point. We're going to have to get clocks like they have in chess. You give them a bang when you start talking.'

'I actually need another few minutes,' I said, 'to finish properly …' Charles looked at his watch and gave a guarded nod.

'Scene changes for a while,' I continued.

At about ten on most Monday mornings, Abe and I sit in the Wanderers Club coffee bar eating toasted cheese and tomato sandwiches, having walked around the top cricket field a few times – not at any great speed, mind you – every now and then Abe breaks into a jog that is slower than his walk, but it doesn't faze him. 'Just to make my body think it's joggin'...' Then there's a retaining wall where we do press-ups at a 45-degree angle, but it's nice to get to the coffee bar and talk, mainly about sport and old friends, some of whom have died – kicked the bucket, as Abe says. 'Jesus, Forbsey, we mustn't go too near any buckets' – and when I once asked him how many friends he had, he wanted to know if he could count the dead ones. 'Otherwise there's only Tony, Sol, Hilly and Ruby. And you, come to think of it. So that's five I can think of, offhand.'

Then, as it happened, just as I finished telling him all about Peter Waters, on the coffee bar TV, Djokovic began playing Nadal in the finals of somewhere or other. As our coffee came, we saw what turned out to be the longest rally of the match. Fifty-nine strokes it was, about twenty-four topspin forehands, twenty-eight two-handed backhands, two drop-shots, two volleys, a good lob and a good recovery. I forget who won the point, but I can tell you, a rally like that in our day would have sent sportswriters to the nearest pub in search of adjectives. Anyway, the crowd roared, and both players pointed fingers at ball-boys, wanting towels. We had to fetch our own ...

'Fifty-nine shots, Forbsey! Hoadie (Lew Hoad, Abe's idol) once said to me, "Don't mess about at the back of the court, Abie, you're no bloody good there. Make your move and get on with it." So my points were over quickly. Fifty-nine shots would have lasted me a whole set.'

Meanwhile the commentators were reading statistics we could see on the screen – fifty-three per cent of Djokovic's forehands had gone to Nadal's backhand, only twenty-three per cent of his first serves had gone to his forehand, the fastest serve had been 235 kph, and so on.

'Jesus, Forbsey,' muttered Abe, 'do we really want to know all that?'

At the changeover, Nadal took swallows from four bottles and ate a banana. He towelled his whole body, pushed his hair behind his ears (although it was already there), wiped his nose, jiggled his legs and rubbed his elbow to remind the audience that he might have an injury. Djokovic had only two bottles, his hair stayed in place and he didn't rub anything. After a minute and a half the umpire called time. The players got up, walked to the back of the court, did their hops, and Djokovic got ready to serve. He bounced the ball eleven times, served his first ball and missed it. Then he bounced it another ten times, giving Nadal time to unhook his pants again and wipe his nose.

'Jesus, Forbsey,' said Abe again. 'Pass the sugar.'

Meanwhile, I'd been doing arithmetic. 'Abie,' I said, 'do you realise what we'd see if we watched the whole match go to five sets? Approximately, I mean. For forty minutes we'd be watching the players eat their bananas. The twenty-five second break between each point would add up to nearly two hours. We'd see Djokovic bounce the ball 2570 times, Nadal unhook his pants 360 times, and wipe his nose 700 times. And if he decided to have an injury, we'd have to watch for another ten minutes while they rubbed stuff on it.'

Abe stirred his coffee for a long time, then put on an expression he's used ever since I first saw him – as if he's squinting into the sun.

'Listen, Forbsey. I often watched Laver playing five-set matches, and his pants never once stuck to his arse. He drank Coke out of one bottle, ate no bananas, served without ball-bouncing, never wiped his nose, never sat down at changeovers, and never had an injury. When he finished his singles, he'd have a cup of tea, then play doubles with Fred Stolle, and then mixed doubles with Darlene Hard. Then he'd go up to the little players' pub and have a beer with his friends. If you asked him how many forehands went to his opponent's backhand, he didn't know. "I only decide where I'm going to hit the ball just before I hit it …" Let's have another cup of coffee.'

Just then there was another amazing rally, and one of the commentators announced that the career prize money alone of Nadal and Djokovic was over eighty million dollars each. We both contemplated this intelligence in silence, and then Abe said: 'Did Waters ever pay back your pound?'

7

Harvey

A frequent topic at the Table is the large amount of mammon earned by modern sportsmen, and the luxury of their lives in contrast to our day, when tennis was an amateur sport and we all had to travel the world on the smell of an oil rag.

'Nowadays, oil rags are obsolete. In tennis, anyway,' Tim had remarked, and then asked a question: 'How on earth did you chaps manage to pay your way?'

'Each tournament used to pay a portion of our airfares,' I replied, 'and offer us accommodation, breakfast and lunches. We could only fly at the back of planes, and our main worry was having to pay extra for overweight baggage. If it hadn't been for Harvey we'd have been in serious trouble.'

'Who was Harvey?' asked Charles.

'That would mean another story.'

I thought he'd forget, but as soon as Richard's Irish coffees arrived, he asked again. 'Who was Harvey?'

'He wasn't a living creature,' I said. 'More of a procedure. There was this Australian fellow named Candy. Don Candy. Like Ulrich, a most unusual fellow. He told Ian Vermaak and me about Harvey.'

'Who was Ian Vermaak?'

'A good friend and a good player. We toured together for a year, he got to the finals of the French Open at Roland Garros, and he liked his steaks with a fried egg on top of them. Anyway, Don Candy had seen a movie where James Stewart had an imaginary friend he called Harvey and that was what gave Don the idea.

'Weight worried us all. We'd accumulate masses of clobber, having to lug tennis gear, jackets and ties, rackets, books, music machines, tuxedos. In those days they held prize-giving balls and we all dressed up ...'

'Okay, okay, so you had too much baggage. What about Harvey?'

Well, I continued, Candy discovered that with a strong coat hanger and a raincoat, he could create a thing that looked like a coat, but that weighed nearly as much as a suitcase. Then, if he carried it casually over his arm it never got weighed. He called his invention Harvey. In it, jackets covered pants, sweaters hung inside, pockets could be filled with heavy things, and his raincoat covered the whole thing up. The trick was to make Harvey flexible enough not to look as though he was a dead body. Planes in those days had special coat cupboards ideal for hanging Harveys, but if the planes weren't full, Candy used to put Harvey on the seat next to him and talk to him. 'Better buckle up, we're taking off.' 'Get ready, they're serving drinks.' 'Get some sleep.' He'd even borrow Harvey's handkerchief to blow his nose.

Ian and I took Candy's advice and became specialists. Our Harveys were perfect in every way, and the only mishap we ever had was once when Ian hung his Harvey up with a jerk and the coat rail collapsed.

The lusty Lufthansa lady who bent to pick it up staggered as she took the strain, saying to Ian over her shoulder, 'Zis is ze heaffiest coat in ze whole vorrld.'

The Table listened patiently, smiling as Harvey got heavier and the air hostess turned out to have a sense of humour.

Of course, I added, these days the players would eschew Harveys, and in any case you'd never get a good Harvey through the security check. Then it was easy. I once bought a hunting knife in Munich and sat in the plane with Ian, carving slices off an Italian salami they'd given us in Rome the week before. Both the knife and the salami had been in the pockets of my Harvey and no one took the slightest notice. It was a good salami – even the air hostess had a slice or two. No one had yet worked out how to hijack a plane with a knife …

'Maybe you should stick to writing about tennis after all,' said Richard.

'You don't think Harveys have a future?'

Something to do with tennis cropped up at most lunches. 'Young billionaires' is what the Other Peter calls the modern young players, and with this in mind, he once turned to me with the question: 'If you had to play a Grand Slam final, would you play a better match with fifty dollars in your pocket, or twenty million in your bank account?'

Oddly enough, although asked in jest, it was something I'd often wondered about. Throughout my own career I was never without a nagging worry about how I would make a living when it ended. What made it worse was that playing international tennis, even in those days,

Stefan Stockenburg (Sweden), Ian Vermaak and Jean.

Ian Vermaak in the Tropics.

Don Candy (centre) with Jean (right).

accustomed you to a life of reasonable luxury, travel, and excitement – a life you knew would have to come to an end. And one of the most worrying things, when you reached the age of thirty, was that although you could still play well enough, you knew that time was running out and you'd better stop playing and try to make some money.

'I'd probably play better with twenty million dollars in the bank,' I said.

'I'd write better with twenty million in the bank,' said James. 'Even ten. Pass the bottle.'

'Writers are more productive when they're hungry,' Charles pointed out. 'Too much money and they lose their edge.'

'It's a chance I'd take even if it meant a blunt edge,' said James. 'And while we're on the subject of young billionaires, what on earth do they put into those massive tog bags they carry on court with them?'

Here I was at a loss.

In our day, I replied, players carried all they needed for five-set matches in tennis racket head-covers (and racket-heads were smaller in those days). A few salt and glucose tablets, Band-Aids, sweatlets, a handkerchief, lip-ice, an aspirin or two, and, for safety's sake, all the money we had. I find it hard to imagine Federer carrying all his money on court with him for every match. Now, players' needs seem greater than ours used to be. Bananas and bottles. Spare shirts. Vitamins, energy bars, lotions, things left over from the match before. Sunglasses, iPhones and iPads, headphones. A bagful of rackets. Perhaps a small spirit stove in case they feel like a hot snack …

Richard frowned. 'If you'd had the best new equipment and a coach like Boris Becker, do you think that on a good day you could beat, say, Novak Djokovic?'

Although my answer should have been 'no', I took a leaf from Abe Segal's book.

'Quite possibly,' I said with a straight face. 'I don't see any reason why not. I'd have to be on form, of course.'

A bold answer, if one considers that I added no pre-emptive conditions, such as if pigs had wings or the sun rose in the west – and they all seemed content with it, nodding sagely and sipping their Irish coffee – seven ex-warriors, pleased to have in their midst someone who might, in his day, have beaten Novak Djokovic.

That lunch, the Other Peter had just returned from Mogadishu, where he'd been supervising the saving of an endangered bird species that lived in swamps. He's always just been somewhere, or is about to go somewhere – a trip to Antarctica to study penguins, mountain climbing in the Andes, a trans-Atlantic boat race, a conference in Davos, an assignment in Somalia – and is always planning new and more daring adventures, such as swimming the Channel, river-rafting down the Colorado, skiing to the South Pole, or trying to communicate with gorillas. There are also many notable things that he nearly does ... once claimed, with a straight face, that as a younger man he had very nearly climbed Mount Everest. 'Had it not been for an unexpected knee injury, I would have,' he said.

'Aren't all injuries unexpected?' James asked. 'I mean, I've never heard anyone saying, "I won't be able to climb Mount Everest too soon because I'm expecting to injure my knee next Thursday ..."'

8

An Urge to Write

Richard's book on Smuts is going strong although, like all writers, he has his moments of introspection. Lately he's been reading Boris Johnson's book on Churchill and is worried that Johnson's prose is more flamboyant than his, giving as a wry example a paragraph where Johnson writes about soldiers waking at dawn to find 'a cavalry charge come tootling over the hill at them'.

'I could never get cavalry to tootle,' he says glumly. 'For me they're either at rest or full gallop.'

'Smuts wouldn't want cavalry that tootled,' says Tim soothingly. 'And he wouldn't want fancy prose either, so don't worry.'

'Why don't *you* write another book?' Richard asked me one day. 'You seem to have a few stories left in you. If Abe Segal can paint at seventy, then surely you can write at eighty. Include your silly humour if you must – people will put up with it provided you write about modern tennis. Aren't you always being asked for another book?'

'I do get hundreds of requests from one or two people,' I admitted, then told them of Sergio Segalla, our Italian factory manager in my business life. Salt of the earth. If ever I complained that his production was holding up our sales efforts, he would get angry. 'You are-a always passing me the bucket! Trying to make-a me chew more than I can bite off!'

'Another book might be trying to chew more than I can bite off,' I said lamely, but Richard wasn't deterred. When we were walking to the car park, he stopped and said as a sort of postscript: 'Don't write about tennis if you don't want to. Just write for the fun of it.'

His advice stayed in my mind as I drove home – and came back when I awoke in the early hours of the next morning. 'For the fun of it' gave writing a different slant, although my English teacher once told me that the essential thing about writing a book was knowing what it was to be about.

*

'When we were children, without such things as TV, movies, iPads, computer games and so on, reading aloud on long winter evenings was one of our favourite pastimes,' I once told the Table.

Although we avoided the heavy classics, the lighter ones were essential, and we loved to branch out into the simple fiction of the time – Zane Grey, Clarence Mulford (Hopalong Cassidy), Leslie Charteris, P G Wodehouse, Mark Twain, even Oliver Twist got a show in. Every month my mother would visit the town library and come home with a pile of books, and every evening in front of the fire, we'd float down the Mississippi with Huck Finn, rescue aristocrats with The Scarlet Pimpernel, rope steers with Red Connors, or win dog-fights with Biggles. I got to love stories, and from a young age wanted to write one of my own.

'Why didn't you?'

'I actually did,' I replied.

On the tennis circuit, where there was a lot of spare time, I used to labour away, ending up with the most unruly work ever written. I called it *Nor All Thy Tears*, and filled it with such strong characters that they ran amok at the drop of a hat – fist fights instead of discussions, a funeral instead of a ball, a murder instead of a love affair. My characters drank heavily and were all highly sexed, with the result that no matter what I'd planned for them, they always ended up sleeping with each other. There were rapes, snakebites, plagues, suicides, murders, mad dogs ... The hero got rabies, and the heroine, vital to the ending, got leukaemia and had to be kept alive. She received bone marrow from a lesbian donor, and although it cured her, she became one herself (a lesbian, not a donor). Her lover, in a fury of revenge, turned gay and fell for his boss. A virgin gave birth to twins, causing confusion among those awaiting a second coming. Could God have two sons? And what if one turned out to be a girl? The book flatly refused to end, so I finally took it home and put it on a shelf.

'Sounds like a best-seller,' said Charles. 'You should publish it and let readers make up their own endings ...'

'Moths have eaten some of the best parts,' I said.

'A new way to edit,' said James. 'Allow moths to decide.'

'It was my sister Jean's suggestion that I make notes about people on the tennis circuits so I'd remember to tell her. I'd sit with a pencil and a rubber, scribbling away.'

'Yes, yes, yes, it's happened to us all,' said the Other Peter. 'I once nearly wrote a whole book that way. But, as I've said, urges to write always desert me at the last minute.'

9

What's in a Name?

Richard and I would sit in the bay window of my house with a tray of tea and exchange ideas. We agreed that writing books was a lonely business, and that talking about them often helped clear the mind.

'A writer once told me that it's easier to write a book when you've given it a title,' he said. 'A title gives direction – a destination. You can't go anywhere until you know where you're going. Have you got a title for your book?'

'I haven't got a book, let alone a title!'

'That's the point. Apparently a title helps.'

It was then that I thought of Don Candy again. In the old days, before tennis matches began, we used to toss for side or service by one player spinning his racket and the other calling either rough or smooth. (Rackets, then, were laced with what was called 'trebling' – fine nylon lines that gave a 'rough' or a 'smooth' side to the upper and lower racket strings.)

'*Rough or Smooth*,' Richard mused. 'Isn't that a good title?'

WHAT'S IN A NAME?

Cautiously, I agreed. In every life there were rough and smooth patches, and as we talked the age-old ritual flashed through my mind –

'Rough or Smooth?'

'Rough.'

'Rough it is!'

'I'll serve.'

'I'll take this side.'

I'd said those words hundreds of times over and they brought back another set of memories. Candy and I used to practise tennis together and one day, to get started, he'd spun his racket as usual, I'd called 'rough', won the toss, chosen to serve, and as I walked off to my side, he stopped me.

'Now – look – here – Forbes …' In certain moods he had a way of saying each word separately, and beating time by tapping my shoulder with his forefinger. 'Just – one – minor – point. You called rough. Now if the racket ended up standing on its edge, what do you think would happen?'

'You'd have to spin it again, of course.'

'Wrong. You'd have lost the toss.'

'Why?'

'Because your call was incorrect. To win, you'd have had to call "rough or edge". All – you – called – was – "rough".'

'Hypothetical,' I said. 'Rackets don't stand on their edges. Now let's play tennis!'

But for a strange epilogue, I said to Richard, I'd have forgotten about that little event. But one year we went to Bucharest to play Davis Cup against Romania. I had to play the first match against a guy called Ion Tiriac – even in his youth, a bear of a man with a fearsome moustache and a master of every tennis trick in the book. Now he's one of the most successful businessmen in Europe. He got ready to spin his racket, and I saw that it was one of the old white Slazenger jobs with a heavy head and a square grip. A veritable club of a thing.

'What you say, Forbey?' he said, and I called 'rough', as I always did.

He gave the racket a twirl, it spun around for a while, bounced about, teetered, and to my amazement stood on its edge. I didn't mention Candy's thesis, and with a laugh he picked it up and spun it again. I won the toss and lost the match, but we managed to beat the Romanians 3-2, and get ourselves safely back to London. Romania was behind the Iron Curtain at the time and, being South Africans, we all (especially Segal) had visions of being held hostage and ill-treated. Back at the Cumberland Hotel Abe said we'd come in from the cold. 'Jesus, Forbsey, there's nothing like a cup of English tea.'

'*Rough or Smooth?*' mused Richard. 'It may just work.' But it got condemned by the young publishing people who said the words were used to advertise a certain make of condom. Nevertheless, this book was nearly called *Rough or Smooth*.

※

Apparently chronology is important when one is writing a book. My sister Jean once ordered me to read a poem where the beginning was the end, the end the beginning, where time past and time future all existed in time present, and so forth – the poet obviously getting carried away by some notion that must have come to him in the night. I didn't understand it at first, but the words stuck in my head, and following them up I imagined the act of walking down a street and meeting an old and special friend; it's early evening, we embrace fondly and sit down at a table in the village square.

'A glass of wine, perhaps?'

'What a good idea!'

A waiter listens, nods his head, comes back with wine of the region, opens the bottle and fills our glasses. Delighted, we look into each other's eyes and take the first experimental sip … that exact instant is the present! The waiter opening the wine is in the past, the next sip we take will be in the future, yet we smile, touch glass to glass and say, 'How fortunate we are to share this moment!'

This moment, past, present, future, all in one! May not the question be asked: If they can merge together for a moment, why not for all our lives – which are, after all, a moment in eternity? Jean's poet may be right.

'It's hard enough coping with the present,' said James. 'I wouldn't like past and future descending on me in one fell swoop.'

10

Bird Calls

There was a lot of tennis taking place at the time of one lunch – the Aussie Open, Roland Garros, Federer playing Djokovic, Nadal injuring his knee, Sharapova developing a new shriek, a new Russian chappie with a big serve, a bad-tempered Australian, and so on – so my misgivings about modern habits kept coming to the fore and I began to feel the Table might be starting to agree with me.

'Okay. Okay, you're right,' someone said. 'In cricket also there's too much hugging and spitting. They'll be kissing each other next, making love at mid-on! Can you imagine Don Bradman punching the air? Or Graeme Pollock hugging Barry Richards?'

But we all knew that, in the modern way of things, both spectators and players loved this show of swagger, and sportsmen themselves got a kick out of it.

Richard had come to visit me that afternoon, and we'd put the TV on the tennis channel as we talked. Instead of men, we found two of the leading women playing a singles match. These days, I often enjoy watching women's tennis just as much as men's, so for a while we sat back and watched them.

'You know, Richard,' I said, 'more and more it strikes me that the women of today are so much better than the women of my day – more so than the men of today are better than the men of my day. If you get what that means. They seem taller, stronger and more athletic, and all of them have good service actions – amazing to me because in our day most women used the service simply to get the ball into play. These days some of them serve and smash nearly as hard as the men.'

'They are also noisier, don't you think?' Richard said.

One of the women that day was Victoria Azarenka. The match was a close one, and she'd perfected such a long and melancholy howl to go with every stroke that I worried about her vocal cords. Out of interest, I did a quick calculation and revealed it to Richard.

'If she does 1 howl per stroke x an average of 10 strokes per point x 8 points per game x 10 games per set x 2.5 sets per match,' I said, 'say 3 matches per tournament, that's 6000 howls per tournament. If she plays, say, 25 tournaments per year, that would be 6000 x 25 = 150 000 howls per year. That's a lot of howls. Maria Sharapova must be in about the same bracket, only her howl is more of a scream.'

'That's also a lot of screams,' he said thoughtfully.

When at the next lunch we disclosed our findings to the Table, James was first to comment. 'I don't suppose that howling or screaming consumes much energy in younger people,' he mused, 'but it does in older ones. The other day when I caught my finger in the car door, I gave a single howl that left me tired out. Now, if I had to do that a hundred and fifty thousand times a year …'

'You'd have to give 410.9 howls per day,' interrupted the Other Peter. As usual, he was busy on his cellphone calculator. 'About 29.35 every hour, allowing ten howl-free hours' sleep a night.' Then Mark wanted to know how you gave .35 of a howl.

The One Peter muttered about this being another example of the depths to which our inanity had descended, but it got worse when the Other Peter, an authority on bird calls, announced that it should be possible to identify women tennis players by the calls they make.

He gave several examples. 'A long melancholy call would be the purple-breasted Victoria ... a shorter yelp, the crested Maria ... A deep, throaty call, the greater helmeted Monica.'

'In our day,' I noted, 'there were no bird calls in that sense. One had to be in visual contact to identify women players. If one of our lady players had suddenly made sounds like that, she'd have been hospitalised and sedated.'

'Surely there are rules about noise,' said the One Peter. 'What if players complain?'

'I've been reading Alan Mills's book,' I said, '*Lifting the Covers*.'

Alan was elected Wimbledon referee in 1983, and endured for about twenty years, so if anyone knows, he should. One of his chapters is called *It's All Gone Bananas*, and it deals with both grunting and tennis players eating bananas. (The record banana consumption during one match, apparently, is nine.) He also throws light on grunting. Apparently it crept up on tennis in about 1990 via Jimmy Connors and Monica Seles. They were the first to make sounds. Before that, players grunted silently, having been told by their coaches to inhale as the ball approached, and exhale when they hit it. When grunting became audible, officials realised they had a problem, but it was too late. Various measures were discussed and there was even talk of a gruntometer to measure decibel levels. When Maria Sharapova advanced grunts to howls, she had to defend herself before the referee at Roland Garros, but by then they'd decided to apply a thing called the *Hindrance Rule*. Players could be penalised only if it could be proved they were grunting deliberately to upset their opponents.

'A bit of a farce, really, don't you think?' I asked the Table. 'If an umpire asks Victoria Azarenka, "are your grunts deliberate?" she's unlikely to say, "yes they are". Oddly enough, even Alan seems ambivalent about grunts and screams.'

'Perhaps you should suggest introducing a bird call rule for women players,' said the Other Peter, 'allowing them only a signature cry.'

'When you caught your finger in the car door, James,' Tim wanted to know, 'did you howl deliberately, or was it unavoidable?'

James didn't deign to answer. All he said was, 'How do you give a silent grunt?'

As I was thinking about another book, I began writing tentative paragraphs, to see what would emerge, and after a few months I gave some pages to Tim and Richard to read, in case I was flogging a dead horse. Richard cautiously proclaimed that they showed promise. Tim scribbled comments in red ink on almost every page. His writing is small and unkempt but luckily, for my seventy-eighth birthday, Frances had given me a magnifying glass with a lens strong enough to make his words legible. On the last page he wrote: 'Not only do you fling inverted commas around with profuse abandon, or omit the little buggers completely, but you are also extraordinarily profligate with et ceteras. There is a diarrhoea of them! Best avoid them, for they are said to be what writers use when they can't think of anything else!'

'But you haven't answered my question!' I cried. 'Must I continue?'

'At your own risk.'

Frances and I have an old farmhouse in Plettenberg Bay, a holiday town on the southern Cape coast of South Africa, where we spend time and where for more than twenty years, the whole family has gathered for Christmas holidays. A few weeks before our next lunch, Frances reminded me that we were due to drive to Plettenberg Bay, so for a while I'd had to set aside lunches and books to make ready. One of my jobs was a board meeting. Among other report-backs was the young sales manager announcing that as a result of a quiet month, he'd had to put his leave on the back burner, and work overtime.

'Our business is too vertically integrated,' he explained. 'If we were more horizontally enabled, I could rollout the sales budget and keep everything going forward.'

When I told that to the Table, one of the older members muttered: 'Bloody hell, don't we all …?' then stopped and glared round at the others.

'Don't we all what?' asked the One Peter.

'Wish we were more horizontally enabled, dummy!'

11

Intellect at Sea Level

On the following Thursday, Frances and I began the long drive from Johannesburg that would end at the Old Farmhouse on its little hill.

'We travel to Plett quite often during the year,' I told the Table, 'but it is over the Christmas holidays that the place comes alive. Too alive, really. Holiday crowds, matric raves, boats, beaches, bikinis. For older people, I can tell you, it's no laughing matter. Our whole family gathers and even Abe arrives in January to stay with Tony and Gisela Bloom for a week or two. They have a lovely house on Beachy Head, glorious beach, blue sea, dolphins surfing the waves and a chef who makes mince on toast for Abe in the mornings, so he doesn't have to go to the golf club to get it. He claims that very few Beachy Head chefs really understand it.

'Prawns, lobsters, goose liver, yes, but mincemeat makes them nervous,' he said to me.

Tony and Abe watch the Arsenal soccer games in Tony's theatre and eat Cadbury's chocolate when play gets slow. Once when I went to join them I found them with Sir Dominic Cadbury, yes, a genuine Cadbury

Schweppes heir – Eton, Cambridge, Stanford, the whole nine yards – although, going by his modesty you wouldn't think so. Salt of the earth type of fellow. Tony's big bowl of Cadbury chocolate came into its own, and I had a chance to talk to him, Sir Dominic, I mean. Asked him if he liked his chocolate and he said he did; said South African Cadbury's was particularly good, and that no two countries' chocolate tasted exactly the same. Something to do with the milk. Odd talking to a man who's made your favourite chocolate for two hundred years …

'You digress,' complained Mark. 'Your road to Plettenberg Bay is strewn with mincemeat, chocolate and British aristocracy …'

The road to Plett is the same road that you take to go to Burgersdorp, my old hometown, I said, coolly ignoring his school-masterly tone. It's a long drive, but we do it once every year because it's an evocative road, lined with memories. And last year, while driving there, recalling the fun of our Rainbow Room lunches made me wonder whether it might be possible to arrange similar lunches in Plettenberg Bay.

I glanced round at my audience to see whether it was paying attention. 'Do you think there might be enough people in Plettenberg Bay with sufficient time, patience, inanity, intellect, and so on, to re-create lunches similar and equal to our Rainbow Room ones?'

'Similar, perhaps, but not equal,' said James. 'Time, patience, inanity, yes. Intellect might be a tall order.'

Tim nodded agreement. 'Moist saline air induces languor,' he said. 'It's hard to be simultaneously languid and profound.'

'You'd be surprised,' interjected Mark. 'I know a little seaside place called Kleinemonde that contains profound people who manage very well on moist air.'

'Really! About how many?'

INTELLECT AT SEA LEVEL

Mark solemnly consulted his fingers. 'At least eight.'

'Well, if Kleinemonde has eight, and Plett is about five times bigger, it must have about forty.'

'Or more,' I said, 'because Plett is full of ex-people, who've made a point of remaining as profound as possible, given the measured pace and moist air.'

'Ex-people? You mean has-beens?'

Only in the sense they have been, I explained. But many of them still are. Ex-doctors, lawyers, professors, academics, businessmen, and so on. Naturally, they're different. If, say, a Johannesburg doctor moves to Plett and becomes an ex-doctor, he changes — sea views, grilled fish, plentiful wine, beaches, whales, all have effect, but he still knows a malady when he sees one. Plett men tend to become mellower and heartier and wear trousers with large side pockets full of useful things. And they can be very clever, especially before lunch.

'The men, you say. And the women?'

'They're quite a different kettle of fish.'

'Odd portrayal,' interrupted Tim. 'Women usually come in gaggles.'

'Oh, Plett women can come in anything — packs, clusters, bevies, arrays ... a full array of Plett women can be an arresting sight,' I said. 'But your typical Plett woman has a slightly windblown look, even on a calm day. Gardening, apparently. Not the part-time women, if you get my meaning, the Swallows, those who come in summer. Johannesburg, London, Munich, even Geneva. They don't garden and they're much more contained, although it's not easy to contain such women.'

'Goes for all women! Which of us can truly say we've contained one?'

'My friend Paolo says that in Italy, women sometimes even ...' I

63

began, but decided against finishing and gave a wave instead. 'Never mind what they do. Plett women are usually younger, and more reliable than men, especially after lunch. But they're hard to get the hang of. Large variety. Long legs on Robberg beach, shorter ones on the Lookout side. Some with dogs ...'

'You'd better stop,' said Richard gently. 'The hole you're digging's getting deeper.'

'To get back to your question,' said Mark, with a touch of weariness. 'Suppose you solve the intellectual side of things, and the women can be contained, is there a Rainbow Room?'

'Not as such, but there are other rooms. Habitable, but not as circular. There are no half-price senior buffets either, but then most people in Plett are seniors, and most Plett lunches cost half as much as they do in Johannesburg, so the effect is the same. Damn good lunches, I might add. A Plett fish knocks a Johannesburg fish into a cocked hat. Chips are pretty much on a par ...'

'But no dyed-in-the-wool buffets. Isn't that a drawback? At this Table, very important ideas often emerge between courses.'

'Plett men need only one course for ideas – so many, in fact, that they often go to waste. Ideas, not courses.'

'This business of being mellow and hearty,' said James. 'More difficult up here. The other evening just as I began to feel hearty, the power went off and our soufflé collapsed. I was wearing the wrong kind of trousers – no torches in the pockets ...'

'Oh, don't worry, the power also goes off in Plettenberg Bay,' I said, 'but Plett people love gas and candles. We were having dinner with Jeremy and Gail one night, and after the starter, Gail looked at her watch and said, "Dammit! The lights are supposed to be off by now.

I've got thirty-two candles burning and I was looking forward to having the oxtail by candlelight." Most Plett people look better by candlelight, and gas is common, both for cooking and conversation. As for oxtail, well, some oxen must be very large, others very small …'

'Thank God we still have hand-operated corkscrews,' said Tim, thoughtfully. 'Imagine being unable to open a bottle because of a power failure …'

12

The Specific Gravity of Lead

Frances and I have been driving the road between Johannesburg and Plett for the last twenty years or more. Long as the journey is, its advantage is that Burgersdorp lies almost exactly halfway, making it the perfect stopover, and allowing us to spend a night or two with my brother Jack. On the way to Burgersdorp we have to pass Bloemfontein, and when we do, more memories abound because Bloemfontein is where Jack and I went to boarding school.

St Andrew's School, it was, and still is, better than ever and with the same simple nobility that it has always seemed able to achieve. Saints, they call it. My father was the one who chose to send us there as boarders, in spite of the fact that Saints was a church school, and he a confirmed atheist.

'It has a good Scottish name,' was his explanation to mother, but he cautiously admitted that a brush with God might do us good. Jack and I marched to the little chapel twice every Sunday and got to know the hymns and services virtually by heart. When the part came that said *'We have left undone those things that we ought to have done and we have done those things we ought not to have done and there is no health in us'*, Jack would nudge me and whisper, 'What do you think Dad would have done if we said that to him when we forgot to do farming chores?'

I once made the mistake of trying to tell Abe about St Andrew's, that it was a church school and that I'd been to chapel every day for four years. 'Jesus, Forbsey,' he'd said, 'shouldn't that help with our doubles matches? I mean, isn't He supposed to watch over you?'

I forget what I replied, but do remember once mentioning (to test his reaction) that the Nunc Dimittis was a canticle to do with St Luke.

'St Luke, hey? Well, leave the Latin to him and try watchin' the friggin' ball ...'

Anyway, last year, Foxy Campbell (ex-tennis player, old friend and schoolmate) and I attended the school's 150th anniversary, and for a long time wandered about the old place, reminiscing. Certain old memories were clear as day, some old classrooms still the same.

'Do you remember old Archie Dunne?' he asked, chuckling to himself.

Archibald R Dunne, true salt of the earth, was our science master. He'd wounded a little finger in one of the wars, and it stood straight out, so he used it for pointing out small objects, adding his forefinger for bigger ones. Once a week we'd go to the lab to do practical work – such things as weighing empty, clean, dry beakers, half filling them with water, then weighing them again. You could then find the specific gravity of, say, a lump of lead, by immersing it in the water, finding the volume of water displaced, applying the right formula, and then working it out. If you didn't get exactly the right answer you were allowed to write at the bottom of your calculation, 'allowing for experimental error'. Muffy Stow's errors were sometimes not small enough to escape notice.

'Try again, Stow,' Archie once said. 'Lead doesn't float. Try removing the air bubbles with a camel hairbrush.'

This was Archie's secret joke. Instead of saying 'a camel-hair brush' he would say 'a camel hairbrush' and then smile to himself when no one noticed. A R Dunne was also our housemaster and his office was the scene of 'getting cuts', as Saints boys euphemised. If you got three bad marks in one week you got 'cuts'. As it was almost impossible to avoid bad marks indefinitely, we all got occasional cuts and had to stand in line outside Archie's office, making nervous jokes to show how brave we were, while wearing as many pairs of underpants as we dared. It was the head prefect's job to give the cuts, while Archie stood by as referee and linesman. Boys would emerge, bums on fire, and do a knees-up jig all the way to their dorm, where they could proudly lower their pants to show off the blue lines.

'I read somewhere that corporal punishment, fairly used, was a good thing,' said James when I told the Table about the cuts. 'Now, of course, it's regarded as barbarous. Supposed to cause all kinds of jitters in later life – anxiety, stress, insomnia, hot flushes, palpitations, even bed-wetting ...' He cast his eyes round the table. 'Wrong, of course. Who of us can honestly say that he never got caned at school? Yet here we are, eating away, fairly sane, none of us scarred for life ...'

'I do have the odd palpitation,' Tim interrupted thoughtfully.

Where the circular lawn used to be, Foxy and I found the little arbour they'd built to hang the two old pieces of railway rail that, as prefects, we used to strike at 6.40 am to wake everyone up. The power of memory! The moment I clapped eyes on those old irons, I heard again their terrible clang of doom, and remembered having to crawl out of a warm bed to stand in line for a cold shower. It often seemed to be winter, and while icy water was the main distraction, occasionally we'd find that morning glories could give trouble. Most boys were self-conscious in this regard and developed cunning ways of concealment, but one cheerful and well-endowed boy solved the problem by simply having no inhibitions. At the sound of the irons he would remove his pyjamas, hang his towel over his sturdy erection and trot to the bathroom singing his song to the tune of morning reveille:

It's a bugger in the morn
When you wake up with the horn,
And you can't get your jockstrap on!

And before leaving the dormitory he would stop in the doorway, turn and make an extravagant bow, his towel still hanging on its hook!

Seeing those iron rails reminded me that schooling was much simpler in those days. There were twenty-five boys in our class, and I can't remember any of them showing any signs of the things that afflict some children of today – autism, dyslexia, motor dysfunction, auditory problems, stress-related complexes, learning disabilities, and so on. Our masters would walk up and down with wooden rulers in their hands, and if you had learning disabilities, a sharp rap on the knuckles cured them.

Schoolwork, too, seemed more straight forward. Nine eights were seventy-two, tea came from China, coal from Newcastle, diamonds from the Big Hole, and reindeer roamed the Tundra regions, providing food and clothing for Eskimos. Our wool went to Leeds and Bradford, where it got made into warm jerseys. Napoleon lost at Waterloo, Lisbon was the capital of Portugal, England ruled the waves, and the Congo and the Amazon were the biggest rivers. Some boys were good at maths, others poor at it. Muffy Stow, the class wit, struggled with Algebra, and the remainder theorem puzzled us all but, predictably, it was Stow who came up with the best solution.

'On our sheep farm,' he explained to us, 'we'll never need the remainder theorem. When we count our sheep there are sometimes a few missing, but we've never had a remainder.'

⁓❊⁓

'Have any of us at this Table ever needed the remainder theorem?' the Other Peter wanted to know. Nobody had. 'Well, there you are,' he went on. 'I nearly got it right, but it didn't matter. If only schools could teach the right things to the right people. Take history. It really doesn't matter any more who fought who in 1066, does it?' and he glared around the Table.

'Historians would disagree,' said Charles. 'To some people it does matter because they like to know. History can be very interesting …'

'We had a history teacher called R A Brown,' I said. 'We called him Rab. A bit of a showman he was, loved history and walked into the classroom as if he was coming on stage. To explain how the Cape Colony expanded and the frontier wars took place, he would snatch up a piece of chalk, make an extravagant U-shaped sweep on the blackboard, then add to it three straight lines that he labelled K, F and S.

'That is South Africa,' he would say, waving at his creation. 'Those

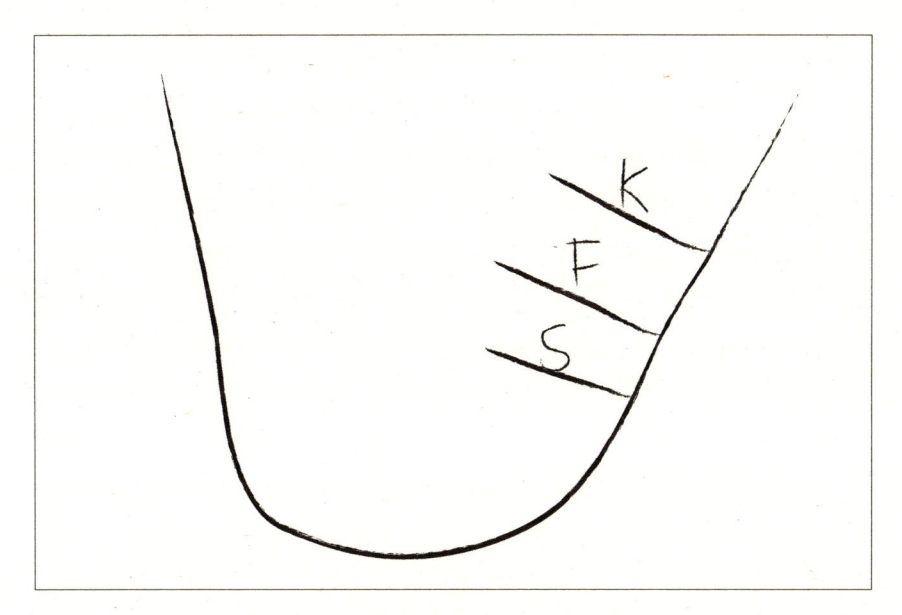

RA Brown's diagram showing river boundaries.

are rivers, all boundaries at one time or another. This whole area is where the nine Xhosa Wars took place. Your duty is to know why, where, and when; who started them, who won them, who lost them, and how they ended. Dates, gentlemen, dates – and I don't mean the things that grow on palm trees in the desert.'

While old Rab did his best to keep his explanations simple, he never quite succeeded. In addition to his three rivers, there were a lot of others, and large numbers of protagonists – the British, the Dutch, the Boers, a few French Huguenots and any number of African tribes, not to mention San and Khoi. Each group had its own leader, and each leader had his own idea about who owned what and where borders should be. Men such as Piet Retief, Sir Harry Smith and Sir Benjamin D'Urban proclaimed one boundary after another, and chiefs such as Cetshwayo, Tsili, Hintsa, Kreli and Sandile all refused to accept them.

A sixteen-year-old prophetess called Nongqawuse added confusion by announcing that on a given day the sun would rise in the west and ancestors would return bearing gifts. There were impis, commandos, platoons, regiments, mounted rifles, horse-guards, Light Horse, observers and scouts, all roaming the same area at the same time, some herding cattle, others stealing them, everyone eating them. One by one the rivers became boundaries, and there were buffer zones in which no one was allowed to be shot at or speared. One problem was that since all the rivers looked the same, no one could tell which was a boundary, so there might be entire armies guarding the wrong river ...

Another problem was to get all parties to know the same things at the same time; which war was being waged; which river they could cross and what they could do when they got to the other side. And then there were the dates. Although everything had a date, only the British knew what it was – with the result that some parties were still fighting the fourth war, long after the fifth one had begun. Some troops fought on after wars ended, others began fighting before they were declared, and on several occasions entire armies discovered they'd won the wrong war. At one point, two British platoons nearly fought each other, each believing the other to be the Boers. Fortunately they realised their mistake just in time and had a barbecue instead of a battle, slaughtering cattle that belonged either to the Boers or the Xhosas. (The British army had no cattle of its own, but its men liked beef.)

We strove mightily to comprehend, and Rab did his best to help, but after one particularly obscure lesson, he put down his piece of chalk, mopped his brow, and looked up at us with a crooked smile.

'As you can see,' he said, 'confusion was the only thing that reigned with any confidence.'

It was then that Muffy Stow, innocent expression in place, stepped in with his typical Stow-like solution. 'Sir,' he said, 'could we not simply say that for a hundred years it was all a bit of a muddle?'

'We could, Stow,' replied Rab. 'And it was. But I doubt whether there'd be high marks for that conclusion.' (In my manuscript, Tim wrote in red ink against this particular section: *Rab and Stow both right. Studied history all my life, never come across a clearer muddle than this.*)

My school yarns were spread over about four lunches, and always had someone saying, 'Oh, not again', but patiently they would let me have my turn.

'It was at Saints that I got my first writing lesson,' I said. 'Not only was English my favourite subject, our English master's name was John Forbes – nicknamed "Dagga" (South African for marijuana) because he smoked so energetically that, like Table Mountain, he had his own cloud. He was an exceptional teacher, dearly loved English, often asked us to write compositions on subjects of our own choice, then sat back to see what we were able to produce.'

From family fireside readings of the 'Saint' books, I was once inspired to write about a private detective modelled on Hoppy Uniatz, Simon Templar's bloodthirsty sidekick. Inevitably I was called into Dagga's office and told to be seated.

'This work of yours, Forbes,' he began, 'though showing faint signs of imagination, leaves a lot to be desired. As you know, I don't like hyperbole and I detest slang. Your private dick would do better as a private investigator – but even as a private dick, he would be unlikely to slay with such abandon.' (This was before movies like *Natural Born Killers*.)

He paused there, his eyes assuming the mixture of superiority, sarcasm, amusement and mild contempt that take most schoolmasters a lifetime to perfect. 'And as I have often told you,' he went on, 'the key to superior writing lies in the art of leaving certain things to the intelligence of your reader. You, Forbes, write exclusively for fools.'

'But Sir,' I exclaimed, 'then the better I write, the fewer people will read what I have written.'

He tested my words for insolence, then said in a tone of sceptical amusement, 'So you feel that most readers are fools, do you?'

'Well, Sir,' I soldiered on, 'if I thought that only brilliant people would read my story, I could merely begin: "Once there was a beautiful woman whose eyes held many secrets", and then leave the rest to them.'

Still he searched for impertinence.

'I wouldn't worry about that if I were you. I doubt whether many brilliant people will read your work. And in any debate, reducing things to absurdities is what they call a "cop out", these days.'

It took a long time for me to realise that in his sardonic teacher's mind he felt that merely discussing my work should give me encouragement. And he was right! I have never forgotten his words, and to this day I can't write anything without wondering whether it will please intelligent readers or fools!

13

Reaching the Top

To get to Burgersdorp from Bloemfontein, one has to pass Reddersburg, Smithfield, Rouxville, then turn right at Aliwal North. I once described to the Table the strange, emptiness of the country, and the lonesomeness of the road we knew so well.

'That dry old country, you understand, meant a lot to me because for the first eighteen years of my life, it was home. Solitary landscapes, sharp horizons, wispy clouds in a faded winter sky. What John Buchan called "the Old Country" – a veld of rocky hills where Boers and Britons fought one another with their Lee-Metfords and their Mausers, while blesbok and springbok stood watching them …'

I stopped for a moment, waiting for the command to get on with it.

Burgersdorp was the town nearest to our sheep farm, and our childhood couldn't have been more simple. There were four of us – Jack was the eldest, then me, then Jean, six years younger than me, then Jenny, the youngest. The farm was our world, and Burgersdorp our town. World War Two was being waged, causing nothing but hardships, anxieties, and thrift. Life on the dead level.

Jack, Mother, Jean and G F.

My father gave us jobs to do – chores such as irrigating the vegetable garden, oiling the lighting plant, cutting the grass, rolling the court, dosing sick sheep and feeding orphan lambs, day-old chicks, dogs, cats and the many baby animals we were always catching and taming as pets. At times there were far too many animals in the house and Father would vent his feelings. 'There isn't a single window sill in this house without a bloody cat on it.' 'Could you ask the bloody dogs if I can have my bed back?' 'Your bloody guineafowl have eaten my lettuce plants.' Every year we'd catch a clutch of baby guineafowl and tame them.

'Jack had a phrase he used when confronted by Father's sterner orders,' I told the Table, 'such as getting up before sunrise on a winter's morning to go to the frosty land where the ewes were lambing, to prevent the pied crows from pecking the eyes out of newly born lambs. "Nothing for it," he would say. *"Let's take the strain."* It has lasted our whole lives, for every crisis, big or small, a tennis match, an interview, an exam, finding a job, having a tooth out – we would always have to *take the strain.*'

'How well we know it,' murmured Tim.

Mother had been a teacher, I continued. She gave Jack and me lessons in the Little Room until we reached higher grades and went to boarding school. She also ran the farmhouse, attended to the garden, looked after Jean and Jennifer, and was number one on the Burgersdorp tennis team. My father, too, played on the team, and as children we would hit balls against the club wall while they played their matches – the reason why, I suppose, I have always thought that by far the best way to begin tennis is to hit against a wall. Our own tennis court was between the house and the vegetable garden, so if balls went out on the far side they'd end up in the cabbages. Most of all, it was my father who urged us to play tennis. He loved the game much more than we realised then, and it was in *our* tennis that (perhaps) he yearned for the opportunities he himself had missed. He was very fervent about it all, and sloppy tennis on our part would be the cause for his feelings to be vented, very strongly at times.

'If you want to get to the top,' he'd rant, walking up and down on the side of the court, 'you'll have to pull your socks up and do a hell of a lot better than that!'

Jenny, the youngest, was the one who started it – questioning the Top, I mean – and for me, anyway, began what was to be a lifelong contemplation of exactly where and what it was. Jenny would listen to his rants, then sometimes dare to throw spanners into his works in the form of questions. It was one of them that started my contemplation – hit the spot, if you see what I'm getting at.

'Tell us, Dad,' she asked, 'how will we know if we reach this famous Top you shout about?'

'Interesting question,' murmured the One Peter.

The Table was quiet for a while.

One of Jenny's points was, I suppose, quite straightforward. In those days there was no thought of actually making a living out of playing tennis. My father may have dreamed of one of us emulating his tennis heroes and winning some big tournament but for Jenny, just then, things like Wimbledon were much too distant. She needed a clearer definition of the Top – making it something tangible that could be reached by careful study and plain hard work. For me, again, it was her simple question that led to the eventual realisation that every one of the billions of people on earth were, in fact, fervently seeking some kind of Top of their own – riches, fame, power, recognition – or perhaps simply a dependable job, peace and happiness, or a place to go. All a bit vast and vague, you may say but there it is …

'What was your father's answer?' James asked.

'He thought for a while, and while he did so, Jenny went on to tell him that in her opinion there was no such thing as a Top that suited everyone – and that her Top might be different from his. When he asked her to explain, her reply actually echoed everything I've just said – amazing, when you think of it, because she was only about twelve at the time!'

'Shouldn't everyone have to find their own Top?' she asked. 'One man's top may be another man's bottom.'

For a few moments there was a thoughtful silence around the Table which, in a way, was typical. They loved topics, those chaps, even well-worn ones that needed re-examining. Where was the Top? I think it

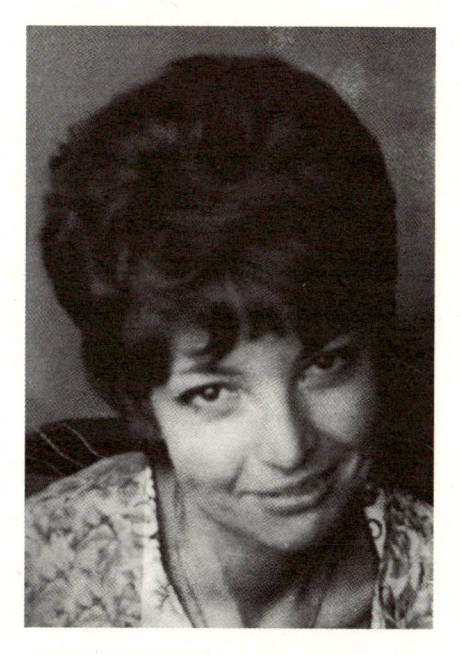

Jenny. Everyone has their own Top.

was the One Peter who asked about my father's reaction to Jenny's theory.

'In spite of his sternness he was a thoughtful man,' I said. 'He had, in his own way, reached a Top of his own, being an energetic, honourable man, a good farmer and a diligent father, with a fine sense of humour just beneath his stern exterior. Perhaps he realised this but he urged us, his children, to aim for higher things, for if ever there was a man who admired greatness, it was he.'

Richard was the first to give an appraisal. 'Jenny was right, of course. There are a variety of Tops, as you call them, and a useful life is certainly one of them. But there must have been others, higher up, that he thought you should aim for – perhaps the kind that Shakespeare had in mind when he wrote *"Some men are born great, some achieve greatness, and some have greatness thrust upon them".'*

As if to test the validity of these words, Charles murmured to himself, 'Some men are born at the Top, some achieve the Top, and some have the Top thrust on them. Not quite the same. You can't really be born at the Top, can you?'

'You can if your mother is Queen Elizabeth,' said James. 'And I suppose Prince William will also have a Top thrust on him. All he'll be left to do is achieve it.'

'Which is the hardest part,' said Tim. 'I have always hoped to have a Top thrust on me.'

'Don't worry, Tim,' said Charles. 'You have reached one of the rarest Tops of all. Trader Horn saw to that!' (One of Tim's finest books, *Tramp Royal*, traced the unique life of Aloysius Smith, alias Trader Horn.)

It was then that Mark stepped in, out of sheer habit, I suspect. 'I think Jenny and Richard are both right,' he said. 'The question goes right back to the Greek philosophers, who separated it into two key areas of thought – *kleos* and *arête*. Their meanings overlap, *kleos* more to do with fame, *arête* with virtue. Socrates, a *kleos* man, believed that unless you achieved fame, something exceptional you see, there was no purpose to your life. Plato disagreed; his doctrine supported *arête*, so he said that an unexceptional person who was hard-working and virtuous had merit, and had also reached a Top.'

'*A* Top, perhaps, but not *the* Top,' mused Charles. 'You can't get to *the* Top by just being virtuous and having merit.'

'Well, according to Plato, you can,' cried James. 'We've all reached the Top via virtue and merit!' He glared at Charles. 'You can't argue with a man like Plato, can you?'

'Perhaps we should simply combine their theories,' said Charles, thoughtfully. 'I think I'm right in saying Richard was right when he said Jenny was right. James's Top may easily be Tim's bottom. It simply depends on how James looks at it.'

'Tim's bottom?' said James, looking deliberately alarmed.

Tim frowned for a moment, then suddenly let fly with a mysterious quotation: ' *"Tee hee," quoth she, and clapped the window to.*'

'Chaucer!' cried Mark, triumphantly. '*The Miller's Tale*! The old carpenter and his bawdy young wife with a lusty bottom ... Fifteen love, Tim!'

14

The Winding Road

Burgersdorp stopovers were emotional interludes, I told the Table. Jack now lives in a Karoo house in the old part of town, but I still sense the presence of the farm, feel the dry, silky flow of summer air, and look forward to days that echo with memories and the latest yarns – for Jack always has a few – like when cousin Sandy sucked on the end of our garden hose to find out why the water wasn't getting through, and swallowed the little brown frog that had moved in. Or mother's foot slipped and she fell into the sheep-dip and got sanitised.

Jack, now eighty-three, has slowed down a bit, but we still have a game of chess, a Scotch and soda, and natter on about the old days. Dunkeld, our farm, had to be sold because it was too close to town. What had once been a blessing became a serious security problem, and with Dunkeld went our childhood memories, our mountain, the old tennis court, the dam, our yacht, the river pools, the Little Room … Well, never mind! The Little Room! The very mention of it brings tears to my eyes. When I paused, Tim asked why.

It was my father's study, if you can call it that, I explained, but for us it was the Little Room. Apart from his desk, and a table for our schoolwork, it had chairs and a sofa clustered round a fireplace, as it was our winter room for family forums, chess games, reading aloud, scoldings, mugs of cocoa. Above the fireplace was a long mantelpiece cluttered with a vase of flowers, playing cards, samples of wool, spare keys, a few shotgun cartridges, chess pieces, a bushman's flint, an orange or two – always comforting in an untidy way. On one wall was a bookshelf, and on the other a rack of guns, a photo of Winston Churchill and a framed print of *If*. God, I still miss that room!

There was silence, so I went on.

On the evening before we left for boarding school, my father called Jack and me into the Little Room, sat us down and solemnly told us that from that day on, life was to be a long and winding road. We'd be on it, he said, steering our own courses, and he'd gone on to give us the kind of messages that fathers used to give sons in those days, but with rare compassion in his voice – almost a sadness, if you know what I mean, for he was a no-nonsense kind of man – life isn't always fair; look people in the eye; remember who you are; never make excuses; look before you leap, fight your own battles, and so on.

'It's uphill much of the way,' he'd continued, getting back to his winding road. 'There'll be straight stretches, but also nasty curves. When you come to forks in the road be sure to read the signposts, and think carefully, "is that the way I want to go?" You may not have the answers, but make sure you ask the questions.'

The occasion was a tense one, I can tell you. One of those moments when you feel life is about to change and you'd much rather it stayed the way it was. I was twelve, Jack fourteen, and neither he nor I had ever before left home. We were too busy with our own woes to realise our parents were just as upset as we were. I remember walking about the old house, taking a last look at things, and wondering what on earth my father had been talking about. Only much later I twigged that the winding road with its signposts was his way of letting us know that we had to think for ourselves. He was one of three brothers, all of whom had joined up to fight in the First World War, all of them ending up as pilots in the Royal Flying Corps. Gordon, the middle uncle, and the one after whom I am named, first joined the infantry and was one of the few survivors of the battle of Delville Wood. He then joined the RFC to be with his brothers and, aged twenty-one, was killed over the English Channel.

'He survived Delville Wood!' cried Tim. 'And was then killed in an aeroplane? If that isn't irony, I don't know what is …' Tim had made a close study of Delville Wood for his book *The Great Silence*.

'I was once very nearly killed in an aeroplane,' began the Other Peter, only to be silenced by James.

'I was once nearly killed riding my bicycle,' he said. 'Tim's talking about *supreme* irony, not the common or garden type.'

※

My father was passionate about his Scottish ancestry, proud, I tell you, always on about James Watt, Alexander Bell, Stevenson, etc. In Scotland, apparently, all roads were winding. He would quote Robert Burns:

> *O life! Thou art a galling load,*
> *Along a rough and weary road,*
> *To wretches such as I!*

Words that made Mother angry: 'Oh for heaven's sake, Duncan! You're not a wretch with a galling load and not all Scots are wandering vagabonds!'

His father, John Forbes, a Latin teacher, had been sent to South Africa as a cure for tuberculosis – consumption they called it, and dry air was the only known remedy. So, part of the clan had ended up in the Karoo, and the two farms, Craigievar and Dunkeld, were born.

My brother Jack's son and daughter still farm near Burgersdorp, one of the best towns in the region. There are signs of wear of course, but the two old oak trees on the Town Square still stand. When Jack and I were children we once collected a hatful of acorns under those trees, and took them home to Dunkeld. My father made us plant them along the water furrow that led to the vegetable patch. I'll never forget what he told us. 'They'll make nice, deep shade and you'll be able to sit under them with *your* children and have *your* tea.' He had no doubt about the longevity of the trees, the shade or the tea, but only whether the acorns would germinate – which they never did, because that year there was a drought and the water furrow ran dry. We were so busy keeping the sheep alive that we forgot to water the acorns.

In certain moods, I could write a book about Burgersdorp as it used to be – warm-hearted, proud of itself, informal and untidy in an organised sort of way. It had character. A mountain with its name on the side of it; two Boer War blockhouses near the nine-hole golf course, two churches, a rugby ground, bowling green, a stockfair every Friday. A Greek café, barber's shop with a sugar-stick pole, post office, general dealer, chemist, creamery and shoemaker. A British tailor named Bill Motley made my father's suits. A baker's shop where ladies with powdered faces could bring their specialities – Mrs Lotter's scones,

Mrs Lategan's koeksisters, Mrs Motley's lemon tart, Mollie's meringues, Hentie's Boston bread, old Mrs Steytler's pancakes and Mrs Slater's white bread. Strong ladies, the wives of strong men.

'Salt of the earth, mainly,' my father used to say. 'Occasionally a bad egg.' His other labels for the menfolk were varied – 'nice old sticks', 'bloody windbags', 'straight shooters', 'fly by nights', 'wets', 'rotten apples', decent enough chaps – and a farmer with a new red Chev thought himself a hell of a lad. But, fortunately, 'salt of the earth' was most common.

'Oh, for heaven's sake, Gordon …' That was Charles. But it was a mild reprimand because he loved the Karoo. In fact, in certain moods none of them seemed to mind my droning on.

You get unusual people in small towns, I told the Table. I had a friend named Ronnie Roberts, who remained a farmer while I played tennis. He and his wife Sheila had five children in four years, their firstborn son was called Ronnie, and his boss-boy, yes, boss-boy, can you believe, who had a son at the same time, also named him Ronnie. When the two Ronnies got a bit older, they reared a baby baboon whose mother was shot in a hunt, and called him Ronnie too, so there were in fact four Ronnies on the farm – *Groot* (big) Ronnie, *Klein* (small) Ronnie, *Swart* (black) Ronnie, and *Bobbejaan* (baboon) Ronnie. For years the three youngsters were inseparable – too many adventures to tell you about, damn funny some of them – but when the two boys went to boarding school *Groot* Ronnie had to look after *Bobbejaan* Ronnie and sometimes took him to the Jubilee Hotel pub where he learned to drink beer out of a bottle. Apparently what he really liked was peppermint liqueur. According to *Groot* Ronnie, that is. Problem was, he couldn't hold his liquor …

'Are you lying to us, Forbes?' interrupted Charles. 'We're gullible, but there are limits.'

'Absolutely not. Go to Burgersdorp and there're witnesses; in fact the chaps at the pub loved *Bobbejaan* Ronnie. Bought him peppermint liqueurs. Even tried to get him interested in rugby …'

'Far-fetched,' said Richard. 'Don't put it in your book.'

'All the farmers had rudimentary first-aid kits to treat minor injuries,' I went on warily, having left a silence in case of other gripes, 'because there would be incessant complaints from workers. *"My kop is seer"* (my head is sore), *"My rug is seer"* (my back is sore) – teeth, chests, stomachs, right down to knees and feet. Treatment was limited to things like aspirin, headache powders, bicarbonate of soda, Vicks Vapour Rub, castor oil, Dettol, bandages and so on. One farmer, Edwards I think his name was, used aspirin only. He then bought Smarties, separated them into colours and displayed them in a row of glass jars. His broad-spectrum cure was a course of aspirin and Smarties, with instructions to take "two white pills, one red pill and one yellow pill three times a day". Funny thing, old Edwards told my father, the red pills worked best.'

'Perhaps they'd cure my hay fever,' said James.

But that was the old Burgersdorp, I concluded. It's still the best town in the area, but it's fighting a losing battle – potholes, plastic bags, old car parts. It's hard to believe that our beloved Dunkeld still lies out there, with its cliffs, its river, the rock pool in the canyon we used to call Sheba's Bath. Even the remains of our yacht must be somewhere, but the dam's broken. No water. I'll never forget the day Jack and I sat high up on that mountain with our father, eating the sandwiches that Mother had cut, and watching a little fire boil our coffee kettle, while two black eagles turned in the sky above their nest.

'Well, at least they can never destroy our mountain,' Father said suddenly.

He must have had a premonition, even then. Our mountain is still there. Probably not the same eagles …

15

The Forbes Family Band

'When you leave Burgersdorp you drive south on a road that runs past a farm named Rosslands. Now there's a memory, if I may say so!'

I'd been telling these yarns while the Rugby World Cup was on the go and the All Blacks were the favoured team. Both Peters were rugby experts and came up with analyses and predictions austere enough to increase the need for Irish coffee. Meanwhile the mere mention of All Blacks caused memories so strange that initially I decided to keep quiet about them. Nonetheless, towards the end of lunch, the mood had mellowed enough for Richard to say to me: 'Well, tell us about this memory, Gordon. If it's not long …'

'I've always wanted to be a musician,' I began. 'A good one, I mean. Mother was an accomplished pianist. Father played what he called "the fiddle", and we used to have musical evenings around the piano. Then one day Father went to East London to a wool sale. It must have been a good one because at the music shop where I'd bought the Benny Goodman record, he bought a saxophone, a clarinet and a set of drums. We were ecstatic – set up the drums near the piano and, from that moment on a variety of noises came out of our living room, sounds that went on for months, to some extent moderated by my mother's piano playing. Then we had a windfall.'

The half-brother of Ronnie Roberts, I continued – yes, exactly, the same *Groot* Ronnie who taught Baboon Ronnie to drink beer – was a young man named Mikey de Villiers. Different fathers, I suppose. Mikey was a proper dance band musician who worked in Bloemfontein, and had taken a sabbatical to help his stepfather on the farm. Musical to the core, he was. Played piano and sax and was happy to teach us, and lead our motley group with his saxophone, while mother played her stride piano and we tagged along behind. Jean played the drums. She was around eleven at the time and, amazingly, she was able to copy the drummers on our gramophone recordings (Father had by then got used to Benny Goodman, Glenn Miller, et al. – even Count Basie). We slowly got better, so that after a year or so, when Mikey had to leave us, we found we could manage – badly missing him, but keeping a beat and finding ourselves playing for country dances and show balls. The Forbes Family Band we were called – the only band for miles around, and we played for the fun of it, didn't dare ask for mammon.

In 1949 the All Blacks toured South Africa. It was the last time that they would travel by sea, and sports teams in those days made the most of tours by playing as many games as possible – tests, provinces, and games against Barbarians, universities, and so on. Our area was called North-Eastern Districts and we had a rugby team. Following the game, the evening's entertainment was left up to the Burgersdorp people, who organised a grand ball in the shearing shed of Rosslands – a sheep farm with a big shed that had inside it all the space and impedimenta needed for shearing sheep but, if cleared, it had plenty of room for music, dancing, eating, drinking, and in fact all that country folk needed to give it what they called a serious thrash. Anyway, a ball was given, the two rugby teams were invited, and the Forbes Family Band was asked to provide the music.

Jack and I practised like mad, had our hair cut and our tuxedos cleaned. The shearing shed was lined with bales of hay and festooned with leaves and flowers, and our band was set up in the small pen reserved for injured sheep. A more serious problem was to find enough girls. The NE Districts hadn't an unlimited supply, but urgent calls were sent out with surprising success, and even a few younger married women offered their services. Everyone donned party clothes (the All Blacks wore blazers and ties) and the party got under way.

When we began to play, Jean, with her urchin hairdo and winning way, caught the fancy of the New Zealanders, and spent the whole evening surrounded by huge, burly and good-natured Kiwis who teased her incessantly, while the rest of us gamely played our repertoire of simple songs – *In the Mood, Twelfth Street Rag, Beautiful Dreamer, The Blue Danube, Whispering, Bye Bye Blues,* and two Scottish tunes, *Annie Laurie* and *Bonnie Dundee,* that my father liked and that Mikey had helped us alter from Scottish folksongs to foxtrots.

I'll never forget that evening. There was a huge barbecue and plenty of beer ...

It was James who first responded. 'Well, it just goes to show,' he said thoughtfully.

'What does it go to show?' Mark wanted to know. As a true headmaster he liked definition.

'How things have changed. I doubt very much whether the All

Blacks of today would go to a shearing shed near Burgersdorp on a Tuesday night to dance to the music of the Forbes Family Band.'

'Mammon,' muttered the One Peter. 'Sportsmen will do virtually anything, if they get enough of it …'

'So will writers,' said James.

After Steynsberg, the road runs out into the veld between the iconic mountains Teebus and Koffiebus (Tea-pot and Coffee-pot) and gets to Middelburg, where my grandfather was first sent as a cure for his consumption. From here on the distances seem greater, the road straighter, running through an immense sort of emptiness – profound Karoo landscapes, yes, the word does apply, huge cloud patterns and pastel colours. Graaff-Reinet, Aberdeen, Willowmore. At last Uniondale, from where it's really only a hop, step and a jump to Plett, if you risk the Prince Alfred Pass. In earlier days we would always go that way, revelling in the simple gravel road and superb mountain views. Now that road is too unpredictable, so we go the long way round, through George and back down the coast past Wilderness, Sedgefield, Knysna, to finally reach Plettenberg Bay.

16

The Beautiful Bay

Our old farmhouse is a home from home. When the family arrives this year it will be the twenty-first time we've all gathered together for Christmas. Both my children, Gavin and Ashley (James is unmarried) have two sons each, now aged between fifteen and twenty, and the old house, the lagoon, the beaches, the fishing spots, in fact the whole of Plett has become their own. As small children they liked to wade in the lagoon (then a wetland of sea-grass, mullet, turtles and hermit crabs), always needing adult protection to guard against the water-potamus and jelly-bottles that lurked there – the water-potamus was their own invention, and the jelly-bottles a combination of the jellyfish and bluebottles that came in with the tide, occasionally to sting unwary children.

From the veranda of the house you can see waves breaking, and nearer by the lagoon with its sand faults, seabirds and fishermen trying their luck. We love the beauty of the place. Once, long ago, when Frances and I had braved the pass, we came to a particular spot where the view opened up. It was late afternoon, with a summer rain shower

The Old Farmhouse in Plettenberg Bay.

Gavin and his wife, Venetia.

on the go and shafts of sunlight streaming through the clouds – and suddenly, there it was, the whole bay, gleaming like a jewel in pure white light. On arrival we always go to The Lookout Deck for a piece of fish and a close-up of the sea, and when all is well, the first night in Plett is a sigh of relief …

⁂

True to my word, I pursued the elusive Rainbow Room Syndrome. It suddenly occurred to me that what already existed in Plett were coffee clubs where groups of men met to sort things out, and I wondered whether coffee and buns could give the same stimulus as wine and bivalve molluscs.

With this in mind, I decided to investigate a coffee bar called the Double Shot, where an ex-architect called Angus apparently arranged philosophical gatherings on a regular basis. I used to call on an Angus at Anglo American Properties to sell him light fittings; I wondered whether this could be the same Angus, so I went to the Double Shot and, sure enough, it could. There he was, heavier than he used to be, surrounded by about seven men and two women, all at a long table, drinking coffee and knee-deep in philosophical matters. Guardedly, I entered.

'Ah, it's you,' Angus said. 'Not today, I'm afraid. Your prices are far too high.'

'Come on, Angus. Force yourself!'

In a few words we'd resurrected conversations last used fifty years ago. Angus made a place for me next to him, introduced me to the others, and I remember again being struck by the fact that Plett people seemed a friendly lot. As a newcomer, I listened for a while, and began to realise that there was potential. Angus must have been an inveterate coffee club man, because they'd named one of their coffees after him – a 'Brown Angus', they called it – which he insisted I try. When it came, it seemed to contain every coffee-producing ingredient known to man.

'It's got a kick to it,' said Angus in a satisfied voice. 'Have one and you won't forget where you parked your car.'

'Do Plett men lose their cars?'

'Only occasionally after lunch.'

If ever there was a realist, it was Angus. I told him about the Rainbow Room, and asked him whether he thought it possible to emulate it in Plett.

'Absolutely,' he said. 'Some of the best brains in the country end up in Plett. The problem might be that the moment they get to Plett they unwind. Like clocks, in a manner of speaking. They may have stopped, but the mechanism's intact and it's simply a matter of rewinding them. Give them a bump and off they go …'

He went on to warn me not to get too enthusiastic about the men who lived on Beachy Head because they had their own coffee machines and didn't know where the Double Shot was.

'Very few of them ever venture north of the Piesang River. No, Gordon, lower your sights. It's this layer where the truth lies,' and he glanced around the table to underline his meaning. 'We've long since realised it's no use being high-powered in Plett. It's better to be on the esoteric side, read poetry, and become well known for doing untypical things – exploring caves, studying bird-life or walking to the South Pole. People sculpt, paint, collect things, and so on. Some say they're writing books, but very few get finished.

'One thing about Plett men,' he mused on, 'they've pretty much perfected the ability to stay calm. Setbacks have to be pretty severe to cause panic. For instance, only the other day in a queue at the bank I heard someone telling his friend that someone had just broken into his car and taken his laptop, his phone, his golf clubs and, worst of all, a Woolworths chicken he'd bought for lunch. "So we'll have to have fish and chips at the Ski-Boat Club." Plett men are happy men …'

Here he paused for a while, then went on in his musing way. 'Some of them are downright useful. Gerry makes the best apricot jam in the world, David supplies the whole coastline with lettuce, John makes olive oil and wine. Joan looks after the environment, Lady Annabel raises money for charities, and there's an Italian chappie out on the airport road who makes Italian ice cream better than Italian Italians. Patience is a virtue. They've been trying to create a small boat harbour since the turn of the last century, but not a sod's been turned. No. You won't get the same kind of man you get in Johannesburg. But you'll get an interesting bunch if you persevere.'

'They shouldn't be *too* clever,' I said. 'One likes to keep up.'

'No need to worry about that,' he replied, assuring me that the minute Plett men got too clever they were taken down a peg or two. 'Old Tom's had to downgrade his conversation. Knew far too much about the Khoi people and their history …'

I continued my observations with growing interest until one of the members suddenly said, 'My treat today. It's my birthday.'

The group began to disperse, my Brown Angus was gratis, and I realised Angus was right. There were very clever men in Plett, but they were of a different ilk.

'What ilk are we?' Tim asked. His question initiated a discussion about the Table's place in mankind, culminating in the Other Peter suggesting that we were not really an ilk at all. More a rare breed. Richard maintained that we were not as rare as he thought we were.

'On the other hand, we might be,' said James thoughtfully. 'Take Tim. You could travel the world and not find another Tim' – to which Tim responded: 'People travelling the world may not be looking for another Tim.' Turning to me he asked, 'Did any interesting discussion take place?'

'Certainly,' I replied. 'Granted, hearing problems are rife, so at times people discuss different things at the same time. Oddly enough, they often reach agreement. There are periods of coherence when serious problems are solved. For example the subject of World Cup Cricket arose and it was agreed that the Proteas (the South African team) would win if they could avoid choking at critical moments. Simon's view was that they by now must have realised that choking didn't work. Nic mentioned that there was no need to worry because the Proteas' coach had made a new game plan in which choking was abolished.'

Choking is not something you can abolish, I added tentatively. I knew a tennis player who thought he'd abolished choking, but the very next time he had a match point he tossed the ball up to serve and it went sideways.

'Writers can also choke …'

Meanwhile, the term 'game plan' had struck a chord in my mind. These days, game plans in sport are very much in fashion – usually contrived by crafty coaches and managers after careful study of relevant videos and opponents' tactics. The theory is that if players don't have game plans they don't know what to do next. In our day the term didn't exist. We would watch our adversaries playing their matches until we thought we knew their strengths and weaknesses, and then adjust our own games as best we could. If, for example, you were up against Butch Buchholz, you'd avoid his forehand; it would be silly to attack Rosewall's backhand, or try to lob over Pancho Gonzales's head. In a way, I suppose, these were game plans, but we never really wrote them down. Perhaps we should have …

17

The Game Plan

'Talking of game plans,' I said to the Table, 'one of the best game plans was made by Arthur Ashe when he beat Jimmy Connors to win Wimbledon in 1975.'

I felt on safer ground because it was within my bailiwick.

Now I've never liked the new meaning of the word 'cool', I continued, mainly because I like the old one better – a cool breeze, or a cool day, or even a cool reply to a leading question. Now you hear of cool dudes, or cool music being played by cool groups wearing cool jeans with holes in them. Arthur Ashe was cool – not in its old meaning (he was the same temperature as everyone else) but in its new – polite, clever, warm but aloof, in a place of his own. The archetypal cool dude.

Given all that, he and I were friends. He was a black man, opposed to racism, and committed to getting rid of hostility between whites and blacks; I was a white South African, and despite the fact that he took for granted that I too was opposed to apartheid, I sensed a covert reserve whenever we were together. One day our fragile friendship was given an unusual boost.

THE GAME PLAN

Virginia Wade, and her legs.

In those days the BBC used to end their daily Wimbledon coverage with a 'Match of the Day'. One evening, as guests of an American businessman, Arthur and I found ourselves together in the TV room watching these highlights, on this occasion featuring Virginia Wade in a match on the Centre Court. We watched for a while, making only the usual monosyllabic remarks common to players watching tennis together. I had always felt that Virginia was one of the most striking players, and there we were, Arthur and me, watching her play, when after one spectacular leap I happened to murmur to myself, 'heavens, what legs!' – at which Arthur looked up at me with a sudden, warm smile and said, 'd'you also think so?'

Now one may not immediately think of Virginia Wade's legs as being able to soothe latent racial feelings, but the fact that they appealed to both Arthur and me somehow made us comfortable with each other – if you see what I mean …

'We're trying our best but it's damned hard to get a conclusion out of you,' muttered the One Peter. 'What about the game plan?'

The Wimbledon final when Ashe beat Connors must rate as one of the most cerebral tennis matches ever played, I said. You must remember that Ashe had never before beaten him, and that at age thirty-two he was well aware of it. Yet in that match he had the nerve, not only to target winning, but also to make plans and carry them out. Granted, surprise was on his side. No one, least of all Connors, expected the astuteness and determination of Ashe's attack – although he should have been forewarned by Ashe's path to the final.

To win Wimbledon you have to win seven matches in a row and, quite naturally, they become increasingly harder. That year Ashe beat Bob Hewitt in the first round, Brian Gottfried in the third, Marty Riessen in the fourth, Bjorn Borg in the quarter-finals, Tony Roche in the semis and, as it turned out, Jimmy Connors in the final. Being Ashe, he would have made plans for every round, but the one he devised for his match against Connors must rate as one of the most subtle conceptions in tennis history. The esteemed tennis writer David Gray wrote: *'He approached it almost as though he was to play Connors at chess, with a strategy deeply considered and carefully rehearsed.'*

Gray went on to explain the tactics in detail – a complicated and technically difficult combination of short, angled shots, volleys and lobs, especially designed to exploit a weakness that Connors probably didn't even realise he had. As it was, he was so taken by surprise by

Arthur's tactics that he quickly lost the first two sets, rallied in the third, then lost the fourth when Ashe stuck to his guns. In his book, *The Outsider*, Connors himself gives Ashe credit:

> *Arthur's game was flawless, that day. He had figured out a way to play me. By reducing the speed and length of his shots, he constantly brought me into the net before passing me or lobbing me.*

We were astonished by Arthur's win. Not only is it difficult to make and stick so rigidly to a game plan, but to execute it for four sets, the delicate angles and volleys that Ashe asked of himself, was devilishly hard to do and, with it all, I detected in his manner an abiding dignity and respect for tennis – so different from the cocky demeanour of his opponent. So it was that Arthur won Wimbledon, and by doing so 'had it made', as the other players said. An all-American hero, he was lauded as an icon, awarded virtually every honour his country had to offer. Many believed he would have made a fine presidential candidate, for his diplomatic skills were as good as his tennis. He wrote a moving book called *Days of Grace*, and with a lovely wife and daughter, was destined for the legendary 'happy ever after' ending. But it was not to be. Fate stepped in, apparently unwilling to condone so much good fortune in one man.

One day, out of the blue, this superb athlete was struck down. After a series of mysterious chest pains, an angiogram revealed that the arteries in his heart were all but closed, and he underwent a quadruple bypass operation. There followed complications, a second round of heart surgery, and a few years later, paralysis in his right arm which doctors discovered to be a disease linked to Aids. Subsequent tests revealed that he was in fact HIV positive, the result of a contaminated blood transfusion during his second operation. There were no antiretroviral drugs in those days. He died at the age of forty-nine, showing to the end the same combination of stoicism and courage as in his tennis.

Both Double Shot and Rainbow Room philosophers applauded Ashe's amazing achievements, as intrigued as I was by his game plan, and as saddened by his death.

The Table fellows lapsed into a reflective silence that was finally broken by Tim saying that his game plan was to go home for a nap. Charles said that he allowed Destiny to plan on his behalf, and Richard announced he'd use the same plan he'd used the day before.

'So be it,' said James. 'Pass the bottle.'

18

A Worthwhile Passion

'You can't simply put tennis aside,' said Richard testily, laying down the sheets of paper I'd given him. He'd taken a paternal attitude to my writing, and disapproved when it went off at a tangent. 'Tennis is your life.'

'Tennis *was* my life. I *used* to sit in locker rooms and hear what Ken Rosewall was saying, see Rod Laver whittling at his racket-grips, see Roy Emerson scrubbing his tennis shorts. I'd have drinks with managers, talk to referees, argue with linesmen. Now, it's different. I don't know the game any more – what Nadal says to Federer, or whether Murray wears a jockstrap, or why they need so many rackets. All I have when I see them are flashes of memory – brief jolts of feeling that are of little or no interest to anyone but me.'

'All right, all right,' said Richard mildly. 'However, give tennis a chance. When you have these jolts, write them down before they go away.'

'They can be tedious. For instance, I might suddenly see the old farm court with creepers twined in its surround, and the jug of water that my mother used to place on the sand near the gate. She too wanted us to be good at tennis, but she didn't make a fuss about it. I suppose I must have wanted to be a champion, but I didn't have the powerful calling that, say, Gary Player must have had when he decided to make golf his life. Dedication, discipline, total commitment to his cause – standing in front of mirrors, telling himself he was going to win Grand Slams.'

'I doubt whether any of us have ever been called as powerfully as Gary Player was,' said Charles. 'I'm sure we've all heard voices but, for instance, I've never had a loud call from a burning bush: "Charles! Thou shalt write history!" What about you, Tim? Ever had callings?'

'Only dulcet ones,' said Tim. 'If I'd wanted a burning bush, I'd have had to set fire to one myself.'

'Abe Segal once told me that if he'd stood in front of a mirror and said "you're going to win Wimbledon", the guy in the mirror would have said "who, me?"'

'All very interesting,' said James, 'but what kind of calling gets you from a shearing shed to the Wimbledon Centre Court?'

'Serendipity perhaps,' I replied. 'The whole family went to see Don Budge playing an exhibition match against Bobby Riggs in Queenstown – 1946, I think it was. They were touring South Africa as professionals with two other Americans, Carl Earn and Welby van Horn. I'll never forget the excitement of seeing that tennis. The sheer wonder and surprise of it ... One talks about beauty! Well, Budge's backhand was beautiful – flowing, elegant, even and effortless. In comparison, take Nadal's double-hander. Very effective, of course, but he gives the ball a clout – like swatting a giant fly ...'

'Things *have* changed,' said Mark, ignoring my backhands. 'Can you imagine Federer and Djokovic playing an exhibition match in Queenstown?'

'Mammon,' said the Other Peter. 'Give them enough, and they'd play in Cathcart' (the next small town on from Queenstown).

༺༻

A more detailed answer to James's question would have been that there was enough competitive tennis in the country towns of my youth to create interest and competition. The bigger ones such as Aliwal North, Queenstown, King William's Town, East London and Port Elizabeth, all held tournaments, both junior and senior, into which my father dutifully entered us. There was even a tournament in Idutywa which Eric Sturgess once won. The tennis clubs in those towns got into our blood – silly, I know, but we loved them, loved the excitement of the tournaments, wanted to play and suddenly, as wide-eyed teenagers, found that tennis was our game.

At 10 pm one night in 1951, on the little Burgersdorp station, I caught the train to Johannesburg. I'd been selected to partner a player called Redmund Geach in the Border team to compete in the under-eighteen junior inter-provincial event at Ellis Park. Another street of dreams. Johannesburg was vast, and the Ellis Park stadium seemed very grand, as did the Parktown house of people called Sacco, who had agreed to be our hosts. Mr Sacco, the tennis people told me breathlessly, owned mines, played tennis and was an important businessman. Mrs Sacco was very nice, and there were two bouncy children, Desmond and Sally – so friendly and natural in that palatial home that I assumed all Johannesburg people lived that way.

'Johannesburg people are different from us,' I told my mother when I got home. 'They own mines, live in palaces, have two new cars, and side tables with silver trays and whisky in crystal flasks.'

'I don't think that *everyone* in Johannesburg owns a mine, Gordie,' she responded. 'Count your own blessings. We have a mountain and a river and one car, we don't drink whisky, and our wool doesn't have to be dug out of the ground.'

We were well beaten in that inter-provincial. I sat in the Ellis Park stands, watching the finals, and wondering about my game. The Transvaal and Natal juniors were much too good for us, more experienced, more worldly, and I remember the mixture of feelings that came to me up in those stands – admiration, chagrin, doubt, fear, anger, yes, anger, thank goodness for the anger because despite my disappointment it goaded me into taking up the challenge. Those finals egged me on, and that journey opened up a whole new world of glamour and adventure – amplified by the energy of youth, with gusts of excitement that knocked the breath out of me. Youth!

'But you fellows know it, you've all felt it, remember the strength of it!' and they nodded at me, deep in thought, strangely solemn for a minute or two.

Something more must have got through to me on those stands, because I made a few notes, mental ones, I guess. I remember them vaguely and they're still valid.

> *I must get better, and I need a weapon. Forget style, find a way to win points.*
> *Serve, get to the net and volley. Don't fiddle about at the back.*
> *Don't make excuses (my father's credo).*

A WORTHWHILE PASSION

Watch him (all opponents were called him). Think. Why is he better than you? Get to know his weakness.
Don't rush.
Watch the ball.

Here, to some extent, I missed the point. Watching the ball was correct, but the most important part was missing. Tagged on should have been the words *and keep your head still when you hit the ball.* Watching it does steady your head, but not enough. In all sports where bat hits ball, the simple words 'keep your head still when you hit the ball' are vital, and would have saved me hours of frustration. Watching the ball alone is not enough — the head might move a fraction of a second before impact, you lift your eyes and you mess it up — and worst of all, it happens more often on 'the big point'!

As with most theories, there is a rider to all that. In 1963, I spent the week of the US doubles championships in Boston, living in the house of Foster Furcolo, ex-governor of Massachusetts, and sharing the guest suite with Rod Laver. Each morning we would go to the club for long practice sessions — it was so easy because Rod was at the height of his fame, and there were always plenty of courts and balls available. Now I've said time and again that Rod had the best-ever 'eye' in tennis and, with Lew Hoad, was the cleanest striker of the ball I've ever seen. (Now, of course, Federer intrudes.) I, meanwhile, was obsessed with 'watching the ball' — to the extent that I spent hours trying to get my eyes to observe that elusive split second when the strings actually make contact with it.

Rod and I would chat when we changed sides, and suddenly I knew that it was a perfect opportunity to ask him how he did it — what precisely he saw and felt at the critical moment. I remember thinking that it would be rather like asking Mozart what he heard when the orchestra struck a chord! Anyway, at an opportune time, I asked Rodney, 'What exactly happens when you play a shot? Do you actually see the ball hit the strings of your racket?'

'Don't know exactly,' was his cheerful reply. 'Haven't really thought about it.' He paused for a little while to think. 'I see the ball coming, and at what seems the right time, I hit it.'

To my credit, I laughed. 'Come on, Rod, there must be more to it than that!'

'Not really,' he replied. Rubbing his thumb and forefinger together like a tailor feeling a piece of cloth, he went on, 'It's a feeling. I kind of know where the other guy is, where the court is, I see the ball, I feel I know what I have to do, so I do it. I guess I must be watching the ball, but I don't really think about it. Come on, it's your serve, let's play …'

I must admit that his words confounded me, but the more I thought about his answer, the more I understood it. In those simple words, he'd succeeded in revealing that tiny, subtle difference that I'd pondered for so long – the distinction between regular faculty, yes, straight talent, I suppose, and genius. All people with genius had a special gift of their own that made skill look easy. Mozart with his music, Nicklaus with his golf, Fischer with his chess, Einstein with his physics. They felt things that others couldn't feel …

MIDNIGHT... AND THE CHAMP TWISTS

Jean doing the twist with Rod Laver the night he won Wimbledon.

19

A Wider World

My true tennis career really began when I got a letter from a lady named Doreen Malcolm asking whether I could accompany the present South African junior champion, Gordon Talbot, on a six-month tour of the English tournament circuit. In those days, travelling by ship was inexpensive enough (Father paid the fare) and in a small way the tournaments helped with expenses (private accommodation and rail fares). Fifty pounds, Mrs Malcolm said, would be enough to see me through, and in a savings account I had at least fifty pounds, so expense-wise, I was home and dry. These days it's hard to explain the thrill of a journey like that ...

Our ship was called the *Winchester Castle*, and the fare included a first-class ticket on the boat train that ran from Southampton to Waterloo. Gordon and I had a compartment to ourselves and were invited to go to the dining car where we were served a full English breakfast by an English steward in white livery and black bow tie. Bacon, eggs and sausages, served on thick British Rail plates, with white cloth napkins, tea, toast and marmalade. 'How do you boys like your eggs? Coffee or tea, sir? Will that be all, sir?' Two eighteen-year-olds being pampered by a middle-aged Englishman doing his job with pride. We left Southampton at seven and when we arrived at the King Charles Hotel on the Cromwell Road another Englishman carried our bags up three flights of stairs and in the small hotel dining room they served us another breakfast.

'I know a place where they serve sausages and grilled tomato with bacon and egg,' said Richard. 'And coffee in white china coffee pots ...'

⁂

My tennis life was full of friends and friendships but as a tennis player, I'm ashamed to say, I concentrated on tennis-playing friends more than the good people who organised our lives for us. In those days it was normal for young players to be accommodated with local families – in Sutton with Mrs Parsons, in Paddington with Mrs Walters, at Surbiton with Mrs Harding, and so on. Then there were the people who ran the tournaments – the referees, groundsmen, umpires, lines-people, even the ball-kids – salt of the earth but, for us, peripheral. Thank God our mothers had taught us to be well-mannered and to write thank you letters.

In Manchester, one of the bigger tournaments, we stayed with Mrs Marjorie Goodwin, an heir to the Cussons Imperial Leather cosmetics company. To our naive minds she was simply a nice old lady (of about fifty) with a Rolls-Royce and a mansion that seemed much too big for her. But it had a table tennis table and a snooker table in a vast basement, and a garden big enough to jog in. Meanwhile, she was the consummate English lady, with all the old-world attributes of such ladies combined with pure nobility and not a hint of ostentation.

Each morning her chauffeur would drive us to the tennis courts in the Rolls, and each evening he would fetch us home. To this day I remember those drives – the soundless purring, the Winged Lady on the bonnet, the soft 'chunk' of the doors closing and the voice of the chauffeur wishing us luck. Every evening we dined with Mrs Goodwin, fine food and silver cutlery; she watched our matches, and the first Sunday afternoon took us to her club for a proper English tea.

When we left she gave us each a ten-pound note 'to buy your tea on the train' (although it cost only two and sixpence) and, unbeknown to us, she must have followed our progress because when we qualified for Wimbledon, she invited us to dine with her at the Savoy Hotel. When, as a parting gift we gave her a small box of Cadbury's, she assured us they were her favourite chocolates, and even dropped us a note in answer to ours, to thank us. Thank us! We never contacted her again because we were too busy playing tennis. How's that for stupidity? Never realising that half the people in Manchester would have given their eye teeth to dine with Marjorie Goodwin at the Savoy. I seem to remember ordering steak, and in hindsight I only hope to God I didn't order it with a fried egg on top of it!

'If she was the kind of woman you say she was,' Richard said, 'she would probably have asked for a fried egg on hers.'

'Are we saying,' asked Tim, 'that a steak with an egg on top of it is disapproved of by British aristocracy?'

'Not aristocracy. I think Gordon means that asking for a steak with a fried egg on top of it at the Savoy Hotel is not the thing to do.' James, of course.

'It's three things, really,' said Tim. 'The Savoy Hotel, aristocracy, and steaks with fried eggs on them. Singly, they're fine. Combine them and you get raised eyebrows.'

'Talking of steaks with eggs on top of them,' I said, 'Ian Vermaak, the Harvey specialist I told you about, had a habit that made us laugh. When the SA Tennis Union paid the bill, we'd go to better restaurants, especially in Paris. He'd carefully study the menu, then ask the *maître* to go through the specials – *soupe à l'oignon, coq au vin, poulet à la bretonne*, that kind of thing – then after a period of careful thought he'd say, 'I'll have a steak that thick with an egg on top', using his right thumb and forefinger to show the thickness of the steak, and his left hand to position the egg. I never dined with him at the Savoy …'

Funny how one recalls these moments! In Manchester that year, practising with Gordon Talbot, there were two young Australian boys playing on the court next to ours. I can still see them, hitting a white ball back and forth with such effortless ease that even at my young age I knew I was seeing something momentous. We stopped to watch them, then Gordon turned to me and said, 'Now we know what we have to aim for.'

The boys' names turned out to be Lew Hoad and Ken Rosewall. I suppose I was young and impressionable, but moments like that were like great shafts of light. After our practices we would go to the club cafés and order Coca-Cola with Penguin Bars – biscuity things covered in chocolate – and nothing could be nicer.

While I'd first met Teddy Tinling at the Sutton tournament, it was in Manchester that I got to know him better. Manchester was one of the

G L Talbot and G L Forbes before a match against G L Paish and G L Ward. Neither team can remember who won ...

bigger tournaments on the English circuit, populated by all the young and promising British players, of whom there was a whole tribe – Billy Knight, Bobby Wilson, John Barrett, Tony Pickard, Roger Becker, Mike Davies, the Ward brothers, Roger Taylor, Mike Hann, and so on. Then there were the visitors, headed by a veritable infestation of young Australians – not only large numbers, but good players too, so good in fact that they became known as 'the bloody Australians'. In tennis locker rooms you'd hear things like: 'The tournament is full of bloody Australians' or 'The final is between two bloody Australians' or 'I'm drawn to play a bloody Australian in the first round'.

No one could explain why there were so many of them, or why

they were so good. Ted Tinling said it was something they put in the food. He had something to say about everything, but was most famous for making tennis clothes to fit women champions. Also, he played good tennis himself; he had one of those do-it-yourself British county games – big forehand, tall, rickety service, safe backhand, quick wit, cunning strategies, and a sardonic way of addressing the umpire as 'my dear man'. At Manchester that year he found he had to play Lew Hoad in the second round.

The British players in those days were more famous for their fighting spirit and good behaviour than for winning tournaments. When they lost, they would seldom say, 'I got murdered or beaten, or killed or trounced', they would simply say, 'he was better on the day' – a phrase that softened the blow, and made the après-match drink more pleasant. The Tinling-Hoad match caused great excitement. Ted had persuaded Lew to wear his clothing for the Manchester tournament (payment was unheard of) so they left for their court in a blaze of white, amid a chorus of 'Good luck, Ted' but not a single 'Good luck, Lew'. In about thirty minutes Ted returned, his hair awry, but all else in place.

'How did it go, Ted?' went the chorus.

'He was better on the day!' was the laconic answer. He'd got one game that Lew had given him as a reward for the clothing.

I once had to play Ted in a small event, and I remember arriving at the courts at eight so as not to be late for the match scheduled for eight-thirty. Agitated, Ted arrived at about 8.35, apparently having had to work through the night on an urgent design for one of Britain's top lady champions. He was in the habit, as he worked, of playing Frank Sinatra songs, in those days recorded on 12-inch LPs.

'My dear boy,' he said, as he put on his tennis gear, 'my humblest apologies! I'm a little punch-drunk, you see, because I've worked all night and listened to seventy-two straight inches of Frank Sinatra!'

From that day on, I've had in mind this mad notion of music by the yard. 'Six feet of Beethoven, two yards of Oscar Peterson, a furlong of Mozart, half a mile of Mahler …'

Those smaller tournaments were simple things. There were no ranking lists or qualifying rounds so any good club player was free to enter, with the result that there was a wide range of competitors in the first round – lords, colonels, viscounts, professors, commodores, doctors and so on, most of them club champions who loved the idea of competing with top-class players.

The early rounds of such tournaments often produced unique styles in both play and attire and, in particular, some astonishing service actions. I remember playing a first round match against a tall, thin squadron leader who wore cream-coloured flannel 'longs', a silk shirt with a frayed collar, cufflinks, a white golf cap and neckerchief. He arrived on court carrying with him only a small bag of resin, a face-cloth, and one well-worn racket in a press.

When we began our hit-up, I noticed that he had a good forehand, and a very 'cut' backhand that sizzled over the net like a frisbee. For his first service he used a 'hammer' grip that resulted in one of the astonishing actions I mentioned. After carefully securing his footing and giving his shoulders a few twirls, his left arm would flick a ball high into the air, while his right fist, clutching his racket, would leap up and position itself just below his chin, the racket head stuck out sideways, ready to strike the ball on its way down. He practised this service action several times in the warm-up and, to my surprise, it always managed to sort itself out in time to produce a flattish, military service that sent a ball flying past me at a respectable pace.

Tournament play often produces an attack of nerves, and the one that assailed the squadron leader must have been a bad one. I won the toss, chose to serve and won my service according to plan. We changed ends, he wiped his face with his little cloth and got ready to serve, holding three balls in his left hand and settling himself on the grass behind the baseline. His undoing came on the very first point. His flick-up went well enough, but his right fist, gripping his racket, came up too fast and too high, giving his chin an uppercut so sharp that his cap fell off. The blow must have surprised him because for a minute or two he walked in a circle, rubbing his chin and talking to himself. Then, approaching the umpire's stand for a drink of water, he looked up and said: 'False start I'm afraid, old man. I'll have to start again,' and to his great credit, the umpire allowed him to play a let.

Umpires were more lenient in those days. One of the big differences was in their attitude towards weather. In our day, both referees and umpires looked upon it as part of the game. How often did Gordon Talbot and I not find ourselves playing a match in light drizzle on a wet grass court, with sawdust on our racket grips, slipping and sliding about, pretending anger but secretly enjoying the fun of it?

'These days it would be unthinkable,' I told the Table. 'Play would stop, the court would be covered. Not a drop of water is allowed to fall on the court, in case one of the young millionaires sprains an ankle, because sprains these days seem worse than they used to be, more expensive and easier to get. In the old days, tournament referees were often ex-military men, all with a deep love of tennis and so steeped in the cause of duty that abandoning a tournament because of rain was a grave humiliation.'

Gordon Talbot and I both managed to qualify for Wimbledon. For the week of the qualifying rounds and the Wimbledon fortnight we stayed at the Austin Hotel in Lexham Gardens, Earls Court, where the tariff was ten shillings and sixpence each (10/6, bed and breakfast) allowing Gordon, James Farquharson (son of Norman, the famous South African champion) and me, to share one large room. The American player Hugh Stewart also stayed there, having a room to himself, and coffee for breakfast instead of tea. Down the passage from our room was a bathroom where you had to put a token into a slot to get hot water. There was a separate toilet with an old wooden seat and a long chain which, when pulled, released a spectacular explosion of water that swept away everything in its path. English breakfasts were served in the basement, a room so full of aromas that if one breathed deeply enough one hardly needed to eat. The menu was generous. Oatmeal porridge, bacon and eggs, toast and marmalade and big enamel pots of strong English breakfast tea. It was here that Hugh startled the British residents by rinsing his mouth with his last mouthful of coffee before swallowing it. At Wimbledon the lunches and afternoon teas were free, and round the corner from the hotel was a restaurant where English dinners costing three shillings were served by waitresses in white caps and aprons – soup to start, cottage pie or mutton stew, with stewed fruit and custard for pudding.

A WIDER WORLD

G F playing mixed doubles with Valerie. Wives partnering husbands can be tricky, and there have been cases where arguments had continued after matches ended. One husband reported that in the middle of the night after a close match, his wife had sat up in bed and shouted, 'Mine, you fool!'

There was great comfort in those twenty-one days of the Wimbledon season – a warm and a timeless sense of security. Life was safe, Lyons Corner House a friendly place, and London a home from home. If you saved up you could have tea at the Ritz. Simpsons of Piccadilly was a friendly store where you collected the two pairs of Melton tennis shorts every player received as a reward for competing at Wimbledon. The Underground cost a few pennies, you could practise at Hurlingham, visit the Tower, have a special lunch at St Katherine's Docks and row a boat on the Serpentine.

Father's road didn't wind; it went dead straight, without a sign of danger.

20

The Competitors' Enclosure

'Simply walking on court at Wimbledon for the first time was a Top for me,' I told the Table. 'The grass was so perfect that I stepped carefully, and the first few shots I hit were as if in a dream …'

I lost in four long sets to a Canadian called Bob Bedard, an ice hockey star with a rock-solid game and legs like cement columns. Nonetheless there were still the two doubles events to come and I had secured the treasured competitor's badge that awarded me virtual membership for the 'Fortnight'. One of the great things about the All England Club members was the way that they quietly honoured the Players – seemed pleased to welcome them, even pay homage to them – and not only the winners, but also the ones who battled away on the outside courts. We were treated with kindness and respect and we all had our place in the sun and darn good lunches and teas. (These days the players' restaurant is a five-star place with food of every conceivable kind.)

'In addition to the badge,' I told the Table, 'we also got a complimentary guest ticket giving entry to the Centre Court Competitors' Stand for a friend or relative.'

Selling this ticket was of course a cardinal sin, but the Club recognised that many of us were hard-up, and allowed us to sell our guest tickets back to the Club for an amount of twenty-five pounds. The tickets then became prized by those who either purchased or were awarded them, because access to the Competitors' Stand was (and still is) exclusive and special.

That year Gordon and I took up the offer. We never knew who got our tickets, but I often found myself watching the Centre Court matches with Peter Ustinov sitting beside me. Already a star of stage and screen, he continually invented his world of humour. We became acquaintances, then friends, and I got used to his frequent impersonations, in which he would imitate players contesting line-calls, or umpires laying down the law, in one of the six or seven languages he spoke – imitations so perfect that I found myself stuck between laughter and astonishment. He'd met Abe the previous year, and was no doubt pleased to find a quieter South African who made a more ordinary kind of conversation.

'Is that how he came to write the foreword to your book?' asked Richard.

'Fundamentally, yes, but via an amazing stroke of luck. Chance moves in a mysterious way, you know.'

All through my playing days, I'd had happy reunions with Peter Ustinov, but for a long time we lost touch. Some twenty years later in 1977, the tennis notes I'd made finally ended up as a manuscript called *A Handful of Summers*. My lighting business was going well by then and in it we had an old Irishman called Charles Murphy who'd been in the printing industry and who created our catalogues and leaflets. He took my manuscript under his wing, printed it, bound it carefully and designed a cover that had a bright sun on it, and on a business trip to London, I tucked it into my briefcase, to reread on the plane.

THE COMPETITORS' ENCLOSURE

At Heathrow with several samples to declare, I found myself standing in a queue behind a man trying to get through Her Majesty's Customs with a whole smoked salmon he'd bought in Paris. To my utter astonishment, it was Peter. After standing stock-still in surprise for a moment, I tapped him on the shoulder. He turned his head, immediately put on his famous pouting expression and his first words had a French accent because I think he was pretending to be an agitated Frenchman trying to explain his fish.

'Gordon! *Mon dieu, C'est toi!* Zey wish to take away my fish!'

His sulky frown was exactly as I remembered it, and although I hadn't seen him for years, it was as though we'd been together the day before. After further negotiations in an astonishing mixture of French, English and agitation, both he and his fish were allowed into England. We shared a cab into London, and in the course of conversation it transpired that he was on his way to see his publishers about his new autobiography, a lovely book called *Dear Me*. On impulse I pulled my manuscript from my briefcase.

'You couldn't perhaps ask them to look at this?' I enquired tentatively, explaining it as best I could. I think it was Charles Murphy's work that did the trick.

He looked at the manuscript in surprise, and without hesitation agreed. 'Of course I could. Which doesn't mean they'll publish it. But I can certainly get them to look at it. But don't hold your breath. Publishers take their time ...'

'That's all I could possibly ask!'

Except for a lunch at Franco's in Jermyn Street, we hardly saw each other again before he went back to Geneva. I returned to Johannesburg, became absorbed in my work, and after a period of about two weeks I received a telegram from Peter.

Peter Ustinov and Valerie.

```
NNNNVX                                              32
ZCZC FRS639 ZTC687 TTC816
SAJN CO FRXX 055
PARIS TELEPHONE DE BOULOGNEBILLANCOURT 55 10 1014


GORDON FORBES POBOX 11280
JOHANNESBURG2000


DEAR GORDON DELIGHTED TO SAY FIRST TWO READERS VERY PLEASED WITH
BOOK BUT SUGGEST CERTAIN AMPLIFICATIONS SO FAR SO GOOD STOP
WILL GIVE THEM YOUR ADDRESS STOP CONTACT IS PUBLICITY CHIEF
NIGEL HOLLIS C/O WILLIAM HEINEMANN PUBLISHERS 15 QUEEN STREET
MAYFAIR LONDON W1 SHOULD YOU WISH DIRECT COMMUNICATION EVER
        PETER
```

Peter Ustinov's telegram regarding A Handful of Summers.

At the A Handful of Summers *book launch. Left to right: G F, hosts Monty and Jane Wolpe, Fred Perry, Frances, Brian Young, and Abe.*

Well, I can tell you, it was another Top, and I was thrilled to the core — not a novel, but at least it was a book, and until the publisher put a copy in my hand, I couldn't believe it had happened. I had to get permission from every character I'd written about, but none seemed to mind. Abe Segal was the easiest. Without reading his consent agreement, he simply said, 'Anything you write is okay, Forbsey, as long as I don't end up in jail,' and he signed the paper I put in front of him.

'What a remarkable coincidence,' said Richard, when I told him the story. 'Twenty years later, you travelling from Johannesburg, he from Geneva, and you end up standing behind him in a customs queue in London, with him on his way to his publishers. Heavens alive! Make sure you enter the lottery. Much shorter odds!'

And as the Table folk heard my story, I had the distinct feeling that they shared that long-ago moment.

21

Segal's Knack

Abe had an astonishing faculty for meeting rich and famous people and making them sit up and take notice.

'You disarm them,' I once said to him.

'Oh, I disarm them. I never realised they carried guns.'

'It's purely figurative,' I said, knowing it would irritate him. 'You say things they don't expect.'

'Jesus, Forbsey,' he said. 'Like what, for instance?'

'Well, you might tell a mogul if he doesn't lose weight he'll end up in a wheelchair. Or when his fancy wife serves you quail for dinner ask her why she's givin' you birds.'

'I never said any of those things!'

'I know. But you might have.'

Anyway, accompanying him, I'd find myself watching Muhammad Ali from a ringside seat, at the London Palladium with Sammy Davis Junior's friends, playing tennis at Brenthurst (the Oppenheimers' home), in a box at Lord's or Ascot, in Sol Kerzner's plane, or eating *foie gras* at Tony Bloom's house in Plett ...

'There's this friend of mine, Forbsey,' Abe used to tell me, in a matter of fact way, 'wants us to go on his boat. He's some kind of a director …'

'What does he direct?'

'Who knows, Forbsey? Does it matter? He's a rich Greek, an' it's a big boat.'

Two such exclusive people he met in South Africa were Gordon and Mary Richdale who lived on a marvellous estate in Morningside. They were more British than the British and had a Rolls-Royce and a twenty-acre garden. On the eve of our doubles final at Roland Garros, they came over to Paris and took us to dinner at La Tour d'Argent. I had fish, but Abe ordered a steak, well done, no egg on top, but with tomato ketchup on the side – a request which, for a few moments, confounded the *maître d'*. He'd finally recovered and brought it in a white bowl.

Next day we lost the final to Roy Emerson and Manuel Santana – a blow to our careers but not something we could blame on the Richdales who seemed as upset as we were, so we had dinner again, but not at La Tour d'Argent.

We used to play tennis on the Richdale court and dine in their house at a long table that had flowers in silver vases and a bronze eagle in the middle of it – the dinner served by a splendid man in white who wore a fez and a crimson sash.

Abe and his wife Heather finally decided it was high time to reciprocate, so they invited the Richdales to dinner at their house in Bryanston. Valerie (my first wife) and I were ordered to attend for moral support. Abe and Heather had made a friend of one of the petrol attendants at the local filling station and, needing someone to tend their house and garden, they'd employed him. He was smiling, jovial and efficient and, because he'd worked at an Atlantic petrol station, Abe and Heather called him 'Atlantic'.

For the dinner party, without telling Abe, Heather had bought Atlantic a white uniform, a sash and a fez, and taught him how to serve wine from a bottle placed in a basket with a white cloth over it. The big night came, the Richdales arrived, we all fell over ourselves to welcome them, and at last it was time for dinner. Heather seated us at her table and Hilda, her cook, served the first course. Then Atlantic appeared with his basket of wine, all decked out in his new outfit.

'Jesus, Atlantic,' exclaimed Abe, 'I didn't know it was already Christmas!'

Grinning widely, Atlantic poured a little wine into Abe's glass, and stepped back.

'What's happening?' asked Abe. 'Why are we havin' samples?'

'Taste it, Abe!' said Heather urgently. 'See if it's good.'

'Listen, Mouse. It's all we've got so it better be!' Abe used to call Heather 'Mouse'.

When Ian Vermaak and I played in a tournament in Beirut, we were each presented with a full Arab sheik outfit, complete with tassels and headgear, and when the movie *Lawrence of Arabia* came to Johannesburg Mary Richdale wanted to see it but Gordon didn't, so I offered to take her to a matinee. My car at the time was a red Volkswagen, and when I went to pick her up, as a joke I put the Arab outfit over my suit, intending to remove it before reaching the theatre. She laughed, of course. On the way into town I removed the Arab outfit, we saw the movie, and I drove her home. Meanwhile, Gordon, returning from work, found the house deserted. The Richdales had a very English lady named Madge

Hannah who looked after the huge garden, and in desperation Gordon asked her what had become of Mrs Richdale.

'She went off with an Arab in a red Volkswagen,' came the reply, so haughty as to imply she may never return.

22

The Players Who Live on My Shelves

That first trip to England set the course for me. Both Gordon Talbot and I had become better players, and found ourselves candidates for the 1955 Davis Cup team – into which I just scraped. For the six months before the team left, I took a job selling sports goods at a shop called L F Palmer on the corner of Commissioner and Loveday Streets in downtown Johannesburg. Around the corner in Loveday Street was the Rand Club, where the mining magnates made plans, and across the road was an Italian barber named Giuseppe Rossi who, the week before I left, cut my hair as a parting gift.

A new world beckoned and the old farm seemed miles away.

How much can one love tennis? A court waiting, new balls, a sweet spot in a new racket, a good shot, four games to three, thirty love, our ad., the pure fun of it! There was a player in England called Tommy Anderson who everyone loved and who would spend hours on a court with a basket of balls, practising, practising – the same old mistakes, over and over again. He would enter the tournaments, lose in the first round, have his tea, faithfully resume his practice sessions, then try

THE PLAYERS WHO LIVE ON MY SHELVES

again. In a way, Tommy Anderson loved the game in the purest sort of way, for he would never get headlines, never reach a final or face the crowd holding a trophy above his head.

And nor would the people who loved it in a different way – the sports writers who made room for me in the Wimbledon press box; the fans who queued for hours with their flasks of tea and their orders of play; the kids who ran to fetch balls, the officials, the umpires in their cotton hats, the patient linesmen, content even after McEnroe had told them they'd need seeing-eye dogs to get them home. The small folk, like Bernie Schwartz, who saved up each year to come over from New York for Queen's and Wimbledon, roaming the courts with his Brownie camera and packet of toffees. Alan Little, the curator of the Wimbledon tennis museum, who knows every tennis fact and artefact that ever was, whose latest Wimbledon compendium of 572 pages is in itself an astonishing piece of history, art and knowledge. Thank God for the Bernies, the Tommys and the Alans of this world! There can be nothing so noble as loving a game for the reasons they do. Any game, really, even those played on a quiet village green. You can't but love the words of Sir Henry Newbolt:

> *And it's not for the sake of a ribboned coat,*
> *Or the selfish hope of a season's fame,*
> *But his captain's hand on his shoulder smote*
> *'Play up! play up! and play the game!'*

❧

'You chaps love books, and you know them much better than I do,' I said to the Table, and of course they all muttered denials, but it was true – they loved books in the proper way, knew them, venerated them, liked good writing that captured elusive things between the lines.

'They're living things, words,' Charles once said, 'but it's when you're lucky enough to find the right combination! That's when they really come alive ...'

'There was a man named Archibald T Halliday who must have loved both books and tennis,' I told the Table one day. 'Did a great deal for tennis in South Africa before my time: counsellor, benefactor, patron and so on. A very good man, they tell me.'

Anyway, I continued, when he died, to my surprise, one of his daughters contacted me to say her father would have liked me to have his collection of tennis books, and did I want them? Well, did I ever? Most of them were written by players who had played long before my time – simple old books, each one presenting earnest, carefully documented accounts of treasured ambitions and achievements, and love of tennis. *I wonder if it's right to confine such a joyous game inside the covers of a book,* began Lili de Alvarez, the most glamorous of the early lady champions. On the flyleaf of each book, Archibald Halliday had written his name, and just below it, an odd little adder that made me suspect that he loved books more than ever I realised:

Archibald T Halliday
his book

Tim told me that, over time, this old habit had changed to become simply *Archibald Halliday's Book*, but to me it had a special ring to it. Of course it meant that the books were his, but there seemed deeper meanings in those two words: 'His game', perhaps, or 'his players', 'his youth', 'his world'. Even, possibly, 'his life'. Archibald Halliday must have loved those books – but even more, the people who wrote them, the players who populated them, and the simplicity of the game they described.

Now, long afterwards, having contemplated them, read many parts of them, and been moved by the lives of the people inside them, I see more clearly just how old, sensitive and complex tennis must be, and how, from its vantage point in time, it must look down at the modern game with a knowing smile.

The books duly arrived – hundreds of them, big to small, old to new, each one telling of some tennis lover's triumphs and disasters. From the very beginning I liked the feel, smell, and tone of them, and spent happy hours unpacking them, pausing now and then to give thanks to Archibald T Halliday. And, I suppose, it was natural that as I worked I thought of Jean.

The sudden death of Jean at a relatively young age had devastated me. Later I realised that when you'd taken too much for granted the deep love of someone, the true depth of such love struck home only after they'd gone. I miss every single thing about Jean, and often find vivid memories emerging from simple moments. For example, when we were young, one of our favourite pastimes was sitting together at the old farm piano, strumming away at what we felt was thoroughly modern music. It was the time of the great American songwriters, and we were entranced by the charm of their melodies and the deftness of the

Jean.

lyrics. One of the songs we came upon was called *The Party's Over*, with music written by a man named Jule Styne. We loved the music – but it was the words that moved us, taking on a new guise each time we looked them over. Now, nearly fifty years later, their meaning is more poignant than ever:

> *The party's over, it's time to call it a day*
> *They've burst your pretty balloon*
> *And taken the moon away ...*

– a lover has gone, leaving a broken heart –

> *The party's over, the candles flicker and dim ...*

THE PLAYERS WHO LIVE ON MY SHELVES

Jean and I would look across at each other and she would give me the knowing glance that I loved so much.

> *Now you must wake up, all dreams must end,*
> *Take off your make-up,*
> *The Party's Over,*
> *It's all over, my friend.*

And then, even as teenagers, we would allow ourselves to suspect that in addition to lost love, the words also alluded to 'The Party of Life' and that like all parties it, too, would one day be over. At that time, of course, 'one day' seemed far enough away as to be of no real concern. But soon afterwards, when her young school friend was killed in a car accident, Jean was, for a while, at a very low ebb. In an attempt to comfort her I remember saying words that I judged to be a suitable mixture of grief and logic.

'There is nothing for it, I suppose. You'll simply have to accept that she left the party early, and that she's having a darn good rest.'

And Jean, after a reflective pause, replied in her typical way: 'There might be nothing for it, but that's cold comfort' – adding after another pause: 'except the part about the good rest. I'm very glad that you said that!'

Well, I am positive that Jean is having a good rest, for no one was as nice as she ... I could never keep count of the number of people who stopped to tell me what a lovely sister I had. Tennis players, academics, politicians. At Wimbledon, the officials, most of the tennis writers and many of the players seemed to be in some kind of love with her. And even today, I am often accosted by people who tell me that her classes (for some years she

I'LL TAKE THE SUNNY SIDE

The Jean Forbes Story, the cover of The Outspan, *1955.*

lectured English at Johannesburg's Witwatersrand University) were among the highlights of their learning. Her words inspired people – the result of some instinctive desire to make small folk feel good about themselves. She loved the great writers – what made them great, what they meant, why they put it so well. When I'd leave on one of my tennis trips, she'd give me books to read: 'Dip into that if you have the time.' 'Try *Gatsby*. Try Durrell. Read Eliot, if you can, and there's this new bloke, Salinger ...'

While unpacking Archie Halliday's books, I felt the familiar surge of pure sadness. How she would have loved to help me. Her wry comments and contented laughter were so tangible that, with tears in my eyes I allowed myself to make-believe that she was with me, that her voice was real, and her death simply a bad dream.

Together, we found the old world rubbing shoulders with the new. One of the first books we unpacked happened to be a thick, dark green one, titled *My Story* by Fred Perry. As children when we invented matches on our farm court by 'being' the great players who we'd heard of, Fred Perry always came first.

With due reverence I opened the Perry book, finding on the first page the faithful *Archibald T Halliday – his book* inscription, and then, on the title page, Perry's handwritten: *To Archie, with my sincere good wishes, Fred Perry.*

'And you can be sure that he meant them.' Jean's voice. 'He was that kind of a man. You can tell by his very first lines.'

> *With the pen as well as the racket a good beginning is heartening ... So I should dearly like to jump straight into our Davis Cup story at its climax – that glorious afternoon in Paris when we British stood, full of joy and pride, on the centre court of the Stade Roland Garros while*

a vibrant French throng was sporting enough to cheer four Englishmen for wresting the Cup away from their country ...

'That says it all,' said Jean. 'He'd won Wimbledon three times, yet he chose to begin his story by playing for his country.'

Aged fifteen, she had met Perry during our years of playing the British tournaments, and in spite of their age difference, they'd got on very well. I could see them together at some tea table, he with his deep voice and healthy suntan, smoking his pipe and being amiable – for he was the most amiable of men. She, absurdly young, sitting beside him, chatting away, pressing him into telling stories about tennis, for she had a way of making people feel that she really wanted to know.

So far, I have only dipped into the books, savouring their simple prose, and admiring the respect for tennis they all seem so quietly to project. One talks of loving tennis. In those days there seemed no need for swagger. Tennis was enough. Players were content to travel about on boats and trains, stay at small hotels, dress in old-fashioned white clothes and play for their lives on modest centre courts.

As we worked, Jean and I found ourselves re-examining other tennis books that, over the years, we had bought or been given.

'This one fits in very well,' said Jean. She had come upon *Champion in Exile* written by Jaroslav Drobny (Wimbledon champion, 1954), a book purchased by me at Wimbledon in 1956. Somewhat the worse for wear, it had travelled the world with me and contained the autographs and remarks of nearly all the 'big' players who I'd known and admired. Hoad, Rosewall, Seixas, Emerson, even Gardnar Mulloy and Herby Flam had signed it. Of course, Drobny himself had autographed the title page, while the others simply found a vacant spot, most of them wishing me such things as *good luck*, *happy hunting* or *every success*. And in 1957, when Althea Gibson (the first black woman to win Wimbledon) had won the Ladies Singles, I find a note written by Gordon Talbot in admiration: *Like Althea said to me, dancing with the Duke of Devonshire is a long way from not being allowed to bowl in Jefferson City.*

The inimitable Don Candy wrote, *Anything you'll sell I'll buy – my price of course –* leaving out such things as good wishes. 'They go without saying, Gordon lad. We all wish one another well …' I can see him still, pursing his lips, tapping his front teeth with the pen, and then, as he finished writing, tugging at my jacket sleeve. 'How much do you want for the jacket?' It was a new suede jacket I'd bought in Barcelona a few weeks before, and I doubt that he really meant to buy it – but then, with Don one never knew. At the right price, he might have bought it, and stranger still, at the right price I might have sold it.

Jean adored Don. His verbal antics fitted so perfectly her love of what she called 'delicious humour', that she would sit and smile delightedly at the monologues he so often muttered – not so much to other people but more, it seemed, to amuse himself, for he'd position himself heroically, and speak in a dramatic voice. For instance:

'There I was on the Steppes of Russia, surrounded by thousands.'

'Thousands of what?' Jean, playing his game.

'Steppes.'

'What did you do?'

'I took the elevator!' And he'd always give his juicy chuckle.

Or: 'I was crossing the road this morning and a beatnik in a hot-rod knocked me down. I thought he would apologise, but all he said was, "While you're down there, brother, could you please check the tyres?"'

'I went up in a plane that was a cross between a tiger and a moth. A

Lieut. Peile's instruction book

Tiger-Moth ...' (one of the most famous of the biplanes).

As I unpacked the books I didn't know whether to laugh or cry.

⁂

A number of them were old and rare. Jean came across one called, simply, *Lawn Tennis* written by a Lieutenant S C F Peile, BSC, in MDCCCLXXXV (1885, Tim says). It was a small book of about eighty-six pages, with a faded red cover that had on it a drawing of an ancient player with a deerstalker on his head.

THE PLAYERS WHO LIVE ON MY SHELVES

Lieutenant Peile had done more than just play tennis. He'd served as Inspector General of the Burma Police from 1854-95, been promoted, become a colonel, was awarded the King's Police Medal (GVR), had suffered a gunshot wound in 1902, and also written other books, one of them called *A History of the Burma Military Police*.

The book was notable for its naive instructions, old-fashioned prose and gentle gallantry, especially when it came to those he called 'lady-players', who were apparently making their presence felt just about then. He explained to the reader that 'an underhand service, cut from left to right', produced 'twisters', and went on to say, 'I have noticed how "lady-players" are, as a rule, much puzzled by twisters.' He advises these lady-players how to deal with twisters 'without sprawling', by developing anticipation and making sure they 'start in time', pointing out that on occasion 'a ball will come over the net and only then, and not until then, do some players make frantic rushes, all arms and legs. No sprawling player can ever place a ball, because a sprawler is generally a person whose occupations, before he or she took to this noble exercise, were sedentary ones.'

But even in those early days there must have been a hint of Women's Lib in the air, for Lieutenant Peile hastens to add: 'Now, Ladies! Do not accuse me of calling you "sprawlers", for I have purposely applied the masculine "he" to that class of player. But I have noticed, with a few exceptions, that ladies never seem to know exactly where the horrid ball is going, and they hardly ever take up their position for the return stroke until it is too late. (He'd never seen the Williams sisters!) I attach a few simple hints that may be of use to them as well as any male sprawlers of the game.'

He goes on to advise all players to 'watch your adversary well – both the position of his bat with respect to his body', and also the direction of his eye because, he points out, 'there are players who can disguise by their motions where they are going to send the ball. But by watching their eyes you will know, as they will almost invariably look last at that spot to which they intend to send it. There are very few players who can look one way and send the ball another. This might lead to the question whether a glass-eye might not be an advantage, but on the whole, I think not.'

Can he be serious? Probably not, but the entire book is made up of such delightfully naive instructions that he just might be. He talks about 'the best weight for a "bat",' so as not to get 'tennis arm'. How to toss up a high lob when you find yourself 'in a hole', or the best time to take 'a bisque'. (Apparently in those days there were certain rules that allowed a second chance, such as are sometimes allowed in friendly golf games, where bisques are usually called 'mulligans'.)

Imagine John McEnroe or Jimmy Connors serving a double on break point and then saying coolly to the umpire, 'I think I'll take my bisque now!'

One can tell that in those days tennis was regarded mostly as a male sport, for Lieutenant Peile includes only one 'Chapter for Ladies' towards the end of the book. Nonetheless it is a gallant chapter and it begins with suggestions about what ladies should wear. Short dresses were, apparently, just coming into fashion, and he obviously approved of them because he wrote, 'Short dresses are far better than long ones, because the long dress will spoil your play, and the play will spoil your long dress.'

⁂

The other old manual in the collection is also simply called *Lawn Tennis* and was published in 1895. It was compiled by H W W Wilberforce, who was once 'sec. to the AELTC – the All England Lawn Tennis Club' and who, in 1887, with Hon. P B Lyon, had been the 'four-handed champion'. He was a barrister-at-law, and although he had never run a police force or had a gunshot wound, his tennis instructions were good. Also a little book, it doesn't say exactly what a four-handed champion is, but it must be referring to the doubles game, although Jean mentioned that in many of her singles matches she could have done with four hands!

H W W Wilberforce claimed that tennis was just the game to 'fill the want of Englishmen and women'. In doing so he compared it to cricket, pointing out how frustrating it was if, while waiting to bat, one was suddenly 'possessed with a frantic desire to run about!' Again, the writing is delightfully old fashioned. There is also much debate about 'the implements of the game', a debate that reveals just how much modern implements have changed.

'There are rackets with square heads and oblong heads; with fluted handles, cork handles, grips for the hand and little machines for marking the score. Let players eschew all such, and choose instead, ordinary rackets.'

Wilberforce's instructions are less picturesque than Lieutenant Peile's. The illustrations he uses are placid, even for those early days. The forearm stroke on page 146 is almost contemplative in its mildness.

The backhand, more modern, but still never adopted by Federer.

His book is also permeated by the love of the game, the best way to play it, the excitement of simple tournaments, the beauty of tennis venues, *'Let him leave the fogs of London and go to the Beau Site Hotel at Cannes. He plays in a lovely garden, the blue of the Mediterranean beneath him,'* and one of his lines inadvertently reveals one of the most important qualities of the true winner: *'If he pants for the struggle of a tournament, he can spend a pleasant week in Dublin.'*

Forehand half-volley near the net.

Backhand half-volley near the net.

23

Panting to Compete

The ability to relish contest is a gift. Every great player I ever knew loved to compete, almost all of them revealing it in a different way. Some were aloof, others reserved, while still others flaunted their bravado – like, for instance, Bob Falkenburg who, when serving, sometimes showed his opponent only one ball, then served an ace with it. The interesting thing about such bold acts was that if they didn't come off, the protagonists didn't seem fazed! They'd simply laugh it off, and get on with the game, thus revealing yet another part of the winner's make-up – an ability to forget the immediate past, and think only of the next point.

'This question of panting to compete,' I told the Table, 'always bothered me. Oh yes, sometimes I got it right, but never to the extent of the great competitors. I've thought about it a lot since those days, even rediscovered some lines I'd written in *A Handful of Summers* that threw a bit of light: *In every close match ever played, you always fought two things – your opponent, and the fear inside you, and the worse of the two was the fear.* Plaintive, hey? If only I'd said, I can't wait to get at him, but instead I wrote: *There are those days when nothing goes your way. You fight, you sweat, you kill yourself, but fate, luck, tennis itself seems to have it in for you.'*

Makes me bloody angry, you know. But also underlines the two ways to compete – playing to win, and playing not to lose – short phrases, miles apart. I've known a lot of guys playing not to lose, but not one of them won a Grand Slam. And it doesn't mean if you play not to lose you don't fight your heart out. You do – you fight, sweat, kill yourself trying not to lose, some days succeeding, on others finding that fate, luck, tennis itself seems to have it in for you. Yet you keep at it, hoping against hope …

'Cometh the hour …' said Richard, giving his wave.

'And hopeth the man cometh.' Tim, I think. 'No good having the hour without the man …'

'It's no good you fellows wallowing in self-pity,' said the Other Peter in the voice of someone who played to win. 'Were you allowed to take hipflasks on court with you? A shot of brandy before a match point might have done the trick.'

'Never thought of it,' I said. 'All I now know is that I would have had more fun figuring out how to win than how not to lose! And, I might add, there were many players who pretended to relish competition but had inside them this same lurking fear – stupid when you come to think of it.'

Once, in the locker room at Roland Garros, having lost a match I should have won, I asked Tony Trabert, the great American player, whether he'd ever had doubts. He had the locker next to mine and he was preparing for his match (he won the tournament that year).

'Not if I'd done everything possible to prepare myself,' he replied after some reflection, for he was innately forthright. 'If I can say to myself, "I've done all I can in preparation, I can't do more", then I feel ready to compete.'

Simple, hey? And there was I, trying to decide who I should pray to!

In locker rooms all over the world I would watch the preparations of other players. Some went about their business quietly, others with shows of bravado. Still others took refuge in deliberate calm; there were busy ones and fussy ones; those who made jokes to show that they had no worries.

The Swedes were methodical, arranging all their paraphernalia in neat rows, double-checking their rackets, stretching their muscles, combing their hair, being polite to one another. The British were brisk and businesslike, talking in short, implacable murmurs, like soldiers waiting to 'go over the top'. Americans, in the main, were surprisingly normal. Budge Patty soaked his elbow in hot water; Art Larsen, half dressed, wandered about, chatting to his friends. Tony Trabert was simply unhurried; Victor Seixas, inscrutable. Even Gardnar Mulloy was stoical. The young Australians were noisy, loosing off the odd expletive or guffaw, poking fun at one another, sometimes taking refuge in remarks about women competitors: 'That new Italian chick. Bloody great legs. Could take her home to tea (tay).' 'Mimi. Great backhand. So small you could put her in your back pocket …'

Abe Segal, brusque and impatient, behaved more or less as the mood took him. Outwardly fearless, he too must have felt certain inner anxieties because he once searched for his tennis shorts for some time before realising he was already wearing them. An impulsive chap, was Abe. At Bournemouth, before the doubles final of the British Hard Court Championships against Bobby Wilson and Mike Davies of England, we walked past them on the way to the centre court. I smiled in a friendly way, but Abe said, 'Don't forget to bring your arses along because we are sure as hell going to beat them off' – a remark that I could never have made.

'Are you sure you should have said that?' I asked him.

'Why not, Forbsey? Give them something to think about.' (We did beat them, but their arses stayed in place.)

In locker rooms, the top Australian players – Hoad, Rosewall, Laver, Emerson, et al. – behaved exactly as if they were preparing for a friendly game of doubles. Laver fiddled with his racket grips, Hoad chatted to the players near him, Emerson would sing the odd ditty, sometimes using one of the current advertising jingles; he once produced a freshly washed tennis shirt, and as he pulled it over his head he sang to himself:

It's good,
And clean,
And fresh, tra la la –

Then, when his head emerged, he looked around, grinned at everyone and said, 'I use OMO for that extra whiteness.' 'Emmo' had an imaginary friend he called Hardway Joe, who apparently always did everything the hard way. 'Used to make love standing in a hammock,' Emmo would explain. He once walked into the locker room having lost his match (which didn't happen very often). 'Got my arse beat,' he said. 'Played like Joe.'

The crux of any tennis match is 'the big point'. In most any sport, inevitably comes the time when the whole match hinges on one stroke – a match point at Wimbledon, a six-foot putt at Augusta, a vital drop kick at Ellis Park, a penalty for Arsenal. In an instant, a player can either be famous or seen as a choker – a moment of crisis far worse in his own mind than in anyone else's.

Here the great champions have in their make-up the gift of calmness and confidence. But for the wannabes who get only rare opportunities, the tension is immense. There comes the lonely moment, when silence falls and you long for an arm round your shoulders. In doubles matches, Abe would often come up to me, always with the same instructions. 'Relax, Forbsey, and watch the ball' – simple, familiar, and comforting. But singles matches were no laughing matter. Many players in many sports, at vital moments simply pray to God, and I must say that I envy their inborn belief. I finally decided that the best person to pray to was myself, as I was the one who had to make the shot.

Whatever the case, the question of winning and losing has been on my mind for half a lifetime, and one thing seems certain. To win a big point you can't be cautious. You have to *screw your courage to the sticking place*, take a deep breath and say, let's do it ...

24

Stout of Heart

At last the job of unpacking the books was done. There they lay, content on their new shelves, the players inside them no doubt happy to know that time was no longer their enemy – that for them it had come to a standstill, past, present, future, all in one. Perry would forever hit his forehand, Lew would serve, Tilden would volley, Borotra would bound and Lenglen would leap. On a given page the scoreboard at the All England Club would show that Don Budge and Gottfried von Cramm were even at two sets all; rain would stop falling before it hit the court, the umpire was fixed in his chair, and the players were at peace.

'They no longer have to worry about filling the unforgiving minute,' is what Jean would have said. To go through the books more carefully we'd decided on alphabetical order, immediately finding ourselves confronted by Andre Agassi's book, *Open*. It was, of course, not one of Archibald Halliday's books, but one that our neighbour Colin Brayshaw had recently given me. Momentarily surprised, I contemplated its slick appearance, its orange spine, Agassi's intense face with its designer beard and shaved head, the whole ensemble seeming to cry out, 'Look at me, I'm a superstar!'

It wasn't an Archie Halliday sort of book. To further prove my point I stood it beside one of his simple old books called *Tennis with Hart* by the 1951 Wimbledon Champion Doris Hart. Nothing matched. If ever I'd searched for a visual and literary difference between tennis players then and now, I couldn't have come across a better example. On one hand, Agassi, one of the fittest, healthiest and most colourful players of all time, unfolding a saga of stress and pain, and, between the lines, a worry that life may suddenly let him down. I savoured his sharp bursts of superb prose that so dramatised his story, but nowhere could I find a love of tennis; rather, in the very first chapter, cleverly headed 'The End', he'd actually written, 'I hate tennis, hate it with a dark and secret passion, and I always have.' I had greatly admired him as a sportsman, and loved watching him play, but that line spoiled it. Those two books, lying side by side, seemed to epitomise all my differences between the old world and the new.

In contrast, on the first page of Doris Hart's book she writes 'Tennis has meant everything to me. With all my love for tennis, I offer this account, hoping that it will inspire a few who might be needing help and encouragement, as I did ...'

As a child, at a very young age, she developed a sinister infection in her knee:

> *At fifteen months, when I was trying to master the difficulties of walking, my parents noticed that my right knee-cap was badly swollen. The first diagnosis of rheumatism was incorrect. A strange infection spread rapidly up my leg and my doctor feared that gangrene would set in.*

Two other specialists were consulted, Doris's life was declared in danger, and amputation of the leg was advised. Her father, supported by their family doctor, a Dr Todd, could not bring themselves to consent. Their decision was so controversial that they were afraid to move Doris to a proper hospital. With the help of her father and mother, Dr Todd and his nurse sterilised the kitchen table in the Hart household, laid Doris on it, and performed an operation to open the infection they had diagnosed, and to allow the poison to drain.

Thus began months of anxiety, medication, therapy, massage and exercise. To the family's infinite relief, the infection diminished, but their daughter nonetheless took years to achieve even an unsteady walk, her right leg gradually becoming usable, but remaining weak and permanently deformed. But she hung in. 'From a sickly, not-likely-to-live child,' she writes, 'by the age of nine I had developed into the tomboy that my two devoted, older brothers wanted me to be.'

The two brothers were also responsible for beginning and maintaining her tennis career. With a limp and a deformed right leg, first as a junior and then a senior, she fought her way through all the rigours and pressures of competitive tennis, until, in 1951, she was able to win Wimbledon. And to me it is strange and wonderful that although Doris Hart made no money from her tennis, she ends her book with the words: 'What the future holds for me I do not know, but you may rest assured that I shall never stop loving the game that has done so much for me.'

To return to Andre Agassi: In spite of his ranting, I sincerely believe that a man who played as well as he did could not possibly hate tennis. To his credit, he ends his book with an exquisite description of a game he plays for fun against his wife, Stefanie (formerly Graf, one of the greatest women players). Here, at last, emerges a true love for tennis that goes perfectly with his love for Stefanie and their two children – a proud love he makes no secret of. Let's hope that he loves tennis for what it is, the nicest game of all. Because *we* love both Andre and Stefanie. Between them they have given us as much pleasure as any two tennis players could ever do.

How often have well-meaning friends not sympathised with the fact that in our day there was no money in tennis? And how often don't they end with words of consolation: 'Never mind. You had much more fun than they did?'

'That all depends how you define "fun",' I usually reply.

In our day, for instance, when we played at Roland Garros, many South Africans, Australians and New Zealanders would stay in cheap hotels near Étoile. In the evenings we would gather on street corners and discuss restaurants giving the best value in *Steak Frite*. Prices of menus would be carefully compared – a tricky business, because the thickness of steaks and the volume of accompanying vegetables had to be taken into account …

Agassi and friends, on the other hand, might have a limousine waiting for them in front of the Plaza Athénée Hotel. Their main problem would be to decide which five-star restaurant to go to and, once there, what would be for starters, and whether to have the sea bass or the langoustine. In Las Vegas, where Andre lives, instead of a limousine, he would boot up his jet, then fly off to Beverly Hills, perhaps to some new French place that George Clooney had recommended.

'So when you say that we had more fun,' I told the Table, 'the trick is to define the word "fun". It wasn't much fun carrying Harvey about and pretending that he weighed very little.'

'That's the whole point,' said James. 'Harvey was all part of it. You met air hostesses, your friend Candy had someone to talk to, there was salami in Harvey's pocket ...'

'However, there might be something to be said for private jets,' said Tim. 'I've never owned one, but they can't be *too* bad. I saw a bloke getting into one with his girlfriend, and they both looked perfectly happy ...'

Slowly at first, but with gathering speed, my handful of summers came to an end. I never realised quite how precious those years were until they were past. Youth, they say, is wasted on the young. Among the notes I kept I found scraps of verse that I must have written when my tennis career was about to come to an end:

> *For suddenly my day will fade,*
> *And of the game that once I played*
> *I'll find that only memories remain –*
> *Like echoes of a favourite tune, or*
> *Shadows from a waning moon.*

25

The Next Signpost

'What happened when your tennis career came to an end?' asked James. '1964, I think you said it was. There must have been a gap in your life. How did you manage to fill it?'

We'd finished our dessert by then, there was a little wine left and Richard had ordered Irish coffees.

'Yes, James,' I said. 'Now that you mention it, there was a gap, and your question brings back the feeling I'd had when I knew my tennis was over – an ominous sort of mixture – weariness and anxiety, as far as I can remember.'

I was thirty years old, and after Val and I had rented a small furnished flat, I had enough money to last five months. I'd rigged up a desk and book shelves using bricks and planks – in those days the mark of the would-be intellectual. In the evenings, after Gavin, still small, had been put to bed, I'd sit at my makeshift desk, staring at a 'situations vacant' column and wondering what to do about the rest of my life. There were the vague promises made by business moguls; tennis writers talked of journalism or sports reporting; I tried coaching tennis only to find that a forty-five minute lesson took much longer than forty-five minutes. There was the farm. Novel-writing still nagged at me. Wilbur Smith had just succeeded with *Where the Lion Feeds*. I could try again …

On one of the shelves among Jean's varsity books was one called *Aspects of the Novel* by E M Forster. 'Try it,' she'd once said, 'it might help you.' So one evening I began reading it, but the pedantic words seemed only to amplify my dilemma. To contemplate writing fiction one passage said,

> *We need a vantage point, for the novel is one of the moister areas of literature – irrigated by a hundred rills and occasionally degenerating into a swamp …*

It didn't sound promising. Further on, was another passage that she'd underlined.

> *Genuine scholarship is one of the highest successes that our race can achieve. No one is more triumphant than the man who chooses a worthy subject and masters all its facts and the leading facts of the subjects neighbouring. He can do what he likes.*

'I was disheartened,' I told the Table, 'because the more I looked for a job, the more I realised I hadn't mastered enough facts. It didn't look as if I'd ever be able to do what I liked.'

'Facts aren't always the answer,' said Tim. 'Take Richard, for example. He's mastered all the facts about General Smuts.' He paused to look at Richard. 'Can you do what you like?'

THE NEXT SIGNPOST

Richard glanced around the Table at the seven of us with our Irish coffees. 'Isn't that what I'm doing now?' he asked, then lapsed into a thoughtful pause while we all waited expectantly. 'The simpler the better. Funny how it grows on you; simplicity, I mean. Age, I have realised, is not only a great equaliser, but also a great appeaser. It comforts one by cleverly turning former passions to milder desire, desire to excitement, excitement to pleasure and pleasure to contentment' – and he gave a wave that seemed to cover any sensations he might have forgotten. 'Make any sense?'

'It does, now that you put it that way,' said James. 'On the beach in my December holidays I was reclining in my chair, a hat over my eyes, a near-empty glass of champagne in my hand, and a girl walked past. One of those spectacular girls, tall, lanky. A lot of moving parts. Sure enough, I felt the surges you mentioned – passion, desire, excitement, ambition – and then, as she passed by, it happened.'

He paused for a moment, and Charles rapped his knuckles on the table. 'What happened?'

'I felt a surge of contentment,' said James, 'pure relief at not having to do anything about her. In my youth I would have got into a state, wondering whether to make a move, what tactics to adopt, how to proceed. Now, I relaxed. Simply lay back and held out my glass for more champagne.'

'Brilliant,' said Tim. 'And when she walked back, you'd be able to get a drop more.'

'The conclusion I've come to,' said Richard, picking up the thread of his original thesis, 'is that age turns the surges of youth into the pleasures of age – the greater the age, the milder the surge, and the milder the surge, the greater the contentment.'

'Richard's Law of Surges,' murmured Mark, determined to put an educational slant on the whole matter.

'I suppose,' said the Other Peter, 'practically, one could dispense with the "s". Richard's law is applicable to both surges and urges.'

⁓✦⁓

'All I asked Gordon,' said James in a slightly aggrieved way, 'was whether there was a gap in his life when he stopped playing tennis. I didn't want a flood of philosophical theory …'

'Oh, there was a gap all right,' I said. 'Fortunately, Abe Segal helped. Told me I still had piss and vinegar in my veins, and I'd better get off my arse and find a job.'

'In life, Forbsey,' he said, 'there's always a deep end. A man must dive in and either sink or swim.'

He followed that up by actually finding me a job – not one I expected, you follow. I became a junior salesman. In those days it was much simpler. You took a job – any job – and if you did it well, you got a better one. I managed to stay afloat, and after a few years I remember wishing he'd come up with his piss and vinegar thesis during our tennis days. All in the past. Over eighty, gaps don't need taking, the deep end is shallower, surges abate …

I looked around the Table, suddenly afraid I'd been talking too much. 'Sorry about all that …'

'I've always wondered about the origin of that phrase, "piss and vinegar",' mused Charles. 'You'd think they'd be the last things you'd want in your veins …'

'Steinbeck, I fancy,' said James. '*Grapes of Wrath*. An old Grampa in the book said he was still full of it …' He turned to me and said: 'I'm glad you found it useful …'

⁂

My gap was to last over twenty years.

'Looking back down my winding road,' I said, 'there seemed to have been six segments to my life. About twenty carefree years of childhood, schooling and farming; two years standing behind the counter of an arms shop in President Street; eight years trying to be a tennis player; twenty-five years building a business; another fifteen roaming the world, and ten more, getting from seventy to eighty.'

'And which did you enjoy most?'

'The twenty-five in business.'

The impulsive answer gave me a fright. All those years of toil, trying to make enough money to be independent – were they really my happiest? And, if so, why? It took me a while to answer that question, but it was simple enough. Because they were successful. I'd begun in a small way, just as in tennis, but while tennis ended in a whimper, I'd helped to build a terrific business – big enough, when it was sold, to give me independence.

All through my tennis years, I'd longed for the security with which money and independence were inexorably linked. Oh, yes, I'd rubbed shoulders with very rich people all my life, but I never thought I had it in me to be very rich. Sounds odd, I suppose, but I wondered what it was like to be that way; count in billions I mean; and I was puzzled by moguls, already rolling in money, continually striving for more – until one day it came to me that money was their game – simply another way of keeping score. If Martina Navratilova could strive so mightily for a tenth Wimbledon title, then business people could strive for the next billion. The cars and yachts and planes and big houses were, in fact, simply scoreboards – games for them without scoreboards were no fun – Myron leading Dexter by two Maseratis to a Porsche. Howard one yacht ahead of Kramer, Henry and Maurice at one game farm all. I, meanwhile, enjoyed looking for the best deal in demo-model cars and wearing my old tennis shirts on weekends with beige pants from Woolworths.

'That's the farmer in you,' was Charles's comment when I divulged these thoughts to the Table. 'In fact, that goes for us all.' He looked round the Table and asked in a challenging way, 'None of us have ever wanted to be very rich, have we?'

'Only occasionally,' said the One Peter.

'The root of all evil,' said Tim, shaking his head. 'I suppose if riches were thrust on me I'd have to find a way to cope. Buy a modest yacht. A small plane …'

'I nearly decided on riches,' said the Other Peter. 'Then bird-life interfered …'

James, meanwhile, had lapsed into a reverie of his own, leaving the rich to fend for themselves and musing about life being divided into eras.

'There appear to be three basic stages,' he summarised. 'Young and foolish; middle-aged and busy; wise and relaxed. We at this Table must surely agree that the last is the best. We are wise and relaxed but still able to do the things we did in our youth – the only drawback being that we can do them only one at a time.'

The silence that greeted this intelligence must have persuaded him that further clarification was necessary.

'Well, for example,' he said, 'a *young* man might work all day, play three sets of tennis, do a bit of gym, drink three beers, phone a girlfriend, have a big dinner with wine, walk her home, and still have the energy to go through whatever further activities may be required. He then could have a good night's sleep, and next morning make a running start and do it all again. We can do only one of the aforementioned things before having the good night's sleep, after which a running start might be a challenge. Old age is really just an endurance test …'

'Hang on,' said Charles. 'Most of us could manage more than one of those things in moderation. For instance we could work for a while, have at least *one* beer and then, if we had one, phone a girlfriend, and have dinner. That's already three. As for later activities, well, that would depend entirely on what was called for. A good night's sleep shouldn't be a major problem …'

'But a running start might be.'

26

The Excitement of the Chaste

Despite all the hard work it entailed, business life could also have its moments. As our business grew, we developed ties with lighting companies all over the world, and travelling took on a quite different cast. To begin with, we could at last afford to travel business class, so I no longer needed a Harvey. And it wasn't simply a case of airports, tennis courts and restaurants. Now there were also industrial areas, meetings, business lunches, exciting new products and the thought of getting orders for them.

Often it was I who had to do the travelling, because apart from being accustomed to it, in many countries there were tennis friends who often had useful contacts. Whatever the case, I saw the world through new eyes, and continued with my note-making about places that intrigued me. Once, on a business trip to Italy and Switzerland and Spain, I recorded the whole adventure in a notepad I bought at the airport bookshop. I'd taken a Swiss Air flight to Zurich and a connecting one to Milan, leaving Johannesburg on a bitter winter evening in July and arriving in Italy in a heatwave. Some fancy writing describes my

THE EXCITEMENT OF THE CHASTE

arrival, for I was a bit full of myself at the time:

I am at the Milan airport at the mercy of Italians. It's very hot, I'm still wearing a thermal vest, and I have to get to the *Milano stazione* for my train journey to a town called Recanati, somewhere down the leg of Italy. So, a taxi! Standing next to my little pile of luggage, I give an exploratory hail. A Fiat pulls up in a cloud of diesel, and we set off for the *stazione*. After the quiet of the DC10, the Italian landscape has about it the quality of a Fellini movie – dreary highway, curls of dust, a hot grey sky, and the town of Milano growing slowly out of endless, hazy suburbs, littered with the very stuff of Italy – *Agricoltura*, *Gelateria*, a hundred *Mottas*, *Pirellis*, *Cinzanos*. Piles of melons, stalls with pennants, bars with flashing signs offering *Cocktails*. The Italians use the English word, but on this road it has an Italian flavour to it.

At last, the *stazione* – a massive organisation of marble, its architraves peppered with statues – gods, cherubim, seraphim, assorted saints and martyrs, a chariot or two, and gargoyles gushing water. It is Sunday, everyone is on the move, and one feels that the sheer weight of the building is necessary to keep it from being swept away by rich torrents of Italian, all lorded over by a loudspeaker that never ceases. The *passaggios* are jammed with bodies, moist, breathing, eating, drinking and talking – Italians are not content unless things are either entering or leaving their mouths! Bedlam reigns, and I must find my *treno*.

Tucked into my travel folder is a ticket, all neatly put together. *Milano-Ancona-Recanati*, it says, and miraculously adds, 'Departing 12h00 from Platform 9'.

Surveying the scene, I find it impossible to imagine how my travel agent, tucked away in Braamfontein in Johannesburg could possibly predict the activities of this inferno. Sure enough, my suspicions are valid, *Binario Nove*, as well as *Dieci* and, for that matter, *Undici*, are closed with brown, bare-chested workmen digging things up. It is 11.38. Departure time is 12.00 and my *treno* is lost. No one speaks *Inglese*. *Informazioni* is deserted, the porters push their carts and shake their heads, so I accost the only uniformed fellow I can find, and hurl at him a few random Italian sounds.

'*Trenorapido!*' I cry. '*Bologna, Ancona, Pescara!*' All are names which I have gleaned from my ticket. He pauses, and though I am the taller he manages to look down at me, giving me a broadside of Italian which I can smell, but cannot understand.

'*Treno*,' I say again. '*Treno pour Bari!*' in desperation throwing in one of my French words. It is 11.40 and all avenues must be explored. By now, my plight has become a public affair. With my neat pile of luggage and business clothes, I have become the centre of a growing crowd of Italians who, for the time being, have stopped gnawing at their salamis and are looking at me curiously.

'*Bologna, Ancona, Pescara – Bari!*' I cry again, even more desperately. '*Bari!*'

There is a sigh from the crowd. '*Bari.*' Being the final destination, of course *Bari* is the key. '*Bari! Si, Bari!*' A dozen voices now begin to offer me Italian advice.

'*Silenzio!*' thunders the uniform. *He* must inform the *ignorante*. He hoses the crowd down with another blast of Italian, and they retreat a step or two. Then he turns to me.

'*Bari*,' he says. '*Il treno per Bari in Partenza dal Binario Numero Diciotto.*' Then, having disposed of this wisdom, he glances at his watch, turns away and continues his regal progress through the throng.

'*Diciotto!*' I say, more to myself than anyone else. *Diciotto?* From my tennis days I knew the Italian for fifteen, thirty and forty, but *diciotto* had me beat.

'Eighteen,' says a voice in perfect English. 'The express for Bari departs from Platform 18. It also stops at Ancona.'

I turn to find that my saviour is a tall, thin international-looking girl with tired, intelligent eyes, and a soft voice – the kind of girl you might see at the airport bar with a book in her hands and a straw in her mouth. A mysterious girl. Had her feet not been so low down, I would have kissed them.

'You're a female saint,' I cry fervently. 'Thank you! But am I sure I need a train to Bari? I'm not going to Bari, you see. I'm going to a town called Recanati.'

'Quite sure,' she smiles. 'I am going to Pescara, and I change at Ancona, where you too will change for Recanati.'

'Well, thank goodness for you! I've been near my wits' end, and in Italy wits can end quite quickly.' We both laugh, I a little shakily.

We find seats in the same compartment, and my luggage is safely stowed but, Lord, is it hot – even though a sign in the coach says *Aria Condizionata*. There is an official walking up and down the platform, giving frequent, random and inexplicable blasts on his whistle. The thin, international girl questions him and for a while they thrust and parry in Italian.

'He says we must wait until the *treno* moves,' she says. 'Then it should work. But sometimes a very hot train can't be cooled.'

Nonetheless I am content. To be too hot is one thing, to be marooned in Milano quite another. The *treno* moves at last. There are beads of perspiration on the thin, international girl's upper lip. We close our eyes and wait for the *aria condizionata* to work, but it too seems exhausted by the heat. Suddenly there is a great rattling on the door, and lunch is announced. In the dining car it is cooler, and we sit in comfort at our table, talking about Italy and watching the landscape floating by.

Field after field of *agricoltura*. Ripening grain – wheat, barley, maize and amongst the grain stalks, fruit trees and vines. The warm air coming through a window is laden with protein, heavy with organic smells – earth, hay, compost, chalk dust, and a verdant sensuality so palpable that you can actually taste it. Mile after mile of produce, fodder in fragrant windrows, waiting to be stacked. Rows of trees – apricot, almond, fig, with ripe fruit, bursting open. You can eat this Italy – we are, here and now, eating Italy. The bread roll is the chalky earth, the pasta, the grain, the wine, the vineyards. It is no wonder that the Italians worship food – *cibo!* Their land, like no other land on earth, actually seems edible!

'*Il mangiare fa star bene!*' murmurs the girl, and smiles at me across our table in such a way that I know what she means. We've ordered a bottle of white Chianti that hints at gaiety.

Slowly the scene changes to a new kind of landscape – fields of ancient olive trees and cypresses and suddenly, in the distance, glimpses of the blue Adriatic fluttering with sailing boats. The *treno* runs along the seashore – miles of umbrellas and bathers on the left, and verdancy and fodder on the right. At last a guard rattles the door again and cries *Ancona!* where we must change trains and I must leave the thin intelligent girl, who lives in Pescara. Maura de Luca, her name turns out to be. It is the end of a strange, poignant little interlude of only a few hours, but with a life of its own that seemed to suggest a brief love affair in a passing friendship. Had I been a man in a novel, I could have stayed on the train, and gone south with her. Pescara! Who knows what might have happened there? But I am not in a novel, I'm doing business – I must pull myself together and get to Recanati.

Italian industry establishes itself in strange places and here, near this ancient hilltop town, is a factory belonging to a man called Romano Bonacci which makes the most beautiful light fittings. An old acquaintance, he is standing on the platform of the little station, puts his hands on my shoulders, gives his customary greeting – 'Ciao Gorrdonne!' – takes me to a little hotel, and leaves me to rest.

From my window I can look down on the square. On the right the church tower, on the left a cobbled street so Italian in nature that you feel as though you are living in a postcard. *Via Antonia Calgagni.* Establishments of stucco masonry, arches, a fountain, a tower, and doorways opening directly onto the *strada*. Up and down the street, warm aromas, airs flavoured with centuries of Italian tradition, and at the end, the walled garden with impossibly green fig trees, cypresses and oleanders, all tailored, and standing about the fountain like children's drawings. Gravelled paths, and everywhere the townspeople strolling and chatting. They are dark and heavy-limbed in the main, but here and there one sees a truly handsome specimen – a woman perhaps, proud-eyed and bright as a poppy, swaying with bosom, massive cloud of hair, substantial arms, ankles and thighs, grand of hip and bottom, honey-coloured skin, moist and flowing with nourishment. If there is one word for these Italians it is 'ripe' – a nation of ripe women – some even overripe, the Italian foods tending to ripen even the very soul! In the hot airs of this Sunday evening, cottons hang softly damp and olive

An edible Italian street. (© Shutterstock)

skins are powdered with the finest frostings of moisture. Everyone is talking – rich Italian vowels, as edible as the salamis hanging in the butcher's window.

A window opens, a man's head appears. He calls out. In the street below his handsome wife responds. He needs her! A conversation must be carried on from window to street, a conversation of some significance and velocity. She is dressed in a scarlet halter dress tied at the neck, back bare, a sort of mobile Botticelli, splendid and ample. It is clear that she loves her husband, but also she must treat him like a child. Apparently he must bring a sweater, as it might get chilly. He understands at last, and she throws her mighty arms aloft, blowing kisses, her bosom passionate, her armpits obscured by dense tufts of raven hair like *agricoltura* – what grows must grow and if it flourishes, let it flourish! Eventually, he arrives to join her, as fragile as she is strong, abbreviated no doubt by a lifetime

THE EXCITEMENT OF THE CHASTE

of keeping pace with a woman of her vigour, and one wonders briefly that she didn't eat him after their first mating.

❦

Anyway. Dusk falls, and Romano comes to fetch me. We must eat and I rave on about Italian food and hospitality. Restaurants with festoons of pasta, bundles of onions, grapes, olives and wine in kegs. The long table next to us is taken by an entire family – mothers, fathers, uncles, aunts, children, and a grandfather so old that I wonder whether he will live long enough to eat the food his daughter has ordered for him. But when it arrives, he flares up like a lamp and, assisted by frequent measures of wine, he eats away, slowly subsiding as his plate empties, having to be reawakened for dessert.

Meanwhile, *we* have pasta to start with, and then pigeons – puzzling for me, for they are smallish brown things, but Romano cleans his to the bone, so that only a handful of twigs remains on his plate. Do Italians ever stop to wonder whether pigeons are worth the effort? I doubt it. For them, it is simply another kind of *cibo* to *mangiare!*

After a few days comes the time when business is complete. Put on the right train by Romano I retreat to Milano and, with a sigh of relief, hand myself back to Swiss Air. Zurich is also hot, 30 degrees, the taxi driver tells me, in a state of near panic, but after the ochres and beiges of Italy, to me, the greys and blues of Switzerland seem cooler. I end up in a hotel on the lake, and in the afternoon the water beckons. There is a wooden pier for bathing, a water-world where, to get in, you put a coin in a slot. After the heat of Italy, one feels the need for cool water, so I walk down to the pier. At the entrance, I find myself next to a private secretary-ish sort of girl, also about to go bathing, so I feign ignorance, and ask her for help. Yes, she does speak English, agrees to help, politely shows me where to put my coin, and in we go, chatting away. Once on the swimming deck, she peels off her clothes in a matter-of-fact sort of way, until she is wearing nothing but a small pair of white cotton knickers decorated with strawberries. I am temporarily astonished, but soon realise that Swiss secretaries go topless in the same, efficient sort of way they do their work. She tucks her brownish hair into a bathing cap, and carefully folds each item of clothing, stacking them into a neat little pile. The fact that she has perfect little breasts on show doesn't seem to faze her, there they simply are, two commas on her chest, naive and candid.

We float for a while in the Zurich-See, the lake so cool, clean and clear that one wonders how the Swiss do it. After a while we get out and, sitting at a little table with her still topless, we order two of the Swiss Pils that come in smallish bottles. The conversation is simple:

'What is it like living in Switzerland?'

'Good. Life is very, how do you say, protected. Safe. Predictable. For young people, boring, but for us who are married … And your country? We hear things, read things, what is it really like?'

There seems no hurry, but when the bottles are empty, she tells me that she must go back to her apartment to make dinner for her husband. A pity, I remember thinking, but, on reflection, a blessing in disguise. In the course of a few days, I'd met two girls who'd both ignited thoughts about what might have been but who, instead, would forever remain in the lay-bys of my winding road as friends.

THE EXCITEMENT OF THE CHASTE

On the Friday afternoon I'd finished my business, and on the train back to the Zurich Bahnhof a sublime impulse came over me – one of those rare moments when suddenly life opens up and time beckons. I was alone in Switzerland with a weekend ahead and not a soul expecting to hear from me. I loved trains, especially Swiss ones – sitting on those safe soft seats with the wheels clicking, a glass of wine, nice scenery and the chance of … something, someone, it didn't matter. Things happened on trains. I used to have a few tennis friends in Geneva, so why not go there? A train every hour they told me at the ticket office. It was the simplest of decisions …

The journey took about two and a half hours. Turned out I was alone in a compartment with no interference from girls of any kind, but the feeling created by journeys induced me to compose a simple poem in praise of all those particular women who exist in the mind – in airport bars, on trains, in libraries, street cafés or secluded beaches. In reality of course there are no such women, but in the imagination they can be real, so a poem seemed necessary.

'Every now and then,' I told the Table sheepishly, 'I get these urges.'

A Funny Kind of Girl

Walking on the beach one day,
Beside a shining sea,
I came upon a kind of girl
I'd always hoped could be.

I heard a footstep, caught an eye,
And saw a freckled knee.

And suddenly my heart took note,
Because it said to me:

That's a funny kind of girl, with
A funny kind of walk,
And a funny kind of
Twinkle in her eyes.

With an urchin kind of face,
And a freckled kind of nose
And a shapely kind of aspect
To her thighs.

A cotton kind of hat,
And a denim kind of shirt,
And a wicker kind of basket
For her things,

Two lengthy kind of legs,
Slightly bandy at the knees,
And ten tapered kind of fingers
For her rings.

A lanky kind of body,
With a slender kind of waist
And a gentle kind of fullness
To her rack

THE EXCITEMENT OF THE CHASTE

An untidy kind of hair-do
With an auburn kind of tint
And a heavy kind of ponytail
Cascading down her back.

With that my heart beat faster,
I distinctly heard it say:
For goodness sake don't mess about.
Confront her! Seize the day!

'Relax,' I said. 'Control yourself!
Keep something in reserve,
A sudden act on our part,
Might make her lose her nerve.'

'Don't wait too long,' my heart replied,
'Strike while the iron's hot!
Take a deep breath, collect your wits,
And give it all you've got!'

'I'll do the best I can,' I said,
'To give that girl a go, but,
I mustn't make a move until
My ducks are in a row!'

'It's not the time,' my heart replied,
'To worry about ducks,
When your priority should be

To cut straight to the crux …'

'Just saunter up,' I told my legs,
'Let courage have its way
If nothing's ventured, nothing's won.
But saunter please,' I said, 'don't run!
You'll frighten her away.'

My legs agreed to do their best,
To help me with my fling,
'Relax,' they said, 'don't agonise,
We're good at sauntering.'

'I'm very glad,' I told them both,
'To hear that you've agreed
To saunter. Now my vocal cords
Are what I'm going to need.'

So, while my legs both did their bit,
My mouth called out: 'Good Day.'
'Yes, isn't it?' she answered,
In her funny kind of way.

'A sunny kind of day,' she said,
'With yesterday so wet, that
To give myself something to do,
I made myself a bet:

THE EXCITEMENT OF THE CHASTE

That if I walked along a beach,
All on a summer's day,
And came across a man like you,
I'd have something to say.

So if you're lost and all alone,
With nothing much to do
There might be something off the cuff
That I could do with you.'

'How very kind of you,' I said,
'I happen to be free,
For anything, from making love
To having morning tea.

And though I have experience
At doing other stuff.
I've never really tried my hand
At being off the cuff.

I often find things off the cuff
Are what I like the best,
So if our day looks promising
We'll put it to the test.

Let's start by having morning tea,
And if we find that works,
We go on to investigate

The need for other perks.'

We wandered to a beach café,
That happened to be near, but
Instead of having tea for two,
Decided to have beer.

It came. We drank it. Then she said,
'Another would be nice.
They say beer comes in handy
If one wants to break the ice.'

'It's summertime,' I said to her.
'The weather's warm and nice,
I somehow doubt we'll find a need
To fracture any ice.'

'Although you seem to have,' she said,
'A very honest face
A second beer seems just the thing
For me to drink. In case …'

And halfway through her second glass,
She said, 'My name is Pearl,
And in case you haven't noticed,
I'm a funny kind of girl.'

By the time the train got to Geneva that evening, the poem was more or less finished. I booked into a nice hotel with a cluster of old pine trees and a view of the lake – I was determined to do it right, if you see what I mean. There is something about being alone in a strange city, a feeling of anonymity that makes the mind run free. I walked a lot, in the streets and by the lake, and had a ceremonial lunch of fried perche in a restaurant under trees near a little lakeside shop with postcards outside it. There were odd moments when company seemed possible, but for those two days, being alone was almost an addiction.

27

Out of Ten

Oddly enough, it was James who first mentioned Mark McCormack, another close friend who let me down by dying. We'd been discussing the Masters Golf in Augusta, and how good it was to see Arnold Palmer, Jack Nicklaus and Gary Player make the opening shots, when James suddenly emerged from one of his reveries and startled us by knowing exactly what we'd been talking about.

'Those three golfers were Mark McCormack's fellows,' he said. 'Bloody busy chap, that McCormack. I read one of his books last Christmas – *Hit the Ground Running*, it was called, and it had an odd effect on me. Made me feel guilty, so to get rid of the feeling I wrote a column about it.'

'Send Gordon a copy of it,' said Richard. 'He and McCormack were friends, you know.'

'I'll see if I can find it,' replied James, 'but I must warn Gordon that high achievers put me in a bad mood, so I might have been a bit hard on his friend.'

He found the article – it arrived in my email labelled 'busybody'.

Apparently the book had persuaded him to make a New Year's resolution that required him, too, to hit the ground running – 'Or if not actually running,' he'd said, 'at least moving in a forward direction. Writers are not natural runners ...' and he tapered off, muttering that writing and running were not of the same genre.

'Well, we cycle pretty well,' Richard reminded him gently, 'so if writing and cycling go together, I can't see why writing and running shouldn't.'

'Because cycling is different to running,' James explained. 'That's why McCormack didn't call his book *Hit the Ground Cycling* ...'

'By the way,' I asked, 'are things different *to* or *from* other things? I've never been quite sure.'

We all looked at the headmaster for clarification. 'Some English scholars consider *different to* problematic,' said Mark, obediently. 'The argument is that things differ *from* each other. They don't differ *to* each other, so *different from* is the logical conclusion.'

'So cycling is different *from* running. I must say that different from seems different from different to. Sounds a bit Irish. Never mind ...'

The article he sent me was typically James, so gently wry, sardonic, mocking that you could almost see him at it, chuckling away to himself.

> *I flew to Cape Town last month after having just read management consultant, Mark H McCormack's book,* Hit the Ground Running *– 'an insider's guide to air travel'. I decided to make the flight a demonstration of how seasoned writers travel, saying to myself, 'This day, I am going to hit the ground the way writers hit it ...'*

He goes on to tease Mark about his advice on travelling. For instance, Mark recommends an elaborate 'survival kit' for travelling. James claims *his* kit is much simpler. A piece of string. A safety pin. Enos. Aspirin. Band-Aid. Banana. Air ticket. Wallet and loose cash for tips. He then goes on to describe hilarious accidents that have befallen him on journeys – things that couldn't possibly happen to someone as organised as McCormack.

> *In truth one begins to hate McCormack soon after chapter two. By chapter four he becomes perfectly insufferable, but one is fascinated that somewhere out there, there's a man who can cut through airports like a hot knife through butter. But, I say, no matter how seasoned an air traveller I become, I know in my heart of hearts that if ever I were to hit the ground running it would be because they forgot to put the steps up against the aircraft door.*

'I did warn you,' he said glancing at me. 'These sudden energetic visions have strange effects on me ... A friend of yours, was he?'

'More than a friend,' I replied. 'We were quite different people, but we got on, and had some good times together ...'

❧

James's question brought a flood of memories. Mark was an exceptional man, no question of that, one of a kind – a ten-out-of-ten sort of man in many ways, one of them being that he loved giving points out of ten to things – events, sportsmen, holidays, restaurants, tennis matches, and so on. On one of our holidays, for instance, he even suggested that when people were asked how they were, they were simply to give a score out of ten.

'Saves time,' he said. 'All we want to know is how they are, not their medical history.'

It became a game, and in the mornings I would ask him: 'How are you this morning?'

'Eight. You?'

'Three. Too much red wine and crème brûlée. You and your damn restaurants.'

It was a whim that provided us with a lot of laughs (Poor old George, feeling only one-and-a-half this morning. Mixed the grape and the grain at dinner, then got on to liqueurs ...) But its deeper meaning emphasised his passion for clarity, brevity and efficient time management. But I'm going too fast ...

At the Table we have long since agreed that friends are the most important part of life, and in every life there are those who are of particular merit — who have a profound effect, not only on your life but sometimes on the lives of those close to you. For me, McCormack was such a man — not only a friend but a singular man, supportive in so many different ways — taking Frances and me on journeys, giving good advice, working with my son Gavin, to providing tickets to the 1995 Rugby World Cup final, where Joel Stransky made his historic drop kick.

Mark Hume McCormack. His company, the International Management Group (IMG) ran the World Cup that year, so together with him and his wife Betsy, we also attended the Newlands semi-final, when New Zealand beat England.

In Cape Town we often stayed on Sol Kerzner's estate called Leeukoppie because Mark and Sol were, in a way, kindred spirits and, via Abe, I too had become his friend. Sol's, that is. Strangely, although Mark had quite enough money to be a mogul, I never thought of him as such because he was always so straightforward and down to earth – never seemed to stop loving the simple life, no matter how big his deals were and, believe me, some of them were very big. I've got to be careful, writing about Sol, because it could get hard to stop. There's a whole book there, and even then you'd battle to get it all together. Abe and Sol were like brothers – loved having large whiskies and then insulting each other …

'And it's also daunting to write about McCormack,' I told the Table, 'for he was a man of so many parts that adjectives become tricky.'

Rare, exceptional, creative, bold, wealthy, picky, tireless, strict, meticulous, all apply – but above all he was a simple man who liked simple things, such as hamburgers, ice cream, or getting off the Blue Train for a short walk on the main street of Matjiesfontein. And with all that he had an uncanny business sense, a sort of perceptive shrewdness that enabled him to create a vast sports-management empire – invent it really, you could say, and run it via a filing system that began in his shirt pocket.

I can vouch for this, because once, with his birthday approaching, he said to me: 'If you must give me a shirt, Gordon, make sure it has a pocket.'

'What makes you think I'm giving you a shirt?'

'Because you've just said that you're going to Jermyn Street today, and you told me last year that in Jermyn Street they have the best shirts in the world.'

'You don't miss much, do you?'

'Not if it means getting a good shirt.'

It was just as well he told me because I'd indeed planned to give him a Turnbull & Asser shirt, but their shirts didn't have pockets. When I told them it was for Mark McCormack, they said that for him they'd add a pocket free of charge – a relief, because their shirts were expensive even without pockets, and I still have a farmer's thrift in me. Apparently Mark knew this because once when I asked them to dinner, he turned to his wife Betsy and asked her whether she felt like pizza.

'He continually took Frances and me out to the very best restaurants in whatever city we found ourselves,' I told the Table, 'having a way of arranging things so bills never reached our table.'

A head waiter would arrive to ask whether everything had been to his liking. Usually it had. There was never any sign of payment, and Frances and I got used to it quite easily, because we knew that he was backed up by an enormous business and an even bigger expense account. Every now and then we felt obliged to reciprocate, which was when he made jokes about pizzas. Oddly enough, both he and Betsy loved pizza, it was he who'd made the suggestion in the first place, and even at the pizza restaurant, when the bill came, he wanted to pay it.

Anyway, I was able to get him a shirt with a pocket. But now comes another problem. To explain his shirt pocket filing system, I have to explain his business, and to explain his business I have to explain the size of it, and to explain the size of it I have to explain all the things he did, and to do that would take a long time. Each year there was an IMG book called *Calendar of Events*. And even with it, I'd have to explain all the events inside it, which is impossible because there're too many. Suffice it to say that he was better at hitting the ground running than most of his peers.

In the morning he'd get up at five and sit with his PA Sarah

Abe, Mark McCormack, Frances and G F.

James, Ernie Els and Mark McCormack outside Mark's 'tent' at Wimbledon.

Wooldridge, the wife of the famous journalist Ian Wooldridge. He'd take, from yesterday's shirt pocket, cards that were filled with his handwritten notes (he had a terrible handwriting, an absolute scrawl) and give the notes to Sarah – notes that could be anything from the day's directives for his offices all over the world, to a booking for that evening's restaurant. Then he'd refill his shirt pocket with a sheaf of fresh cardboard cards, and these would be filled up with every detail of the new day. And Mark's days were crammed – I was going to say with meetings, but he actually disliked meetings. Although, of course, some had to be scheduled, he enjoyed doing business over tea or lunch, making notes on his cards with the Parker propelling pencil that he guarded with his life (you can't get them any more) – and the whole cycle would start again.

In his world there were no committees. He was the sole owner of his business, he took his own decisions, making what sometimes seemed to me impulsive ones that had in fact been carefully considered. He had the best memory I have ever known in anyone – a frightening power of recall that enabled him to remember anything from the terms of a long business agreement to, say, the first name of a new tennis client's coach's wife, or the latest world ranking of a junior who he thought IMG might sign up. Under his arm he always carried a leather attaché case that contained all the papers he needed – 'I've got something to show you, Gordon, something we talked about last year' – and he'd fish out a cutting or a note …

A born salesman, too, he looked after his best clients himself. His favourite was Wimbledon – for whom he had created marketing – a client that he handled with loving care, fully aware of the value of the brand and the delicacy needed to exploit it. As it turned out, he was so successful that the All England Club committee invited him to become an honorary member – one of his greatest satisfactions.

In addition to the dozen or so books he wrote, there was a monthly newsletter called *Success Secrets* that went all over the world. His love of good restaurants caused him to devote the back page of his letter to comments on the ones he'd visited, and restaurant owners knew this because he got special service wherever he went. In certain moods, he had a restaurant routine that always amused Frances and me. We called it the McCormack Test, and it went like this: If we'd dined at an expensive place (they were usually expensive and there were often six or eight guests), having paid the bill, Mark would always ask, 'Would anyone like anything else?'

Occasionally guests felt like another Sambuca, espresso, port or something which Mark would duly order. Then, if the restaurant brought another bill, Mark would frown while he paid it and make a note on one of the cards in his shirt pocket.

'Penny-wise and pound-foolish,' he once said. 'The biggest mistake any business can make. They won't see me again ...'

Yet if the food and service had been good, he would give the restaurant its due.

28

The Big Book

Mark wrote about eleven business books, starting with the bestseller, *What They Don't Teach You at Harvard Business School*, a title that summed up two key McCormack aspects: his unorthodox but effective way of working; and the fact that in business great things were often accomplished by words or deeds not taught at universities. Overall, brevity ruled, emphasised by the way he asked questions. 'In ten words, tell me your plans for December …'

I once thought I'd catch him out, and in return asked him, 'In ten words tell me your long-term business plan.'

After a moment's thought he answered, 'I want to take over all sports', then laughed delightedly at his answer.

While all his books were successful, his appetite for authorship was not completely satisfied. From the beginning he talked to me of what he called 'The Big Book' – the story that for years existed in his mind and imagination as a book that would tell of his life, his love of sport, his business, the people he knew, his travels, his restaurants – so many things, in fact, that he had difficulty in getting it started.

'Would you consider writing it?' he once asked me, but in a way that made me suspect he had certain reservations. I was right. Later he told me that his publishers had told him that I was quite the wrong author and would never be able to bear the brunt of it.

'They say you're too inexact and whimsical, but that's what I want. I want your whimsy mixed with my gravity. They say you can't do it. I think you can.'

He liked my book, *A Handful of Summers* – an anomaly really, for his world was one of wealth, discipline and superstars, and my book was about tennis and simple people finding their way. But, he told his publishers, he wanted diary notes included, and he wanted himself and the people in his book to be as simple as the characters in my book.

I had a number of interviews with his publishers and his editor, but could always tell that their hearts were not in it, and when I read some of the 'big' biographies by noted authors, I knew why. They were precise, those books, written by meticulous men who did meticulous research, and I was not enough of a 'detail' man. To complicate matters, Mark had vast archives in which were filed every business memo, every note, letter, business deal and diary entry he'd ever done (even those written on a napkin in some restaurant). To write 'The Big Book' I would have had to sift through all of those, and I'm not good at that sort of thing.

My doubts were further emphasised one day when Charles presented me with one of his books – *The Seed is Mine* – the life of an illiterate black sharecropper, healer and patriarch called Kas Maine who lived to the age of ninety-one under the apartheid regime and made the best of it – fatalistic but positive. One of his sayings reveals his entire world in just two lines:

The seed is mine. The ploughshares are mine. The span of oxen is mine. Everything is mine. Only the land is theirs.

Well, I tell you! That darn book, over six hundred pages of meticulous writing, prodigious research and organised thought, gave me quite a turn.

'What are you doing to me, Charles?' I asked, trying not to sound plaintive.

'Put it on your bedside table,' he replied. 'You never know ...'

So far, McCormack's 'Big Book' hasn't happened. Whether or not his three children, Breck, Todd and Leslie, will take up the challenge, is another thing. They were certainly close enough to their father to do so.

***

'You could say he was a driven man,' I said to the Table. 'But driven by an unusual set of forces. He built a huge business, and made a lot of money, but more than any man I know, he did it by doing things he loved to do. In this way his life became the perfect, self-fulfilling cycle – the more money he made, the more he was able to do the things he loved, and the more he did the things he loved, the more money he made.'

'Ideally,' he once said to me, 'money should be the by-product of what you like to do. A means but not an end.'

Yet he was absorbed by the preservation of money, to the extent that IMG had an investment arm, especially established to look after money made by its young clients.

'They're young, and they tend to spend it foolishly,' he said. 'We want to make sure that when they retire they're okay, so we invest their money very conservatively.'

He was naturally interested in finance and investments, and in October 1987, having lunch with him and one of his high-powered American friends at the Wentworth Golf Match Play Championship that IMG ran, we talked about the current state of affairs of the US markets. The American friend spoke enthusiastically of an extended boom, while to me both the Dow and the Nasdaq indexes seemed far too high. Tentatively, I gave my opinion, and the way the American laughed it off caused me, impulsively and imprudently, to bet him ten pounds that by the year end, the indices would be lower and not higher. With Mark an interested observer, he laughed indulgently and took me on. Remarkably, the very next day turned out to be 'black Monday' when the Dow lost about 22 per cent of its value. Well, you can imagine! Mark saw me as a financial soothsayer, and made sure I got my ten pounds, but it was about the only sooth I was ever able to say.

❦

While in business affairs Mark was obsessed with brevity, at leisure he might sit for hours listening to or telling yarns if they had to do with sportsmen or women, or any of his celebrity friends. If they were funny, all the better, for he had a sense of humour that surfaced unexpectedly, like sunlight in a rain shower. One of his favourite characters was his friend Kerry Packer, the Australian entrepreneur.

In 1986 we gathered in Rome for the Italian Open at the Foro Italico stadium, then owned by IMG (the tournament, not the stadium).

Packer had taken over the penthouse suite of the Hassler Hotel, a huge, terraced affair that overlooked the whole city. Each evening he hosted a cocktail party which allowed his friends to drink champagne and watch the sunset, and we would all gather on his roof to discuss the day's matches. Mark and Betsy also stayed at the Hassler, but had a room lower down. On the first evening, Packer took me by the arm, called over to Mark, and led us to a point on the balustrade where we could see the rooms below.

'See that, Forbsey?' he said to me, pointing at two lighted windows. 'That's where Mark dosses down. Can't swing a cat down there.'

The Hassler was the best hotel in Rome, with every room quite big enough for cat-swinging.

'We don't have a cat,' said Mark.

At the tennis we would sit over Italian lunches in Mark's tent. Although there was always pasta, there were also freckled grapes, anchovies, small black olives, lumps of cheese, *ciabatta* and *caffe espresso*, all amplified by the dusty Italian wines in which you seem to taste the vineyards on the limestone hills. It's not hard to philosophise at such times – Mark, Packer, Richard Evans, Abe, Cino Marchese and me mainly, but sometimes my son Gavin (by then working for Mark) would join us and we would each have to announce our ten best tennis players of all time. Chaos would reign until Mark announced himself chairman, and each of us could reveal our choices. Packer and Richard Evans were experts at tennis and cricket, Mark knew tennis and golf like the back of his hand, Abe and I pretended we knew a lot, Cino was an expert on tennis, tennis players and Italian foods, and Gavin knew the young players. (Our lists in 1986 of course could not include the modern stars.)

After endless wrangling, Mark might announce in summary, 'Right. We've got Tilden, Budge, Perry, Gonzales, Hoad, Laver, Connors, Borg, McEnroe' – at once loosing a storm of protests: Come on! What about Jack Kramer? Has Kenny Rosewall become null and void? Are we binning Lacoste, Cochet and Borotra? Never mind Sedgman, Lendl, Becker, they don't count. The Renshaws and Dohertys won only eleven Wimbledon titles between them so they're non-starters. Well, once we're back in the Ice Age, what about Anthony Wilding?

It was impossible to select only ten, and there would be more argument about those left out than those included. It didn't matter that never, on any occasion, did we all agree, only that we had stories to tell, and were having a good time. Periodically we'd adjourn to watch a match – Vilas playing Leconte, Noah playing Becker, Edberg playing someone-or-other, and again it didn't matter, as long as I got glimpses of my youth on those slow, sunken, red courts. In the evenings, Cino would take us to the best restaurants in Rome – he knew them all – and as we entered them with McCormack and Packer, I used to smile when I remembered how, as young players, we would carefully examine prices on menus pinned to doorways of such places, shrug our shoulders and then stoically walk on.

'There were, in fact, three young players,' I told the Table, 'who, when they felt like a really good dinner, would enter one of those high-class restaurants, choose a table near the door, then have a serious blow-out, you understand, order good wine, whatever food they felt like. Towards the end they would draw lots and the one getting the shortest straw would have to wait for the other two to leave. He would then wait his chance and when it came, get up and run like hell, the theory being that tennis players could run faster than waiters. They were never caught ... What's that? You want to know their names? Have a heart! Mind you, they're all old by now, so they'd probably be proud as punch ...'

After Rome we spent a week with Mark and Betsy at Villa d'Este, resigning ourselves to a fearful bill at the end of the week, eating food and wine on luxury boat rides, sipping expensive drinks and assuring ourselves we were having a good time. On such trips there would be tennis matches, often between Mark and Betsy, Frances and me.

Now, on the road to Plett, we stop for the night at the Drostdy in Graaff-Reinet, boil the little kettle on our washstand, make tea, eat the two biscuits, listen to Sinatra singing *That's Life*, then have a good Karoo dinner, usually something to do with lamb and mint sauce ...

29

Luck or Skill?

Recently, going through one of my old diaries, I came across some notes I'd written while watching tennis at Roland Garros, in 1998.

'There you are,' he said to me. 'That's the difference we always talk about.'

Jim Courier, IMG's latest superstar, if my memory serves was playing a Scandinavian called Kent Carlsson. He should have beaten Carlsson quite easily, but Carlsson was one of those temperamental players capable of brilliant tennis, especially when he was the underdog. It was his day, and for a long time the match was balanced on a knife-edge, when suddenly the same old thing happened. They got into a crucial tie-break. Carlsson got a set point, played a courageous rally, then hit what might have been a clean winner, except that it missed the baseline by a few millimetres. A few points later, Courier had a match point. Another rally gave him a shot identical to Carlsson's, except that his shot touched the baseline, and the match was over.

Luck or skill? Mark and I have debated this question ad infinitum, and we still haven't a clear answer. Nonetheless, Jim's shot filled Mark with satisfaction, for it strengthened his theory that what made players great was the ability to make the big shot at the right time and I had to agree with him. I'd seen the same thing happen on countless occasions. The minute differences bothered me, luck always lurked in the wings of my thinking, yet the great players mostly seemed to prevail.

'If you'd had to make that shot, out of ten, what chance do you think you'd have of doing what Jim just did?' he asked.

'About four.'

The answer seemed to satisfy him. He knew well enough that I'd served my time on tennis courts, that I'd had some good results but never been able to break into the world of the greats. Perhaps this was why he seemed to enjoy what he called our 'intellectual discussions', interludes that took place whenever there was time – writing, sport, success, yarns, humour, and so on. He loved analysing the subtle difference between winning and losing, perhaps because he himself had started out wanting to be a great golfer, realised that he wouldn't be one, taken the signpost leading to sports management and created IMG.

'What do we think are the ten qualities that go to making a Pete Sampras?' he once asked.

We started to think up answers, and as we announced them, he wrote them on the yellow pad he always carried, putting certain words in brackets.

Natural talent essential (gift, genius, flair)
Good physique (strength, agility, balance)
Perfect eyesight (20/20 or better)
Perfect technique (improvisation seldom works)

At least one big weapon (service, forehand)
Courage (recovery, endurance, resolve)
Belief (in winning, conviction, patience, composure, persistence)
Love of the game (passion, enjoyment, relish)
Love of competition (fearlessness, boldness, optimism)
Optimism (buoyancy, confidence, hope)

Finally he looked up and said, 'That's ten. What have we left out?'

'Temperament, maybe.'

'That's a combination of the last five. Good balance, this list. Five physical, five mental. What else?'

'Luck?'

'Irrelevant. If you're good enough it comes naturally.'

He sat staring at his list for a while, then said, 'Do you realise that if you remove any one of those ten things, you've lost Sampras. Nine out of ten, and you end up with just another guy battling away on Court 13!'

Although luck always intrigued me, for Mark it did not hold much mystery. When I asked him why Scott Hoch had to miss a two-foot putt to lose the Masters, then watched Nick Faldo hole a twenty-foot one to win it, his reply was pragmatic. 'Depends on the putt. The ball rolls across the green and either goes into the hole or misses it.'

'But what governs such things? Or is it simply pure chance?'

'Call it that, if you like. There's no one up there calling the shots, allocating luck, if that's what you're asking. What happens, happens, and the better the player, the more goes his way. He wrote on his yellow pad again, then added, 'You need a break or two, of course. You know why I'm in this business, and not missing cuts on some golf course? Because one day I saw Arnold Palmer hitting two irons on the practice range, and I knew I could never do that. So I let him hit the two irons while I kept score. My lucky break was to be on the range while he hit his two irons.'

The deal he made with Palmer was sealed with a handshake, never put in writing, lasting their lifetimes and remaining Mark's proudest achievement.

For him there were no pots of gold where rainbows ended, no pies in the sky and no free lunches. Reality and logic were his guiding lights. Although he decided to manage and not play, in all the time I knew him, he never showed the slightest sign of pretension or resentment at not being a sports star. Instead he enjoyed the successes of the great sportsmen and women he knew, admired their skills, and did his best to help them whenever he could.

Having said all that, he didn't much like losing. He liked playing tennis more than golf, making up for his pedestrian game by inventing rules that made him impossible to beat.

'When I come to net, you're not allowed to lob. And you can pass me only on the forehand side!' Then he'd cover the forehand alley.

'Businessmen never lose,' I once said to him. 'That's the difference between tennis and business. Tennis teaches you. When you walk on court you either win or lose. In business, a win makes the boss a hero. A loss is never his fault, because he can always blame sales managers, accountants, strikes, depressions, slow-downs, fires, acts of God ...'

'There are times when I could do with an act of God,' said Tim. 'Someone on high sending me a few bright ideas.'

'You'd need a literary sort of God,' mused Charles. 'One with a good background in history and grammar ...'

'I was writing my column the other day during a thunderstorm,' interrupted James, 'when a lightning bolt hit the house next door. Shook me up no end. Unleashed adjectives I haven't used in years. May have been one of His acts …'

'Unconvincing,' said the Other Peter. 'To help *you*, why would God hit the house next door?'

'Collateral damage. Even Gods sometimes miss the mark …'

30

Give and Take

By the time Courier's match at Roland Garros ended that day, it was nearly one o'clock.

'Lunch,' Mark said. 'It's Gino Santini's day today and he is a punctual man' – and we climbed out of the stand and made our way to his tent.

In Paris, where Mark's people had particularly good relations with the municipality, a very special arrangement had been made. Instead of being among the other corporate marquees, Mark's 'tent' was in one of the greenhouses in the beautiful *Jardins Municipales*. To reach it one had to follow a forest path, and suddenly, among the plants and waterways, a lovely entertainment area was set up, with Mark's lunch table positioned next to some tree ferns in a far corner. That day Gino Santini was waiting for Mark, having made a unique deal with him.

He was the owner of Ristorante Santini, one of London's best Italian eateries, and a favourite of Mark's. One of its starters consisted of baby courgettes still in flower, grilled in some cheesy sort of batter. Mark liked them. Always on the lookout for good deals, when he discovered that Gino was a nice man and a tennis fanatic, he made him

Mark and I had lost our doubles match, and he didn't much like losing.

an offer: Gino could spend two days at Roland Garros every year as Mark's guest, and Mark and designated friends could have free, grilled courgette flowers for the rest of their lives. Gino had eagerly accepted Mark's offer. He would be at lunch that day, and in the afternoon he would watch the tennis from Mark's box. That day, Mark's other guest was Johnny Carson; well, you can imagine, it's not often that Karoo boys meet their iconic talk show host, but Mark was like that. There was often somebody …

Gino never forgot the deal. Some years later when I was in London for my seventieth birthday, I celebrated it by inviting a few friends to Santini's. Sure enough, no sooner had we seated ourselves when courgette flowers arrived, this time accompanied by a bottle of champagne.

Mark enjoyed making such deals. We had lunch one day at the Carlton Tower on Cadogan Place, a short walk from Mark's house in Clabon Mews, Chelsea. Mark ordered a hamburger, and was told that hamburgers were not on the menu. He called for the hotel manager and asked him to make a hamburger, which the manager agreed to do, getting his chef to grind up some beef filet and add whatever he felt was necessary. It duly arrived. Mark pronounced it the best hamburger he'd ever tasted, and called for the manager to congratulate him. He told Mark there was a large business conference at the hotel, and invited him to give an opening address.

'I'll do it for you,' replied Mark, if I can have free hamburgers for the rest of my life' (his talks usually cost quite a lot of money), and so it was agreed.

As we left, Mark said to me: 'If I have starters at Santini and mains at the Carlton Tower, I've finally achieved free lunches!'

31

Rounding the Horn

'We need a journey,' Mark would say. He loved travel. 'Journeys set your mind at rest. No more decisions, something to do with destiny. You have to go where it takes you.'

He particularly liked the Blue Train and the Orient Express. Sometimes there would be sea cruises, and he even liked long air journeys. 'You sit down and they give you a drink and some nuts, you switch off your phone, relax and listen to the wash of sound from out there in the dark …'

The Blue Train was a firm favourite – something to do with the sedateness of its pace, the cosy cabins, and the dining car with the vastness of the Karoo moving past while he had his breakfast. Several times, Frances and I joined him and Betsy on a journey to Cape Town and back.

'Kimberley!' he would call out. We might see the Big Hole, and I could tell him the story about the entrepreneur who bought up part of the Big Hole, then divided it up into small holes and sold them to golf courses all over the world. The idea delighted him.

'Sounds like me,' he cried. 'I'd call them *Arnold Palmer holes* and make a commission.'

In Matjiesfontein the guard assured him there would be time for a walk down the main street, and when we passed the Lord Milner Hotel he wanted to know who Lord Milner was. Frances knew he'd once been governor of the Cape, but all I could say was that he was an *ex*-lord, so Mark couldn't sign him up.

One of his better ideas was a world cruise starting from Buenos Aires, rounding the Horn, proceeding through the Beagle Canal to Puerto Montt in Chile, then onward across the Pacific with its tropical islands to Australia. This was his longest journey yet – more, in fact, than a journey, rather, a sabbatical, a drawn-out punctuation mark in his life. His plan was to invite friends to join him at various stages of the journey, and Frances and I shared the first stage, from Buenos Aires to Puerto Montt. The two guests with us on that first leg of the journey were Colin and Nan MacLaine. Their presence was typical of Mark's innate thoughtfulness, for I had once told him of my family's love of Scotland – and Colin and Nan were about as Scottish as any two people could be.

There we were, moving over an endless sea, always different, yet always the same, and there could be nothing more nautical than the *Royal Viking* – a nice ship, not one of those modern monstrosities that resemble floating blocks of flats. The ship had two bars, one at the front and one at the back – Fore or Aft, the first mate said. 'Mr McCormack has gone For'ard this evening …'

On some evenings he chose the Aft bar, where we'd look out at the receding wake disappearing into such eerie gloom that we'd settle gratefully into the comfort of our seats. But usually he would choose the For'ard bar where the sea was immense and smooth save for its

Mark, Frances and G F. We had stopped to see the Big Hole.

G F and Frances on the Royal Viking, *rounding the Horn. That's the Horn, top right, and we've just rounded it!*

huge, ever-shifting swells, the ship's bow cutting through the water without a murmur. There could be nothing half so satisfying as those evenings on the good ship *Royal Viking*.

During the day Betsy, a fitness fanatic, egged us on to deck games and exercise, and in the evenings there were the interludes in the bar. After dinner, music in the lounges, or movies in luxurious theatres. Colin MacLaine, once chairman, or perhaps captain, of the Royal and Ancient Golf Club of St Andrews, had many golf stories to tell and used to write colourful reports on the British Open. One of them read:

> *… that Severiano Ballesteros chose not to use the course, but preferred his own path, mainly consisting of hay fields, car parks, grand stands and dropping zones, was entirely his own affair …*

Recalling his lines, he added in his broad Scots accent, 'Sevvy was one of the grreatest,' then after a long silence, finally continuing in a musing way, 'so hard to define greatness. This, too, is great,' and he held his whisky against the light, and gave it a shake. 'Aye. Whisky can achieve grreatness, so could Winston Churchill, and so can a piece of fish cooked by a master chef …' He paused when he saw Mark making his way towards us. 'We're trying to define greatness,' he said, as Mark arrived. 'Any ideas?'

'I hit a great forehand in a doubles match against Fred Stolle,' said Mark.

'You could safely say that Ballesteros reached the Top,' observed the One Peter.

To avoid a 'too good to be true' label, I should say that there were two Marks, one of them the man we all knew, and the other a man who lived in a world of his own. I never got to know that man. No one did. All I got was occasional glimpses of someone I thought might be him. Whoever he was, I was stunned by the suddenness of the news that Eric Drossart first gave me. Eric, a little younger than I was, had been Belgium's top tennis player. After his career he had joined Mark's company, IMG, and worked his way up to become head of the European sector.

'Mark's in trouble,' Eric had said when he phoned me that day, and my heart sank because of the way he said it. Mark had always been meticulous about his health. He'd go to the Mayo Clinic every year in about November, spend two days there and undergo every health test known to man. Invariably the tests would show that he was in good shape, and he would phone his friends and brag about how well he was. That November, in 2002, was no different. He was declared fit, and he let me know that he'd invented a new set of rules, and that Frances and I 'better get ready to lose'.

Fair-skinned, he was always concerned about sun blemishes. After his visit to the Mayo Clinic, he would go to see a dermatologist in New York, and 2002 was no exception. A small blemish on his face needed an injected anaesthetic to allow a minor procedure, and somehow his heart stopped. He went into a coma for some months, and never recovered.

For me, that summer died away to a silence that was hard to bear. I traipsed around some tennis tournaments with the odd feeling that Mark would reappear, and for a while in the IMG marquees there was still a table in 'Mark's Corner'. But he'd gone, and a part of my life had gone with him.

On the evening of Sunday 22 June 2003, at Hampton Court (Mark used to stage classical concerts and musical evenings there) just before Wimbledon, a memorial service was held in honour of Mark. It was named 'A Celebration of His Life', and to my great surprise, pride and alarm, I was asked by Mark's family to speak for six minutes about 'Mark, the Friend and the Man'. Sir Martin Sorrell was to speak on 'Mark, the Businessman', Eric Drossart on 'Mark, our Chairman', and Sir Jackie Stewart on 'Mark from a Client Perspective'. Dame Kiri Te Kanawa and José Carreras were to sing arias in honour of him, and his daughter Leslie, together with Nick Faldo and Virginia Wade, were to read poems.

I was nervous. I carefully wrote a speech, but from previous experience knew that writing a speech was one thing, delivering it quite another. In fact, I'd a bad habit of completely ignoring my writing and losing my place. Worried about this, I looked up in various books what to do if and when the mind went blank, and discovered a story about Oscar Wilde making a speech, his mind going blank, and then finding a clever means of escape. I memorised his method, and forever thereafter wrote at the top of any speech notes 'if the mind goes blank, remember Oscar Wilde'.

(Years later, when speaking at some or other function, my mind did in fact go blank. I remembered to look up at the Oscar Wilde instruction, but couldn't for the life of me remember what he'd said. Managing to avert disaster by telling listeners about how I'd forgotten what Oscar Wilde had said was a tactic that allowed me time to collect my wits. Nonetheless, the thought of a blank mind at Hampton Court was quite another matter.)

The evening came around and although it was even more ceremonial than I'd imagined, I managed to avoid a blank mind. Fortunately, the MC was my old friend John Barrett, one of the first players I'd ever met when Gordon Talbot and I had arrived in Britain. His introduction of me at Hampton Court calmed my nerves. Strangely, my depth of feeling about Mark's death made speaking of him easier. Many of the topics I mentioned are included in this book – his love of travel, his shirt pockets, his tennis rules, his hamburgers, his love of scoring out of ten. I revealed his constant search for new promotions by describing how, in the Beagle Canal, when huge ice blocks fell to spectacular, slow-motion eruptions of water and snow, he wondered whether he could sign up the Canal for an ice show. His tennis rules and his deal with Santini evoked laughter, as if that entire gathering yearned for relief from solemnity.

Mark's death had a profound effect on me. In addition to shock, disbelief, sadness and loss, I felt strangely aggrieved because it was not according to plan and would affect me for the rest of my life. I'd lost not only a friend but also an enduring support – a stick to lean on, if you see what I mean. Franny's son, Jamie, was growing up. My arrangement with Mark was that when he had completed his studies at the University of Virginia he, too, would join IMG and work as Gavin's understudy. But it was not to be.

32

The Black Dog

For me the world of tennis would never really be the same without McCormack. Over the years I'd built up a whole set of memories, clear and sharp until time slowly blurred the edges. One of them returned while talking to the Table about McCormack, making me recall a story he'd always laughed about.

'A story about John Feaver's black dog,' I said during one of those lazy moments when lunch was over and insouciance replaced more weighty issues.

'Who is John Feaver?'

'Another tennis player, British this time, very good – one of those players who nearly won a Grand Slam. Plenty about. One should remember that for every player who won a Grand Slam there were hundreds who didn't. A man of many parts, you could call him, multifaceted sort of chap ...'

'I wouldn't mind another facet or two,' said Tim thoughtfully. 'Seventy-one years with only one facet ...'

'Another facet might have brought out the novelist in you,' said

Charles. 'Tim's books are measured works,' he informed us, 'sometimes prescribed by doctors as sedatives. *Read half a page after meals, and two at night.* I remember one reader becoming so calm …'

'Could you please just tell us about John Feaver's black dog,' interrupted Mark (the headmaster) a trifle wearily.

'As I said, John was a top British tennis player. He had the fastest service in the world and a solid forearm, but as in many of us, there were slight deficiencies in other areas …'

Nonetheless, John reached the quarter-finals at Wimbledon, was a member of the All England Club, and sat on most of the British tennis committees. 'Tea at eleven, lunch at one, and tea again at four,' he once explained. 'British tennis has never been short of committees, you know. There was even a committee specially appointed to appoint committees.' John's bailiwick was to promote English tournaments, and once having persuaded Virgin Atlantic to sponsor a new women's event, he had to report to the tournament committee.

'Good news and bad news,' he began. 'The good news is we've got Virgin Atlantic to sponsor a tournament. The bad news is that we're stuck for a name – can't decide whether to call it the Virgin Women's Open, or the Virgin Women's Closed. We'll need a committee decision …'

As a player, John toured South Africa – played in what was then called the Sugar Circuit, fell in love and married a South African girl called Allie, who was the niece of a magistrate from Aliwal North, a man I'd once played cricket against, and who, in Johannesburg, married Frances to me. Aliwal North is a town near Burgersdorp. The odd thing is that there is no town called Aliwal South. You'd think …'

'Please!' Mark was becoming plaintive. 'What about John Feaver's black dog?'

THE BLACK DOG

'Right. Well. Thirty years ago, John and Allie bought a house on Home Park Road in Wimbledon. It was an Edwardian house on a big stand, with a big lawn in front and a copse at the back, so they felt they needed a dog to guard it.'

'What breed?' asked James.

'Non-denominational,' I replied incorrectly.

'Not a religious dog?'

'An atheist. Not a playful dog … Anyway, John had a very British neighbour whose house also had a lawn. On it was a rabbit hutch with a rabbit in it. Although there was a netting fence separating the two houses, John said his dog spent a lot of time staring balefully at the rabbit.'

'Dogs do that,' murmured James.

'Yes, but nothing happened for so long that he became sure the dog had got used to the rabbit. On summer mornings John used to get up at six to go jogging. One Saturday, to his alarm, he saw the rabbit lying on his lawn, deceased, and covered in soil. And under the netting fence was the kind of burrow dogs make.'

'I panicked,' he related. 'No other word for it, but finally I made a plan. I picked up the rabbit by its hind leg, took it to the sink outside our kitchen; gave it a rinse, got Allie's hairdryer, dried it off, climbed over the fence and put the damn thing back in its hutch. Closed up the hole under the fence, had a shower and went off to the Club to play in a league match. Damn lucky the neighbour only got up at nine on weekends.'

When he returned after tennis, his neighbour was waiting for him. He called John over to the fence.

'I say, Feaver,' he cried. 'Dashed odd. Quite extraordinary. No other word for it. Our rabbit. Poor old chap died on Thursday night, we buried him in the garden, and this morning he's back in his hutch.'

'Alive?'

'Good God, no! Dead. Definitely, this time. Must have had a spark left in him on Thursday. Came to and burrowed out. Rabbits do that, you know. Got back in his hutch, cleaned himself up, and died again. Made a good job of it ... I'll have to bury him all over again.'

⁓⁕⁓

That was long ago. More recently, Feaver told me an uncle had died and left him 'a bit of Somerset', as he put it. 'Small farm, actually. A meadow, a small wood, herd of cows, a barn and a bull called Rufus. Put us out a bit because we don't know much about cattle ...'

And he went on to tell me that they were a bit worried about Rufus as he was getting old and starting to forget what he was supposed to do. Or so the farm manager said.

John still talks in these sharp bursts. Anyway, he and Allie have acquired a share in a lovely house in Pezula, an estate near Knysna. Fresh air, marvellous views, trees and things. We have lunch together these days because, as you know, Knysna is near Plett. This year I asked him whether he had any more stories for me, and told him his black dog story was in my book.

'It is true of course?' I asked him. 'Just a thought ...'

'Quite true, as far as I can remember,' he replied. 'You yourself saw the dog. There was a rabbit, it died, got buried, our fellow dug it up and I found it on our lawn. I did clean it up, but I may not actually have blow-dried it.' There he stopped.

'Let's leave it at that,' I said. 'McCormack loved that story and it was so long ago that it could easily have happened just as you said. So let's

G F, Virginia Wade and John Feaver. The black dog wasn't there that day …

agree that it did …'

'Well, I do remember climbing over the fence because in doing so I tore my tennis shorts.'

With that settled, we reminisced about the time he (John) and Roger Taylor played a doubles match against Cliff Drysdale and Owen Davidson in the Wimbledon seniors (the same event in which Abe and I were humbled). It had developed into a long and tense match in which Roger kept losing his service because Davidson had a tricky return from the right court that floated over the net like a feather. He therefore asked John to crouch down in the centre of the court in the modern way, then leap up and knock off the return before it bounced.

Frances and I, watching the match, were sitting at the side of the court, close to where John had lowered himself into the crouch position, his eyes level with the tape of the net. As Taylor got ready to serve, he looked across at us, gave us his wince, and muttered, 'He wants me to leap!'

33

The Prodigal Son

I have three 'only' children, in a manner of speaking, for there are big differences in their ages – which, strangely enough, has drawn them closer together. There are also four fine grandsons, a fact that enables me now and then to pour myself a glass of single malt and drink a toast to my good fortune.

Gavin is my oldest son. His full name is Gavin-mor Duncan Forbes – 'Mor' in Gaelic meaning 'big'; i.e., Big Gavin – a combination of youthful enthusiasm in his parents, and a spin-off of his grandfather's obsession with Scotland. Dutifully, he grew up to be about six foot four. Julia Ashley came next, and James Duncan last.

Valerie, my first wife, and I got married too young, and Gavin arrived on the scene too soon, both events unpremeditated – the impulsiveness of youth, naivety, optimism, enthusiasm, excitement, and blind trust in luck. Now, looking back, we might ask questions, but at the time there was only one. Why shouldn't we? We both played tennis, we got on well, we had plenty of time, could travel the world, meet nice people, see nice places, use tennis as a guiding light. I was twenty-three,

Ashley and Gavin.

and Valerie, one of the country's best young players, nineteen. In those days 'living together' was frowned on, and as we wanted to be together marriage seemed the only option. If we had our lives over, we'd probably do it again.

The fact that Gavin arrived only eighteen months after we married was both a blessing and a shock. To continue our tennis travels, he had either to be taken with us or left with Jack and his wife Lu on the farm. Usually it was the farm, so that Gavin too has in his blood a modicum of the Karoo spirit. Whatever the cause, he went through all the stages of growing up with a panache that combined mischief and innocence that would serve him well in later life.

With a flair for all school sports, he came close to being a very

Gavin, right, with a friend on the mountain where the eagles nested.

good tennis player. Often, as a boy, and against my strictest orders, he would purloin one of my favourite rackets – there were plenty of others in the tennis cupboard and he had several of his own, but somehow mine (there were about six, hanging on their own peg) seemed to have special appeal. In those days we lived in Bryanston and the Bowes family were our neighbours. Gavin often played tennis with Mark Bowes on our court and one day, having taken one of my rackets (always by mistake), in a fit of temper he threw it at the netting fence where it hit a pole and broke in half. After serious discussion, he and Mark decided the safest course of action would be to bury both halves in the garden. I discovered this some twenty years

THE PRODIGAL SON

later on Gavin's wedding day when, at the end of his speech, Mark (his best man) looked up at me and said, 'Oh, and by the way, Gordon, Gavin asked me to mention that your racket is buried between the Weeping Mulberry and the Pride of India.'

Gavin's sister, Julia Ashley, was born about six years after him. He adored her (and she him) but his mischief didn't rub off on her, for she was as gentle as he was outgoing. Then, much later, in 1982, my second wife Frances begat James, her first, and my second son – in spite of the fact that when we married, I'd warned her that two children were quite enough, and that we should guard against more. Thus, when James arrived on the scene, friends, thinking I would wash my hands of him, named him 'Franny's Project'. From the start, both Gavin and Ashley adored her project, and when he got old enough to think straight, he adored them back, treating them as a father/mother/brother/sister combination. In fact, my children get on so well that it always saddens me to hear of those who don't.

Gavin, in his teens and early twenties, went through a period when I thought he had a prodigal streak in him – when he was, in fact, marginally prodigal, but after he'd navigated the shoals of youth, he became as un-prodigal and fine a son as any parent could wish to have.

'To be a true prodigal,' James explained to the Table, 'you have to wander, commit sins, return and repent. And in the right order. No good repenting before you sin or sinning before you wander ...'

'I wandered and returned all right,' said Tim. 'But I couldn't repent because I hadn't sinned.'

'Successful sinning needs balance and finesse,' James again, 'and you have to be careful not to over-sin. I had a friend who sinned so copiously that instead of repenting, he revelled in it ...'

'I was very nearly a true prodigal,' put in the Other Peter. 'I wandered, sinned, returned but so far haven't repented.'

'You can start by paying for lunch,' said James.

⁂

In the seventies, Abe and I used to play tennis on Sunday mornings with various businessmen, most of them moguls (Abe called them mongols). It was an odd sort of tennis school, with enormous variation in quality, especially when we invited people like Fred Stolle, Ken Rosewall, Ray Moore, Butch Buchholz and Graydon Garner to come as guests. With only the moguls present, the tennis was less spectacular, but Abe and I faithfully kept at it, secretly hoping for monetary tip-offs. They never materialised and it took us a long time to realise that no matter how much time we spent playing tennis with moguls, their wealth would never rub off.

'They were interesting, those mornings,' I told the Table.

Tennis and golf are great levellers, and without knowing it those fellows revealed many traits that lurked inside them. They didn't much like losing. One Sunday morning Abe was playing with a mogul against me and another mogul, neither of us aware of our partner's burning need to win. At 4-all, my mogul missed a volley to lose his service, and at 4-5 down, with Abe's service to come, we hadn't a hope. My mogul was playing the right court, and as Abe threw the ball up to serve the first point, he gave a plaintive cry and collapsed in a heap, writhing in pain.

'My ankle,' he cried. 'An old sprain's come back ...'

We helped him off the court and put him in a reclining chair where he sat rubbing stuff into his ankle and drinking beer out of a bottle.

'Poor you,' said his wife. 'What a pity! And you were doing so well …'

One of the occasional players was Clive Menell whose father Slip Menell had founded Anglovaal, one of the legendary South African mining companies. Clive was anything but a mogul. Although a business leader, he was more the intellectual – tall, slender and elegant in Melton flannels and shirts with long sleeves – walking on court as if he'd just come out of a meeting. He had a willowy tennis style, involving a lot of wrist – the very opposite of what you'd call a safe player, stylish and erratic, serving both balls at full speed with a sort of British *savoir-faire* that must have emanated from his years at Cambridge. We became close friends, and it was he who introduced me to fly-fishing, a pastime that I grew to love and treasure. Anglovaal had once owned a gold mine on the eastern escarpment of what was then the Transvaal, a beautiful region of mountains, mists, forests, rock falls, and clear, cold streams. Although the gold had long since been 'mined out', there remained thousands of hectares of scenic mountainous land, crisscrossed with crystal clear streams into which Clive introduced trout fingerlings that thrived and were able to breed on the river's pristine gravel beds.

34

The Sea of Galilee

Clive Menell was a true nature lover. Save for a few stone barriers, the streams were left in their natural state so as to provide true river fishing. The lodge was the old mine manager's house, also left as it was – a warren of bedrooms, a single bathroom, wood-burning stove and boiler that bubbled away in the kitchen when all went well. Clive loved that house, and he loved the way that whoever stayed there seemed to revel in its spartan simplicity. Company directors, mining magnates, captains of industry, even an Austrian Count with a castle, all seemed delighted to forsake luxury for a few days, and get back to basics.

It was in this old house that I spent many weekends at Clive's invitation, soon getting to know that river like the back of my hand – where the trout lay, how to stalk the pools, which fly was best, and how to cast it into the right spot without snagging the overhanging trees. And although the fish we caught at first were seldom more than a pound in weight, I spent many hours lost in the kind of timeless trance that only fly-fishing can evoke.

THE SEA OF GALILEE

Whenever possible, Gavin accompanied me. Then about twelve, he already showed signs of being the born fisherman that he turned out to be. One weekend we arrived to find an illustrious group of guests, all with the elaborate trappings that wealthy fly-fishermen love to accumulate — the best Hardy rods and reels, Panama hats with flies in the band, landing nets that unfurled at the touch of a button, priests, thermometers, waders, Polaroid glasses, waistcoats with numerous pockets for Swiss knives, tweezers, etc.

Such hi-tech paraphernalia used to make me smile, for I always suspected that the best-equipped fishermen often caught the fewest fish. This was confirmed one day when, walking quietly along the river, I came upon one of these chaps fishing one of the deeper pools. Quietly, I paused to watch him. Decked out in full regalia, he was fishing with intense concentration, staring into the water through Polaroid lenses, and tugging gently at his tapered line to make the fly at the end of it more tempting. The problem was that although the line disappeared into the water in front of him, via a series of loops that only an errant fly-line can achieve, it doubled back so that the fly was snagged in a tree behind him. He was having such a good time that to enlighten him seemed the wrong thing to do, so I backed away to another pool in the river. That evening he said he'd had several good bites in that pool ...

I had modest equipment to begin with, and Gavin's was even more modest — my old rod and reel, his school khakis, a floppy hat, an old pair of tackies and a canvas kitbag that Clive had given him.

He, Clive, had organised a good fishing routine. Each man was given a stretch of river that was 'his' for the morning, and at midday we'd all meet at Suspension Bridge Pool — one of the legendary landmarks — to reveal catches, describe strikes and near misses, comment on the river, then go home for lunch and have a glass of something soothing.

That particular day, Gavin was given a stretch of river that had in it a pool called The Sea of Galilee – long, clear, still, and no more than a metre deep. In it was a veritable shoal of trout, among them some of the biggest in the river, mouth-wateringly visible but impossible to catch, because the fisherman was always in full view, with the fish stubbornly refusing to take a fly.

We fished. The Saturday was hot, the river low, and the fish not biting. At noon, when we gathered at Suspension Bridge, not one of us had anything to show for our morning's labour. Billy Wilson, deputy head of Anglo American, who'd fished the Suspension Bridge beat was standing in his underpants, his clothes spread out on the surrounding bushes. Clive asked him gently what had happened.

'Can't say exactly,' he replied. 'I was wading quietly in Rick's Run and suddenly my feet were a yard above my head!' (The water-worn stones in Rick's Run were as slippery as glass.)

As for the others, keep-nets were empty, excuses rife. Last to arrive was Gavin, who came trudging up the path, his rod in one hand, and clutched in the other a forked stick on which hung four large trout, the stick threaded through their gills. I must confess that my first reaction was one of grave alarm – 'Oh my God!' I thought, 'I pray he hasn't been cheating!' and although not a word was said, I knew instinctively that the same thought was going through the minds of all the others.

'How very clever!' exclaimed Clive. 'What fly were you using?'

He stepped forward to look closely at Gavin's rod, and to my guarded relief I saw that there was a large, white fly tied to the leader – I say guarded, because a worm or cricket can still be put on the hook of a

THE SEA OF GALILEE

trout fly, and in fly-fishing the most iniquitous of all crimes is to fish with live bait.

'Very good indeed!' Clive went on, examining Gavin's catch. 'How on earth did you manage to do it?'

'I found a way,' said Gavin, mysteriously. Then, to everyone's surprise, he added: 'If you like, I could probably get another one.'

'You mean that you could actually show us how you did it?'

'I could try,' said Gavin, and as we all began walking down the path towards the Sea of Galilee, he said over his shoulder: 'I hope it works. It sometimes takes a long time. Trout don't always do what you want them to do ... I'll need luck ...'

We arrived at the pool and, sure enough, the shoal was still there, the trout lying with their heads facing upstream, a mixture of small, medium, and big ones. They broke formation as we gathered round the pool, swirled about in alarm, then gradually calmed down and regrouped.

'Stand back,' said Clive, 'and be still,' and we all obeyed, watching Gavin walk a circular path through the trees, unfurling his rod, then stealing back to stand on the river bank in a clearing behind the fish. Intent on them, he made a simple cast of not more than three or four paces, the fly landing in the water just upstream of the fish. They again swirled about in alarm as the fly gradually sank to the gravel bed of the stream where it came to rest – a tiny white spot among the pebbles.

For several minutes nothing happened. Gavin stood quite still as the trout slowly regained their formation, lazily staying in place with just the slightest movements of their fins, the white fly a foot or two in front of them. Another minute or so passed, then one of the mid-sized fish moved slowly towards the fly, and on reaching it touched it

Little James and Gavin. *Young Gavin.*

with its nose – at which exact point Gavin lightly set his rod, and to everyone's astonishment had the fish on his line.

I was weak with relief and I truly think they were all pleased. There were chuckles, shaking of heads, and a round of applause, at which Gavin turned and said, 'I was lucky. The others took much longer …' and one of the men slapped him on the back – one of those companionable well-done-young-man kind of slaps he would never forget.

Strange, these little episodes. Acceptance is a fickle thing, yet that simple incident won for Gavin a thumbs up that would add a tiny layer of confidence to the rest of his life.

'Thank goodness,' I said to Clive, and he knew exactly what I meant.

G F, Frances, Sir Robin Renwick, and Clive. The fish were biting that day ...

He was an unusual man, was Clive, as quiet and introspective as his wife, Irene, was calm and outgoing. A captain in the mining industry, he had a sensitive and enquiring nature that combined such things as creating thoughtful paintings at home, and reading complex balance sheets at work. His sensitive way of life attracted a diverse army of friends.

We'd go on excursions – such as searching for wooden sculptures in Vendaland, where the mission included Simon Sainsbury of the Sainsbury dynasty, and Rudolf and Sonia Gouws. Simon was as rarefied and understated as any Englishman could be, traits that gave everything he said the absent-minded aspect of an afterthought. Rudolf was the economist for a leading bank, a financial soothsayer who contrived to combine humour, irony and ambiguity in such a way that his

Rudolf Gouws, Frances, Sonia Gouws, Irene and Clive Menell, Marie-Josée and Henry Kravis.

prognosis could never really be wrong. For example, after a convoluted session of financial facts, figures and forecasts, he might finish with the profound prediction that 'the rate at which things are getting worse is slowing down'. Sonia, less extroverted, wrote schoolbooks, and had (amongst other things) knowing blue eyes that didn't miss a thing.

One day, Clive phoned to ask whether Frances and I wanted to go with one of his American friends, a fellow called Henry, he said, on a trip to Kimberley and Cape Town.

'Henry has an aeroplane,' he said. 'I've arranged for us to stop in Kimberley to look at some diamonds. Rudolf and Sonia will be with us. In Cape Town, we're all staying at Glendirk.' (Glendirk was Clive and Irene's 'farm' in Constantia, one of Cape Town's best suburbs, bought by Clive's father in the forties – over sixty acres of vineyards and woodland.)

Henry's plane. Rudolf and I realised he was self-sufficient.

We duly gathered at Lanseria Airport and, by the look of his plane, Rudolf and I judged Henry to be self-sufficient. It was only after Clive introduced us that the penny dropped.

'Gordon, Rudolf, meet Henry Kravis.'

'Good heavens,' I exclaimed, and couldn't help adding, 'why on earth are you here?'

'I suppose because I'm nowhere else,' he said, with a smile, and introduced his wife, Marie-Josée.

I suppose I was a bit disappointed because he was not as one would imagine a true Barbarian at the Gate. Rather, he seemed too nice to be a ruthless corporate raider, although I suppose … And oddly enough, he didn't seem to be a mogul. If anything, he seemed … Anyway, we sight-saw a good deal, ate well, drank good wine, and both Henry and Marie-Josée seemed to like everything about South Africa. When we visited the great wine estates I remember thinking that it must feel strange to travel the world knowing you are able to buy virtually anything you see.

Back at the house that afternoon Clive produced a set of boule, and we invented a new game. Instead of playing on the boule-pitch, we walked down the gravel road, throwing the cochonnet ahead of us, then playing to wherever it landed. What secretly irritated Rudolf and me was the fact that most of the time Henry won. Pure luck, we thought, because of the unpredictability of the rough road. It was eerie how often Henry's boule bumped along and ended up closest to the cochonnet – something that he seemed to take for granted as skill and not luck. I remember being sorry that Mark McCormack wasn't there to bear witness.

35

In Search of a Niche

To get back to Gavin. These days, more and more often I hear of parents worrying about their children growing up and having difficulty 'finding their niches' – something my father used to call 'getting a decent job'. For a while we too worried, for as a teenager Gavin seemed to find that sport, partying and fun was as good a way as any to search for niches. Valerie and I had secretly hoped he'd be a tennis player, and while we'd tried to give him every opportunity, we'd been determined not to be the kind of parents who paced up and down the courtside shouting advice.

'His game was so brilliant at times,' I told the Table, 'that it led me to believe that he had it in him to be a star.'

'It just goes to show,' said James, who paused, then quickly continued when the headmaster raised his eyebrows, 'that if you want to be a star, not only do you have to have it in you, you have to find a way to get it out. I've a friend who's had it in him all his life. He's just turned seventy-five, and it's still in him …'

And for a while we discussed people we knew with great things inside them that wouldn't come out.

If only Gavin had realised how much we cared about his tennis, he'd have tried harder. As it was, our warnings about pulling up his socks and getting to the Top didn't seem to upset his partying mode. After he matriculated, I was probably the only father in the country who secretly welcomed his army call-up (compulsory in those days), believing that a few mindless orders that *had* to be obeyed might do him a world of good. At worst, I knew it would get his hair cut. When the summons did come, he did three months of basic training at the Air Force Gymnasium in Pretoria, then returned to tell us proudly that as he'd talked his way into working at the Atlas Aircraft factory at Kempton Park (reasonably close by) he could continue living with us at home. Could he please borrow Frances's car to get to work – a navy-blue Mini Minor that she loved. It was the kind of request that could lead to argument, but Frances rose to the occasion and agreed.

'Good Lord!' was my measured response. 'What could you possibly do at Atlas Aircraft?'

'I count things,' he said. 'Apparently quantities are important. They tell me that when the new computer gets installed, I'll be redundant.'

It apparently took a long time to install computers, for he never became redundant, and after two years of counting things and playing tennis for the Air Force team, he got a tennis scholarship at the University of Texas at Austin. By then, Jean had married Cliff Drysdale and together they'd moved to the Lakeway World of Tennis, also near Austin, where Cliff had been appointed resident professional.

For four years the Hill Country of Texas became a second home for Frances and me. Lakeway was situated on the shore of Lake Travis, a vast dam on the Colorado River. Lamar Hunt, of the famous Hunt

Cliff Drysdale coaching young Gavin on the sand at Dunkeld (the sheep farm, that is …).

family, had recently bought his way into tennis, apparently intent on 'taking the game over' – a mission in which, for a while, he partially succeeded. Part of his plan was building resorts for tennis lovers.

The scenic Texas Hill Country was the setting for the Lakeway World of Tennis, where Cliff had been appointed the first resident professional, and where such tennis legends as Jimmy Connors, Rod Laver, Billie Jean King, Chris Evert and Martina Navratilova would play periodic exhibition games. Tennis was quite the thing just then, and rich people would buy the best clothing and equipment, some of them apparently unaware that equipment alone wouldn't do the trick. Nonetheless, Lakeway was a success, World Championship Tennis (WCT) became a household name, and the 'Handsome Eight' was the name given to the professional squad in which Cliff played for several years.

Gavin naturally spent many weekends at Lakeway, and for four years Frances and I would spend a month there every springtime, ensconced in the condominium of Hassie Hunt, one of the brothers who never used it. In retrospect, those years were unforgettable, for I could be with Jean again for weeks on end, quite oblivious of the fact that for her the party would soon be over. We could play tennis, and enjoy what used to be the land of our childhood cowboy stories – cottonwoods and coyotes, blue-bonnets, live-oaks and dusty roadside Mexican restaurants. At rodeos we wore Stetsons and cowboy boots, at steakhouses we wrestled with belt-busters and grits. Russell Seymour, my doubles partner before Abe, was the teaching pro at Lakeway, assisted by Billy Freer, also a South African, because Lamar Hunt believed that South Africans were the best tennis teachers.

Gavin, meanwhile, didn't allow the University of Texas to interfere with his partying, but he passed his grades, played tennis on the college team, and managed to acquire a lemon-yellow Chrysler of uncertain vintage which was known as the 'Yellow Peril'. While it produced a wide variety of internal noises, it always started when he pressed the button, and it never let him down. American cars, he maintained, were good at being old.

He finally graduated in about 1975, and got capped and gowned, and for several years travelled the world, working at tennis academies, universities, summer camps, and at GreenSet, court builders and suppliers

IN SEARCH OF A NICHE

Abe, Russell Seymour and G F. Russell became head coach of the Lakeway World of Tennis.

of championship courts in Europe. Periodically, he would come home to see us for a month or two but, for the time being, niches were still in short supply.

36

People, Parties and Persuasion

I had become close to Mark McCormack by then. Of course, I told him about Gavin – his life, his tennis, his studies at UT, and his way with people. In 1986, during Gavin's GreenSet period (its headquarters was in Versailles), he and I were having lunch with Mark in his Roland Garros tent and I was joking about Gavin and his wanderings, saying that although he had majored in real estate, much of his skill was in people, parties and persuasion – Gavin Forbes, BA, PPP! After lunch, together with one other IMG manager, we went to sit in Mark's box on the centre court to watch Boris Becker against a player called Mikael Pernfors of Sweden. Mark, always proud of his tennis judgement, understandably stated that it was a foregone conclusion that Becker would win.

'Oddly enough, on this slow court I'd take Pernfors,' said Gavin, unexpectedly. 'I've watched his progress ever since his college days [Pernfors attended the University of Georgia]. He's shrewd, brave, and he doesn't miss a ball' – and as it turned out he didn't. Astonishingly, he beat Becker in four sets, 2-6, 6-4, 6-2, 6-0, and went on to reach the finals of the singles, where he lost to Ivan Lendl (as did nearly everyone in those days). Gavin had opened his score, and only a few days later Mark offered him a job.

'His knowledge of tennis is astute, and his way with people is a gift. In combination they are just what IMG needs,' he would say to me, and to this day I smile at the irony of the very qualities in Gavin that worried me being the ones that led him to find his niche!

'It wasn't as simple as I've made it sound,' I told the Table. 'He had to go through all kinds of interviews and aptitude tests.'

Gavin survived them all, and his first job was observing and assessing upcoming junior tennis players, getting to know and befriend them, then identifying those he felt were potential IMG clients. He worked from IMG's headquarters in Cleveland, Ohio, and lived, rent-free, in Mark's Cleveland house, a huge, rambling affair seldom used by Mark himself. His salary would start at $1000 per month – 'not a world record, Dad', he said to me, but it was typical of Mark who insisted that people who worked for IMG must first prove their worth. Giving young people opportunities, in combination with his knack of fitting them into the right niches, was one of his great pleasures.

Gavin attended all the major junior tournaments and inter-collegiate events and roamed the courts, getting to know the coaches, the players, and trying to assess their games. At the Roland Garros, Wimbledon and US Open junior events I would often join him, and it was then that I came to realise just how good all the top juniors looked, and how difficult it was to identify the next champion. Somehow one had to see past the present, and visualise how youthful brilliance would evolve. Tennis skills alone were not everything.

'They all look good, Dad, every one of them,' Gavin told me. 'I try to evaluate their techniques, watch their faces, their body language, their tactics, to see how tough they are. The smallest detail can give a clue. And, I tell you, it's not always bad to see a broken racket or two. There has to be anger, real anger. The only problem is how much …'

He put together a system that combined things he'd learned from college coaches, tennis academies, his fellow workers and matches he'd played, adding ideas of his own, and finally trusting his own judgement.

'Come with me,' he'd say to me, 'I want you to watch this kid and tell me what you think,' and off we'd go to watch yet another boy or girl. He was a much better judge than I was, and I have since come to realise that predicting a young player's ability to get to the top is an elusive and fickle art.

As time passed, he would get to know every junior player of any consequence – and more than that, he would note every detail – their coach's name, their parents, their wins, losses, what racket they used, what clothes they wore and so on, for Mark had a nasty habit of suddenly asking obscure questions.

'That young Taylor Dent. What is his father's name? Wasn't he also a good player? Who is Lleyton Hewitt's coach? What age is Ivanisevic?' Questions to which Mark knew the answers, I can assure you!

After being caught out a few times, Gavin realised he had to get it right. 'He can scare the hell out of you,' he said to me. 'He'll ask me something, and if I know the answer he'll say, "Good. Let's have an ice cream." But if I get it wrong …'

But he loved tennis, loved his job, had an enquiring mind and a memory much better than mine. Gavin, I mean. His people, party and persuasion skills came into their own. Young himself, he got on with the juniors, partied with them (sometimes to the chagrin of their coaches), befriended them and talked their language. The first players

PEOPLE, PARTIES AND PERSUASION

Jim Courier (left) with Gavin.

he signed up were Pete Sampras and Jim Courier. ('I didn't have to be a genius to do that, Dad.')

'You might say he was lucky,' I said to the Table, 'but we have already agreed that to get a start everyone needs a break!'

Gavin's early successes quickened his progress. 'I told you that partying would be good for me,' he said, not long ago.

He's been with IMG for twenty-eight years now and knows tennis so well that he has been elected to the seven-member ATP Board of Directors that controls the entire world of international tennis.

'Well,' said James, 'it just goes to show ...' And this time, when Mark glared at him, he quickly added '... that American universities are good places to major in people, parties and persuasion ...'

37

In Patagonia

'I once heard Raymond Moore refer to Abe Segal as a "unique item",' I told the Table.

Ray himself was fairly unique – another tennis personality and star lost to South African tennis. Together with Charlie Pasarell, Ray went on to found and establish the Indian Wells Tournament in Arizona, now one of the greatest on the circuit. And as for Charlie – he was the one who played Pancho Gonzales on the Centre Court in what was to be the longest singles match in the history of Wimbledon, eventually losing 22-24, 1-6, 16-14, 6-3, 11-9, after having seven match points! Astonishing, hey? 1969 it was, and there was no resting between games in those days, nor could you have a medic. If you got cramp or pulled a muscle you were on your own ...

Although the Table chaps all knew of the match, they liked to be reminded of momentous sporting occasions – and as both Ray and Charlie were great friends of Abe (and me) there is some relevance, as this chapter is supposed to be about Abe. There can be no friendships as durable as those formed on long-ago tennis circuits, when the players were all one big happy family. Anyway, for interest's sake I looked up Ray's definition of Abe in the dictionary.

Unique: *Of which there is only one.* Item: *Any one of a number of things.* Thus, going by Raymond's definition, Abe was 'one of any number of things of which there is only one'. Not altogether wrong, come to think of it ...

I'd invited Abe to one of our lunches as living proof of himself, and sure enough he lived up to his reputation. There happened to be some really old people in the room that day, several with crutches, others pale and wan who showed only occasional signs of life.

Abe sat down and after a look around the room muttered, 'Jesus Forbsey. We're having lunch in a waxworks!'

After I'd introduced him to the Table, he seemed relieved at its vigour and continued his muttering as he unfolded his napkin: 'Well at least we have a chance of finishing before we keel over.'

At the starter buffet he regarded the large bean salad. 'We got to take it easy with those things. Don't want to go through the roof before the main course.'

He had a thing about beans and wind and must have told me half a dozen times about the cowboy who blew into Kansas City, had a can of beans and blew out. Later that year in Plett I overheard him telling Tony Bloom that I'd invited him to lunch at Madame Tussauds and when he left, to be on the safe side, he'd phoned his doctor.

He has his own way with words, and sometimes alters aphorisms by getting them mixed up. Once in a doubles match when I was questioning an umpire about a service call, he took my arm and said, 'Leave it, Forbsey. Let dead dogs sleep.' If I played very well, I was 'all over the net like a sieve', but if I missed easy shots I was 'worse than a bee in a china shop' – and in his business, when one of his workers once stole money, he'd been caught with his hand in the coffee tin.

That day at the Rainbow Room, he surprised everyone but me by finishing his lunch, taking a last swig of coffee, laying his palms on the table and saying, 'That's it, gentlemen. That was one hell of a lunch, but I've got to go to a meeting' – he didn't say with whom. Just got up and left, leaving me to explain.

'He does that,' I said. 'Never been one for long goodbyes. You won't believe how many times, over the years, we've been at functions where he suddenly finds he has to leave before the end. "Well, I've had a great time …" "Well, there goes the bell …" "Well, it's been nice knowing you …" "Ding-dong, seconds out the ring …" (he loves boxing).'

These have all been exit lines I've heard. One of his more creative efforts happened a long time ago at one of Tony Bloom's birthday parties – a big dinner it was, a bit of pomp and ceremony, upmarket people and so on. When the gazpacho starter was put in front of him, he suddenly pushed back his chair and got to his feet.

'Very sorry, Ox,' he called to Tony (he often called Tony – and me – 'Ox'). 'I've just remembered. My mother is arriving at the airport an' I promised to meet her,' and off he went.

The next morning I called him up. 'Abie,' I said. 'Have you taken leave of your senses? You can't leave lunches just as the starter arrives.'

'Listen, Forbsey. Tony knows very well that woman he put me next to drives me crazy. All those diamonds on her fingers an' then that voice of hers starts telling me what spoon to use for the soup. What does Tony expect? He cast the first stone …'

Abe doesn't say 'soup' like other people. He says 'sup', shortening the vowel to almost a hiccup. Abe liked his sup to be hot, and he's always had a few people in the town he couldn't stand, especially society women who gave him instructions about cutlery.

'You have to be more tolerant, Abie,' I said. 'Learn to put up with people.'

'Tolerant! Jesus, Forbsey, there you go again. You want me to do a ninety degree about-face ...'

The funny thing was that some society people felt it an honour to be insulted by Abe, and bragged about it at dinner parties. 'Abe Segal told me if I took the egg out of my mouth he'd know what I was talking about ...'

'He's a card,' Tim proclaimed that day as he watched Abe leave the Rainbow Room, and for once there was unanimous agreement.

'Don't worry, he enjoyed his lunch,' I said. 'If he hadn't he'd have left earlier. I told him you're all writers, and he's never been a literary man. "I've only read one book in my life," he told me. "It was called *The Young Lions* and I only read it because Irwin Shaw was a friend of mine. It took me so long that by the time I got to the end I'd forgotten the beginning, and I'll tell you one thing. It's a hell of a lot quicker to see the movie than read the book."'

It was not long after that particular lunch that Abe phoned and told me he was going out of town for a few weeks. This, I knew, was one of his habits.

'I'll be away for a little while. I'm just goin' down the road, or round the corner,' he'd say, then mysteriously disappear, sometimes for weeks.

He worked with his father in their women's coat business called Ray

Fashions. When I called on him to play tennis, there was always a great outcry from his father.

'Vhy tennis, Forbes? How much money can you make playing tennis?' and he'd fix me with a piercing look and say, 'How much in your back pocket? Come. Show me!'

'Leave him, Dad,' Abe would say. 'He's poor.' But his father would persist until I'd take out my pound note. He'd then take a roll of bills from his back pocket, wave it at me and cry out: 'See dish? Vhy tennis? Talk to Abie. To you he'll listen. To me, never!'

Although Ray Fashions was a wholesale business, he was always selling coats to individual women. Thus the perpetual roll of cash.

One year we'd returned from our summer tennis tour and Abe had only just re-established himself at work, when he had a call from Pancho Segura asking him to play exhibition matches in LA, all expenses paid.

'I have to go, Forbsey,' he said, 'it's a great opportunity. This Pancho, running about on those crooked legs of his, is something else.'

Here he was right. Segura was not only one of the great players, but, as Abe used to say, 'they don't make 'em like that any more'.

'What did you tell your father?'

'That I was goin' round the corner.'

'That was in 1961,' I told the Table, 'and he still does it.'

Only last month he told me he was going round the corner, disappeared for about ten days, forgot our golf game, and then phoned me up.

'Listen, Forbsey. We'd better go for a walk. You won't believe what happened to me.'

It was only after we'd walked around the field a few times and were waiting for our toasted sandwiches that he began his story. 'This

Garner Anthony has finally lost his mind,' he said suddenly. 'That's the last time I'm goin' anywhere with him.'

I remember once meeting Garner Anthony, very long ago at Wimbledon. As far as I knew he was a journeyman tennis player who Abe had befriended, and together they'd travelled about America playing tennis. Or so Abe said.

'Then Garner's first wife died and he married this heiress, Forbsey, and now he's a billionaire. A billionaire. So he's always sending me tickets to go all over the world and do the things we used to do, except it's not playin' tennis any more. Two years ago I had to go to Alaska to catch fish, and I'll tell you one thing, Forbsey, I never realised Alaska was so far from New York. You take a big plane, then a little plane, then a bus, and you get to a lodge. Next day, they gave us fishing rods and took us to this big river and this guide says to me: "If you see bears, don't interfere with them." Like I'm the kind of guy who interferes with bears ... Then last year he wanted me to go to St Petersburg to look at paintings. Listen, Garner, I says to him, there's no way I'm going to Russia to look at paintings. Come to Johannesburg if you want paintings, there's a guy called Mark Read's got plenty. I know 'cos I've seen them ...'

It turned out that refusing to go to Russia had left Abe with a guilt complex. 'What the hell, Forbsey, I should have gone. It was only for two weeks and they say that these days you can get out of Russia alive. So I'd have looked at a few pictures, drunk a bit of vodka, eaten those fish eggs they get out of that river. Terrible thing. Garner said the food was good, so I should have seized the bullet and gone with him ...'

'Bitten, Abie. You bite bullets, seize days ...'

'Jesus, Forbsey.'

Anyway, he was soon able to make amends, because about six months ago, two more tickets arrived.

'First class, Forbsey, they're always first class. An' no sooner do they arrive when Garner phones me up. "Abie, we're going to Patagonia," he says, "and don't tell me you can't go, because I've already booked the hotel." I didn't know exactly where Patagonia was, but I sure as hell knew it wasn't round the corner, so I say to him, Garner, what exactly are we going to do when we get to Patagonia?'

'When Abe starts one of his stories,' I told the Table, 'I shut up and listen. Do you guys want me to continue?' They said they did. 'Okay. This one goes on a bit, and of course I can't remember exactly what he said, but I swear I'm not exaggerating. Anyway, I know he asked Garner Anthony why they were going to Patagonia.'

'It's a unique place,' Garner said. 'Unique. We get close to nature, see lakes and mountains, go on walks under waterfalls. There are Condors, and also a couple of volcanos, except they're extinct. It's one of the most beautiful places in the world.'

'Then he tells me how high the mountains are,' said Abe.

'Lakes and mountains, Forbsey. I have to go to Patagonia to see lakes and mountains, and extinct volcanos. If they could guarantee an eruption I'd understand ... But, I think to myself, I turned down Russia, so I better go with him to Patagonia, so I say, okay Garner, thanks, I'm on my way. I get on the plane and sit in this big seat they give you, and have a whisky and a grilled sole. Eventually I get to New York and there's this Anthony waiting for me with another ticket. What's this for? I ask him and he says we're going to Buenos Aires. What's happening in Buenos Aires? Nothing, he says, but it's on the way to Patagonia. So what do you think? There I am, sitting with him in another plane havin' another whisky. By the time we get to Buenos Aires I've got a sore back. Okay, Garner, we're here. Now what? And what do you think he says? Now we get on a bus.

'Well, Forbsey. Four hours on a bus, an' we think we've got potholes! The bus keeps dodgin' 'em, and just when I think my back's gone for good, we get to this fancy hotel on the edge of a lake. Anthony gets out of the bus like he's Christopher Columbus. This is it, Abie! This is Patagonia, an' he points to the lake and the mountains on the other side of it, like it's the only place in the world's got lakes and mountains. Garner, I say to him, have you ever heard of Switzerland? You don't have to travel by bus ...

'Well, Forbsey. Luckily, my room's got television, and there's this one channel they talk English on and thank God it's a movie one. It's a nice hotel, Forbsey, I'll say that, so I have a good sleep, I get up in the morning, we have this fancy breakfast, and then Anthony says to me: get ready, we're goin' on a boat. Well, I think to myself, at least there won't be any potholes. Why are we goin' on a boat? To get to the other side of the lake, he says, so I ask him what's wrong with this side? The other side's got the mountains! he says. Are you feelin' well, Garner? I ask him. We can see them from here! Anyway, I went on the boat, and sure enough, there were mountains. And I must say, Forbsey, for once Garner was right, they were pretty high ones. But when you've seen one mountain you've seen them all.'

38

The Ball and the Tortoise

Abe and I met in the Ellis Park locker room in about 1955 and, as he once put it, we've been getting in each other's way ever since.

'We've been friends for a long time,' I'd previously explained to the Table. 'Played doubles together for years, stayed in the same hotel rooms, dated the same girls. He'd pick up women, he was an expert at it, then pass them on to me … "Another Segal hand-me-down," Ian Vermaak used to say. Ian was very formal with women …'

The Table approved of Abe, so that during lulls Abe Segal stories were sometimes requested. Although not all of them involved tennis, still they'd listen.

One day, we were playing golf at Goose Valley, I related. It's a lovely Plettenberg Bay golf course which is also a tortoise sanctuary, full of small, beautifully marked tortoises, and you have to watch out for snakes. Abe cheats a bit at golf. Correction. He doesn't really cheat, he plays to his own rules. If, for example, his ball ends up in a bad place, even in the rough, it becomes ground under repair and he moves the ball to a good place.

THE BALL AND THE TORTOISE

In the game that day, one of his drives went into the light rough on the left and when he arrived to play his next shot, he found his ball in a mole hole with a small tortoise next to it. He took the ball out of the hole and placed it on a patch of grass nearby.

'Why did you move your ball,' I asked him, 'when you could have moved the tortoise?'

'I saw a sign saying "don't disturb the tortoises".'

Fortunately, although unconvinced, I didn't make a fuss, because a few weeks before, I'd had a game with Colin Brayshaw and Steve Murray at the Johannesburg Country Club. Colin told me that the JCC course had recently become the home of a lot of big tortoises that had become too much for their previous owner and, sure enough, as we walked up the eighteenth fairway, there was one of them, plodding along from somewhere to somewhere. It was a big tortoise, a huge one, and it occurred to me that if my ball landed too close to it, I'd *have* to move the ball and not the tortoise.

That day at Goose Valley I wondered if the rulebook said anything about tortoises, and whether there were different rules for big ones and little ones. So I phoned up Don Searle. Don is one of the Plett golfers who, at seventy-five, plays twice a week and sometimes shoots his age. He prides himself on knowing the rules of golf.

'What would happen if your ball fell in a mole hole near a tortoise?' I asked him, and I told him what Abe had done. 'Should you move the ball or the tortoise?'

There was a short silence. 'I'll have to get back to you on that,' he replied. 'It's a tricky one. You're asking about reptiles, you see. For instance, what would have happened if Abe's ball had fallen next to a puff adder? What would he move?'

'Probably himself,' I replied.

Don phoned back in just a few minutes. 'The tortoise is an Outside Agency,' he said. 'And the mole hole is a Loose Impediment, so oddly enough, Abe could have moved either the ball or the tortoise.'

'Dammit,' I said.

Luckily, I didn't make a fuss, or I'd never have heard the end of it. Abe loved it when I was wrong.

39

Segal versus Woodcock

In 1962 there was a tennis tournament in Comerio, an Italian town comprised almost entirely of a factory making home appliances and owned by a wealthy tennis fanatic, the tournament being his pride and joy. It was a lovely little town and we were treated like kings, but apart from an Olympic-size swimming pool and a games room with soccer and table-tennis tables, there wasn't much to do between tennis matches.

While I was able to pass the time reading and writing, Abe became very restless. In this regard, Warren Woodcock, an Australian player, was a kindred spirit. Together they would wander about, inventing ways to pass the time, usually by betting on things – anything from card games, to seeing who could drink a bottle of Coca-Cola the fastest (this followed by energetic burping). As far as their tennis games were concerned they were exact opposites. Abe had a big serve and iffy ground shots and Woodcock had an iffy serve and big ground shots, and each thought themselves better than the other, opinions that resulted in long wrangles.

'With a serve like yours, you'd make a good plumber.'

'A serve is all you've got. Once your opponent gets your serve back, all you can do is swear at him.'

These arguments were ongoing, until one day in Comerio to settle the matter once and for all, Woodcock bet Abie a hundred dollars that he could beat him over one set, 'in any country, on any surface, any time you like, Big Abie. It'll be the easiest money I ever made.'

It was the kind of challenge that Abe loved. 'Sure, Woody,' he said. 'But what I can't figure out is why you suddenly want to hand me a hundred dollars. Has the Italian sun been too much for you?'

'I'm feeling fine. Court three. Tomorrow morning, ten o'clock. Have your money ready.'

What Abe didn't know was that Woody had been out practising his service the day before, and as usual things hadn't gone well. Finally, in desperation, he'd decided to try serving with his left hand. After he'd positioned himself and tossed up the ball, he realised that at ten o'clock in the morning the sun would be directly in the eyes of a left-hander – a blinding sun that made it impossible to see the ball – which, of course, was when the idea came to him. Abe was a left-hander and if he could get Abie to play him at ten in the morning ... He'd waited his chance and thrown the gauntlet at Abe's feet.

By the time they went out at 9.45 the next day, word of the challenge had got around.

'Segal playing Woodcock for big money! This I've got to see!'

By ten, all the other players had gathered round the court to see the contest. When the two walked on for the warm-up, Woodcock made quite sure that Abe was on the side of the court that conformed with the plan he had in mind.

SEGAL VERSUS WOODCOCK

Here I must stop for a moment to add that in our doubles matches, Abe was notoriously lax about the sun, always leaving questions about its position to me. 'Which side must I serve from, Forbsey?' he would ask – a very important question, as a left/right-handed combination always had a big advantage over two right-handers because, with careful planning, they could both arrange to serve without sun in their eyes.

Woodcock was nothing if not shrewd. Well aware of Abe's contempt for his service, he felt secure in asking Abe the seemingly innocent question, 'Is it okay if I serve first?' knowing full well that Abe would at once agree. He was right.

'Sure, Woody,' said Abe. 'If you want to commit suicide, go right ahead.'

So Woodcock began the match by serving on the appropriate side, and sure enough, Abe broke his service. They towelled off, changed ends, Abe positioned himself to serve, tossed the ball up into the sun, blinked his eyes, and caught it as it came down.

'Jesus, Woody. This sun's shining like crazy. Do you mind if I play the whole match from that side?'

'I wouldn't mind at all, Abie,' said Woodcock. 'I'd willingly let you have this side, but the rules say that we have to change sides every odd game. We have to stick to the rules.'

'You don't understand, Woody. There is no way I can serve from this side, because I can't see the ball. I can only play from that side.'

'But Abie, the rules say …'

'Fuck the rules, Woody, you want me to go blind?'

'That's really tough Abie. I do understand, but rules are rules. Hold on a shake. I'll tell you what I will do for you.'

'And what exactly is that?'

'I'll sell you this side for fifty dollars!'

'Jesus Christ, Woody, you're a gonif. A plain, ordinary, straightforward gonif …'

'What's a gonif, Abie?'

'A Jewish thief. Except you're not Jewish. After today, I'm not so sure …'

As it happened, Woody's scheme backfired because Abe, cross and determined, bought the shady side for fifty dollars, and managed to beat him.

'You're still a gonif, Woody,' he said as he took his fifty dollars.

40

The Man Behind the Man

Abe is a few years older than I am, so he always reaches a higher age before I do. Once, long ago, when I was sixty-six and he was sixty-nine we were having a cup of coffee at Wanderers, and he suddenly told me that he needed peace and tranquillity, 'because,' he said, 'I am going to be full on seventy one of these days, an' it's not goin' to be easy'.

In those days we thought that seventy, was a ripe old age, but then we turned eighty, and had to seriously rethink. Ninety suddenly became a new benchmark and even then, judging by the speed the previous ten years had passed by, I suggested to Abe that we allow a contingency of five years.

'Ninety-five, you think?' he said. 'Have a heart! How far can a man walk when he's ninety-five?'

On our walks round the Wanderers cricket field we talk about getting old, then almost immediately switch to sport on TV. There is very little intellectual content to our conversations.

'This Spieth,' Abe might say, 'is somethin' else. How can you be twenty-two years old an' do what he does? I'd like to hit *one* shot like him. Just one, then I can retire.'

'This Wawrinka has got some kind of backhand.'

'This Amla bloke plays great. Maybe if we'd grown beards we'd have won the French.'

'I'm watchin' this Spanish guy, Ferrer, playin' a match against some Italian guy in a pink shirt. Jesus, Forbsey, he plays well, but every point is the same. After a while I say to myself, listen, go and make yourself a cup of tea. Take your time. It's not like anything's goin' to change while you're in the kitchen.'

'I know, Abie.' I sometimes get an opportunity to answer. 'You may as well watch Ferrer digging a trench. I mean, he digs very well, but it's still a trench.'

'An' I'll tell you one thing for nothing, Forbsey. That Hoadie (Lew Hoad) played a lot of tennis in his time, but I never saw him diggin' a trench!'

That kind of thing. Anyway, I was telling you about Abe telling me that at seventy he needed tranquillity, and I got side-tracked.

'What do you know about tranquillity?' I'd asked him. 'In all the years I've known you, I've never seen you being tranquil.'

'Give me time, Forbsey, I've never been this old before. What's that thing monks do on the side of mountains?'

'Meditate?' I ventured.

'Right. Meditate. I need to go somewhere quiet for a week, like that house of yours in Plett. On my own. Just sit there and look at the sea.'

'Meditating's not your long suit, Abie,' I said. 'You won't last an hour …'

'Not my long suit, hey? Jesus, Forbsey …' He gave me a withering look, and we said a few more things to each other, but the upshot was that off he went, and I was right. After the first fifteen minutes he got tired of looking at the sea, and went for a walk/jog on the beach. Then he went to have sandwiches at the golf club; on the way back he bought meatballs at the Spar, and that got him through to about 11 am, with the rest of the day lying stretched out ahead.

'Jesus, Forbsey. There's not a lot going on in Plettenberg Bay.'

'Why didn't you give meditation another go?' I asked him. 'It's like tennis. You've got to practise.'

'I'm done with it, Forbsey. And anyway, I figured out a way to meditate much faster than the monks do. So I went to the CNA and bought a sketch pad an' some "croakey" pens, an' a paintin' set.'

When Frances and I joined him at the end of the week, the whole living room was scattered with sketches, drawings, and paintings.

'What do you think got into you?' I asked him.

'You won't believe it, Forbsey. It's the meditation. It must be, because I'm seein' things that I've never seen before. Look at that lagoon. Birds, fishermen, dogs, boats. Then behind it, you got all those mountains with clouds and things …'

'But why have you made them orange?' I was studying his latest work.

'They started out being orange when the sun rose. Now they've gone green again. I can't keep changin' my colours because the sun goes round …'

※

'It was quite unbelievable,' I told the Table. 'There was Abe with all these paintings, and like everything else he ever did, they were not like any other paintings. Weird.'

I was once talking to Mark McCormack about how he hired people, and he said that he always looked for the man behind the man. When I told Abe that he must have a man behind him who could paint, he said, 'No way, Forbsey. The only man I ever had behind me was the taxman.'

Looking at Abe's work that day, I realised that he must always have had an artistic streak in him. You don't not paint for sixty-nine years, and then suddenly paint like mad and produce a whole roomful of works. When I mentioned it to Abe, he too seemed puzzled.

'When my father had the women's coat factory,' he said, 'I used to sketch coats for him. I've always been able to draw, but I didn't know I could paint. Anyway, these two are for you and Frances.'

And he presented us with two paintings, one of them with the orange mountains, and the other a lovely view through our bay window over the lagoon, except the lagoon had gone purple.

'Thank you, Abie,' I said. 'One day, an early Segal could be a very valuable thing.'

We were delighted with Abe's gift, particularly because, over the years, the various works of art that we collected always had some special meaning attached to them – a journey, a place, a moment in time, a sketch done by a friend. I was fairly sure that Abe's new passion would fade as soon as he returned to Johannesburg but I was wrong. Not only did it not fade, his inherent impatience enabled him to develop a speedy technique, so that every Monday he would arrive at our house with three or four new works to show to Frances and me. He'd found someone to frame his paintings, and his creativity always surprised us, for his paintings had an abstract naivety that was quite different from any other artist's work. I'd rigged up a stand under a spotlight, and we would place the paintings on it, then step back to contemplate them.

'Forbsey,' he would often say, 'that's a fantastic painting, even if I have to say so myself.'

'Abie,' I once replied, 'you're not supposed to say your own paintings are fantastic. You're supposed to wait for other people to say so.'

'So. What do *you* say?'

'Well, okay. This one *is* fantastic.'

On one occasion, driving between Johannesburg and Sun City, he stopped to paint a field of sunflowers in full bloom, and I must admit it was a good painting – a mass of yellow under a blue sky full of fierce-looking clouds. 'There was a storm comin',' said Abe as we placed the painting on the stand.

'It's great, Abe! It's as if it's got a bit of Van Gogh in it.'

'Except it's got a lot more sunflowers, an' I'm not about to cut off my ear …'

Finally there were at least thirty paintings leaning against the walls of our living room, so I phoned Mark Read and asked him to come over. Mark's gallery (the Everard Read Gallery) is one of the oldest, loveliest and most distinguished in Johannesburg, originally established by Everard Read, Mark's father. The Reads had been our neighbours in the Johannesburg suburb of Illovo, and I had known Mark as a young boy so I felt free to try my luck.

'Come and see. Abie's become an artist,' I said to him.

At first he was sceptical. 'Which Abie are you talking about?' he asked.

'I only know one Abie,' I replied, 'and this is the same one.'

'And you say he's done some paintings?'

'Yes. He had a sudden rush of blood.'

'So Abe Segal, the ex-tennis player, has painted some pictures?'

'I think so. Either him, or the man behind him.'

'And you think I should see them? Sometimes one rush of blood isn't enough …'

'Just a suggestion. The worst that can happen is we have a glass of whisky.'

So Mark came over and I gave him some whisky. He walked around the room with a neutral look on his face. Then he walked around it again, and asked for more whisky.

'I'll tell you what we can do if Abe agrees,' he said at last. 'We'll hang his paintings in the Main Gallery, and give a party. I think that an actual Segal *exhibition* might be too much for my older patrons. We'll supply the room if you supply the food and drinks. And by the way, he'll need to do a few more, because what you have here is not quite enough.'

Of course Abe accepted his offer, although at the time he was not familiar with the Read Gallery.

'What's this Read Gallery you talk about, Forbsey?'

'It's famous, Abe. Not everyone gets to hang paintings in it …'

There happened to be a special exhibition on at the time, so I took Abe along to have a look. He walked about for a while with a slightly stricken look on his face.

'Jesus, Forbsey. I can't hang my paintings in here.'

'Why not?'

'Because I'm not an artist.'

'Who knows, Abe? Maybe you are one.'

So Abe rapidly did a few more, and to speed up production he developed a unique painting technique. On one visit to him I found him busy painting a sky, but with the canvas turned upside down so the landscape part was on the top. From memory our conversation went something like this:

> Me: What exactly are you doing, Abie? (We've long since dispensed with formal greetings.)
> Him: What's it look to you like I'm doin'?
> Me: Painting a picture. Except you're painting it upside down.
> Him: The bottom part's not upside down, idiot, but the paint's still wet, so I have to get it out of the way while I do the sky – if that's all right with you.
> Me: But then the sky's going to be upside down.
> Him: A sky's a sky, Forbsey. I've never seen one with a label sayin' 'this side up'.

In the simple, elegant beauty of the Read Gallery, his paintings took on a life of their own. The so-called party was attended by the cream of Johannesburg society and all the paintings were quickly sold – in spite of the fact that in my introductory speech (which Mark Read insisted I make) I warned everyone that the skies in the paintings were upside down, and explained that the reason that sometimes mountains were purple, skies orange-coloured and grass red, was because of the position of the sun. It didn't seem to bother them. Nearly all Abe's works had something odd about them. In his picture *The Ninth Green* (of the Sun City golf course), for instance, he'd painted the green itself red. When he first showed it to me I questioned him.

The invitation to Abe's exhibition at the Everard Read Gallery. I asked him why his picture had so many steps, and he said that Greeks liked a lot of steps ...

Me: You hear of golfers hitting an iron to the heart of the green, but you never hear of them hitting one to the heart of the red. Why do you think that is?

Him: It was a very hot day, Forbsey. If Picasso can have a guy with two heads, I can have a red golf green.

On the day that we took the paintings to the Gallery, a small one of an Italian village (done during his Italian period, inspired by an Italian calendar) caught my eye.

'How much for that one, Abe?' I asked him.

He gave me a price, and I said I'd like to have it.

'I love the sea in the background,' I said.

'That's not sea, that's sky.'

'Dammit,' I said. 'I thought it was sea.'

'For another five hundred, we'll call it sea!'

The party at the Read Gallery was such a success that for a while Abe got painter's block, and had to rest up. But he started up again, and a year or two later had an exhibition at Stephen Falcke's elegant showroom. At that exhibition a lot of his work was done in shades of blue, to the point that we worried that his blue period, as his friends put it, was a sign of depression. Jeff Rubenstein asked him about it, cautiously suggesting that it might be a nervous problem.

'Why are there so many blue paintings, Abe? Any problems?'

'No problems, Ruby,' said Abe. 'The store where I buy my paints was having a sale of blue.'

⁓❦⁓

My problem with Abe is that he said so many priceless things to me I have no hope of remembering them all, so a lot of them will go to waste. The latter part of this book has become a terribly sad job, because he no longer answers when I phone him up. Life without him is not the same. ('Jesus, Forbsey, pull yourself together …')

41

The Small Folk

Our Mark's second book is a sensitive and thoughtful work that explores the many great schools of South Africa. On the first page he tells of a discussion he had with a friend who asked him a question that first seemed simple, but became increasingly profound.

'Thinking back on your life in scholarship, what single thing gave you the most satisfaction?'

Mark allowed himself an impulsive answer, trusting the old adage – first impressions are best impressions. 'The people I've met,' was his reply, one which, even on reflection, satisfied him. It made me recall something that I had said to Richard after we'd talked about tennis.

'As I get older, I seem to remember the people I met better than the tennis I played. The players in those days, you know, were a great league of friends who travelled together, cared for each other in a way, but I wish I'd paid more attention to the small folk.'

I use the term 'small folk', I suppose, because in a play set in medieval times that we studied at school, an old peasant woman made a moving plea to her all-powerful Lord and Master for some hero's life. I forget the exact context, but her words stayed in my mind:

THE SMALL FOLK

Do you realise what it means to the small folk? The small folk, who live among small things ...

The small folk! The truth is that as you grow old you become one of the small folk yourself. In my tennis days, the words covered anyone who wasn't a player – we were so wrapped up in our own world of competition that the people who worked for tennis were incidental. Referees, umpires, ball-kids, tournament secretaries, Bully, the wonderful old Wimbledon locker room attendant: 'Your shoes are ready for you, Mr Forbes' – he really liked giving young players nice clean things and to see them happy, and in return they liked him but took him for granted. To us big-deal players, even the Marjorie Goodwins of the world, the club chairmen, senior members and tennis officials we met were small folk. We were polite, of course, but in hindsight, how wrong we were!

'In the wider scheme of things, Richard, they were bigger than us!'

'I wouldn't get too philosophical if I were you,' he said, always on the lookout for simplicity. 'It's not easy knowing who is big and who is small, or, for that matter, how much tennis players know of life.' And he went on to tell me of the famous West Indian historian, C L R James who, in his book *Beyond a Boundary*, had written: 'What do they know of cricket who only cricket know?' the words actually originating from Kipling's poem, *English Flag*:

Winds of the World, give answer! They are whimpering to and fro –
And what should they know of England who only England know?

'It certainly seems C L R James knew about life as well as cricket,' Richard went on. 'You have only to read his book. But then I suppose he, too, wrote it when he was older. Wiser … Isn't it extraordinary that while wisdom would be of most use to the young, it usually only comes to people when they're old? Some kind of mistake in the design process, it would seem … Of course in this new world the young seem so very, very clever. Sharp as needles with their iPads and phones. But are they wise? …' And he gave his wave.

'A few. Every now and again …'

⁓❦⁓

Neglecting small folk, I came to decide, was like walking over precious stones without bothering to pick them up. Strangely, it was much later in life that a certain incident gave me a lesson on how, in their dealings with stars, small folk must sometimes have felt.

'It had to do with the book I'd written,' I told the Table. '*A Handful of Summers.*'

I'd come to realise that the book appealed to some people much more than others – sometimes, even at Wimbledon, it seemed to induce friends, acquaintances, journalists, even players, to stop and talk enthusiastically about tennis and life. Richard Evans (a friend and leading tennis writer) suggested that it might make a good movie, and when I asked Peter Ustinov for his opinion, even he seemed vaguely positive.

'Oh dear, yes. A movie. Yes, indeed it might. Tricky though. You'd need a very good screenplay. Tennis and movies have never gone together … maybe worth a try …' and so on.

In a burst of fervour I'd bought a book about screenplay writing, and for a while toiled away. A young American screenwriter called Finkelstein gave advice. 'There are some good scenes,' he said, 'but your story doesn't have a dramatic ending. Good movies usually need to end with a bang.'

'Couldn't mine end with a whimper?' I asked. 'Might start a new trend ...'

'It's actually easier to end with whimpers than it is with bangs ...' began Tim, and though Charles glared at him, he finished his thought. 'Many people may relate to it ...'

'Let Gordon finish ...'

'Americans don't like whimpers,' I went on.

Finkelstein suggested that Joseph, my little black friend (in the book, Jack and I lowered him down a cliff to get an eagle's egg), be made into my faithful follower, accompany me on my tennis travels, become a good player himself and then get killed in the Sharpeville riots. My tennis career could die with him. A sort of bang/whimper combination. We never came to agreement, and the screenplay was never finished, but the film idea stayed in the back of my mind.

Years later, during one of my Wimbledon visits, it came out again, and I had a wild idea that I put to Gavin.

'If I gave a book to Roger Federer,' I said, 'and if he read it, and if he happened to like it as much as some people do, and if he were to agree that it might make a good movie, and if he mentioned that to the media, and if the best screenwriters in the world got interested, and if a movie got made, and if it was a good one,' and I went on to mention fame, Oscars and so on.

'Too many ifs, Dad,' said Gavin but, being a dutiful son, he stopped short of warning me about smoking my socks. Instead, he spoke to Tony Godsick, Federer's manager, explaining to him my wild idea. Tony, also dubious, nonetheless spoke to Federer and arranged for me to meet him at the entrance of the players' lounge on a given day at 12 pm, to present him with a copy of *A Handful of Summers*.

I had only three of the original hard-cover editions left, and asked Gavin if I should give one up, or whether a paperback would do.

'In for a penny, in for a pound,' he replied. 'It's a long shot, but you never know your luck.'

So I bought a special pen and practised writing a good dedication. When the day arrived I put on a clean shirt, a navy blazer and my best tie, and waited at the door at 11.50 am – a perfect example of eager small folk. At twelve Federer emerged, with Tony behind him. He was dressed in a beautiful white tracksuit, taller and slimmer than I'd expected, elegant as he always is. Tony introduced us and he said, 'Good afternoon, Mr Forbes' – no noticeable enthusiasm or warmth, if you get what I mean. I handed him the book, thanked him, and said that I hoped he would like it, all the time dying to explain my movie idea. But there was no gap. 'Thank you, Mr Forbes,' he said, then turned away and went inside without another word. Something I'd looked forward to for days was over in a moment.

Now you'd think, I'd said to myself, he might have … but of course not, you fool. Why should he? Still, a warm smile wouldn't have cost much. Silly. Fifteen Grand Slams, a big match to play, and here I am expecting a smile about a book. Serves you damn well right. On the other hand I'm not such a bad bloke …

I walked back to find Gavin and told him of my defeat, adding, 'You never know, he might still …' But he never did.

'Never mind, Dad,' said Gavin. 'We did agree that it was a long shot and at least we tried. What was it Charles Fiddian-Green always said to me? If you don't have a fly in the water you'll never catch a fish. Let's get a bite of lunch at the Last Eight Club. Something we can be sure of ...'

'Damn,' I muttered. 'A paperback would have done just as well ...'

'In one way you were right,' said the One Peter. 'Your movie idea did end with a whimper. Pass the bottle.'

42

Old Lamps for New?

There comes a time in life when you hanker after old familiar things. The other day I went to have my hair cut by Giuseppe Rossi again. He first cut it in 1955 (I think I've already said that) and he now works with about six other old Italian barbers, all healthy, cheerful and masters of their art. They've stuck to the old way, using the same old equipment – camel-hair brushes, talcum puffers, and hand clippers to touch things up. They give shaves and singes, they have pin-ups on their walls and serve espresso in small white cups. Rossi (he's never called Giuseppe) still has the same barber's chair he had when he first cut my hair. ('But it's been re-covered,' he said.)

I parked my car in the yard next to a yellow Lamborghini, and I suppose what made me take a careful look at it was the fact that its presence in that place at first seemed so incongruous. True, like the barbers, it was Italian, but there the similarity seemed to end – parked outside, this sleek car; inside, a team of ancient hairdressers busy with their Vitalis and Bay Rum. Cautiously I opened a door to look inside, finding to my surprise that it was not a car at all, but a work of art – a

Purdey shotgun, perhaps, a Patek Philippe watch, a Tiffany bracelet. By some coincidence, the day before I'd seen a video of the Tesla factory with its array of Robots and, unbelievable as they were, they couldn't possibly have built that Lamborghini – only the hands of master craftsmen could do that. And it struck me then that certain old tennis players, were, in their way, like that car …

'So men come out of their salon with perfect haircuts?' interrupted Charles, his eyes examining my hair. 'I suppose there are exceptions …'

'I closed the car door,' I said, ignoring him, 'and went inside to sit in Rossi's chair and say to him the same words I'd said a hundred times before – 'like always, Maestro. Not too short on top', and when he blew talcum down my neck, tucked cotton wool into my shirt collar and gave me a cup of espresso, I felt that he was not only salt of the earth, but also a perfect example of the small folk I'd been trying to define. He's cut hair all his life. He likes it. He has his daughters, his grandchildren, a fine collection of shotguns, an antique Mercedes, and he's happy.

⁂

'Are we small folk?' Tim asked, looking round the Table as if measuring us up. No one gave an immediate answer.

'Can folk be a medium size?' asked James presently. 'Perhaps they should be classed in the same way as Woolworths underwear. Small, medium and large. Folk, I mean.'

'I've never really thought of them that way,' I replied.

'Well, we're certainly not large folk,' said the One Peter, 'so let's settle for medium.'

We'd all managed to be at the Rainbow Room that Friday at the right time, 12.45 pm. The lunch before, Mark the headmaster had arrived at 1.45, dispensing cheerful greetings and asking us why we were nearly finished our main course. Mark is meticulous about time, so it took us a while to convince him that it was 1.45. Turned out he'd taken his watch for a service and they'd reset it an hour early, so for him it was 12.45. Finally, when the penny dropped, he let out a plaintive cry. 'I've lost an hour of my life!'

'I once nearly lost a whole Monday,' said the Other Peter, soothingly. 'Woke at 2 pm and only had the afternoon …'

'It just goes to show,' said James, watching Mark resetting his watch.

Our table that day was near the window and when everyone (except Mark) was seated, Charles asked if anyone had anything to report. James put up his hand.

'Through you, Mr Chairman,' he said. 'An odd thing happened to me in the car park. As I walked towards this room, I felt a tap on my shoulder, and turned to find a perfect stranger.'

'Oh dear, I'm very sorry,' he said, 'I thought you were someone else.'

He seemed a decent sort, so I told him not to worry. 'And as it happens, I *am* someone else.'

'What I meant,' he said, 'was that you're not the person I thought you were. You're someone else.'

'In that case, you are not the person that you thought I was either, so you're also someone else.'

'I suppose I must be.' He looked puzzled.

'It was an odd conversation, you'll agree,' said James. 'To be on the safe side, when I got to the clubhouse I dropped into the men's room and looked in the mirror to make sure I was who I thought I was.'

It was then that I told the Table about Rossi, how I felt he would have passed my father's 'salt of the earth' test and if so, according to Plato, he must have reached the Top.

'So if one is salt of the earth, one has reached the Top?' Tim wanted to know. 'Are we sure of that? I sometimes worry about Plato's theory. Take Mozart, for example. Churchill. Shakespeare. Smuts. Walt Disney, for heaven's sake! One of five children, began by delivering newspapers and ended up making the whole world happy. Tolstoy. Eleven children, a large estate to run, and he writes *War and Peace* with a quill. No typewriter, no copying machine! Imagine finishing *War and Peace*, wanting a copy, and having to write it all over again.'

There was a pause while we all considered Tim's thesis.

'He'd need a new quill,' said James at last.

'When we were young,' I said, 'Vladimir Vukovich ran a very successful butcher shop in Northcliff and had a house in the Johannesburg suburb of Emmarentia. After I started work, and if after a bad day I was thoroughly dejected, I would go to Vladimir's house, because in its basement hung legs of ham, smoked a special way with wood chippings that his grandfather sent him from Yugoslavia. While Rossi, Denys, Ronnie, Boris, the Beretta bros, and I sipped Yugoslavian schnapps, Vlado fed us thin slivers of cured ham, and I would soon begin to feel better. Vladimir was the husband of Bernice, who had twice won the South African Open – once as Miss Carr and once as Mrs Vukovich. She, oddly enough, understood small folk best of all. Used to have tea with the umpires and linesmen, club secretaries, referees, parents of opposing players, sometimes even offered to buy the umpire a cup, after the match …'

There was another of those thoughtful silences, until Tim mused, 'It does seem that we're all small folk …'

When I was a child, the value of mammon was so different from what it is today that it is impossible to get my own grandchildren to believe what I say about it. The moment I begin with the words, 'when I was a child', I lose them, but, being respectful children, they sit politely and listen, their thumbs all ready to get back to their phones or their iPads. Who can blame them for not believing that in 1957 two rands' worth of petrol would fill my red Volkswagen? Putting my words in story form sometimes helped.

Every year, I once told them, our mother and father would save up and take us to East London for three weeks. We'd stay at the Hotel Woodholme, from which you could see tugs guiding liners into the harbour. Each morning at eight we'd walk down to the Orient Beach with our buckets and spades and play until eleven. There was a corner shop on the esplanade that sold penny buns with raisins inside and icing on the top, and one of the holiday treats was to buy them, carry them back to the beach and eat them under our umbrella with the thermos of tea that our mother brought along. Jenny, the youngest, would first lick the icing off her bun, then dig for the raisins with her fingers, and only then eat the inside part.

Further along the esplanade there was a milk bar and on every third evening or so our parents took us there for milkshakes. One evening, the two young men sitting at the next table were having a quite different kind. When I asked about them, they told me they were called double thick malteds. Then when I asked my father if we could also have double thick malteds he looked at the menu and said, 'Not tonight. Wait until Saturday. Money doesn't grow on trees, you know.' The regular milkshakes cost ninepence and the double thick malteds cost one shilling and sixpence.

'They must have been very small malteds,' said one of my grandsons, I think it was Daniel.

There was something lovely about those old days and the way they lingered, allowing life to unfold at a pace so measured that a new kind of milkshake was a special treat. I was about ten at the time, and my father's words embedded in my mind a permanent awareness of thrift so that even now, seventy years later, I still find myself instinctively weighing up cost and value – the conservation of time, the nutrition in oatmeal, the quality of hand-knitted socks or the craftsmanship in a good old split-cane trout rod – never mind that it might be less wieldy than modern rods. I even put out lights.

⁂

'I've just watched Adam Scott (another bloody Australian) win a tournament using a short putter again. Thank God the PGA came to their senses. There is something wonderful about keeping certain things the way they've always been. Take the Swilcan Bridge at St Andrews, originally used by shepherds to get sheep across the burn. It's been there for seven hundred years or more – imagine if they suddenly decided to demolish it and build a new one out of yellow carbon-fibre! Or if the London Philharmonic musicians arrived on stage in coloured T-shirts and Mohican haircuts and played Beethoven with a beat ...?'

'Young audiences would love it ...' began Tim, but stopped when Charles glared at him.

'Tennis has been played in white clothes since it began,' I went on. 'Even in the sixteen hundreds when it was called *jeu de paume* and the French played it with the palms of their hands, they wore white. Or so they say. So why not leave it white? Tennis is an elegant game, and what can be more elegant than the green and white of Wimbledon?'

The Table must have resigned itself to my tirades about the old days, because the diners sat quietly, eating away, sipping their wine and waiting for the next stanza.

Anyway, I went on, I've surrendered to colour. It's only sometimes, when I see players in really outrageous gear that I still get a sudden longing for white. Silly, right? Colour is the in thing. They say it's because players get paid so much for wearing clothing that the manufacturers are compelled to use it to highlight their brands. Mammon again. But for me the white Lacoste shirt with its little green crocodile, speaks volumes.

I was only too pleased to leave it at that and listen to the One Peter telling us about the latest political moves in South Africa – he has extensive knowledge and an instinctive feel for such things. Then there was what Donald Trump and Theresa May had just done. Federer had somehow won the Australian Open, aged thirty-five, James's book *Overkill* was finished and needed a cover, the Irish coffees were about to arrive …

I drove home after that lunch feeling remorseful about my grumbling, but back in my office I decided to email the chaps to see what they really thought. To my surprise, they generally agreed.

One Peter *One in white the other in colour.*
Other Peter *White was a delight, elegant, sporty, sexy. Colour not so.*
Charles *White for a sporting contest, colours for being merciless.*
Richard *Don't care; more important to go back to wooden rackets.*
Mark *Tradition vital so white on lawn, please.*

James *I'm all for white and good old Wimbledon's tradition.*
Tim *Ask the old, they'll cry white. Ask the young, they'll cry colour.*

'Tim is right of course,' I said as we recapped at the next lunch. 'It's a technicolor world and there is no going back. But apparently a yearning for simplicity has been going on for some time,' and I took out the piece of paper I'd put into my shirt pocket for the occasion.

In 1609 Ben Jonson wrote:

> *Give me a look, give me a face*
> *That makes simplicity a grace*
> *Robes loosely flowing, hair as free:*
> *Such sweet neglect more taketh me*
> *Than all the adulteries of art*
> *They strike my eyes but not my heart.*

'I thought you said you were nearly a farmer,' said Charles.

'I'm afraid I cheated,' I said. 'I looked it up. But even tennis matches in the old days were simpler things. More informal. More personal, in a way. In one of my old diaries I found an entry that revealed this to perfection' – and because there wasn't much else on the agenda that day, they wanted to know what it was I'd found.

'We've talked about how, in all sports, lady luck is a capricious woman. On any given day, instead of playing fair, she might allocate all the luck in a tennis match to one player, leaving the other high and dry. I found some notes I'd made at a tournament in Hilversum, Holland – typical of those days – a bashed-up stadium holding about a thousand people, canvas backstops to the outside courts, clubhouse with a veranda, teacups all laid out ... But good players. Rod Laver won it that year, beat me in the semi-finals. Emerson, I think, won the year before ...'

Anyway, I continued, my notes are about a match Ramanathan Krishnan played against Eddie Rubinoff. Complete opposites they were. Krishnan, the great Indian champion, was like a fakir, cunning as a closet rat with a quiet, spiritual sort of game that often surprised the very best of players. Rubinoff, on the other hand, was one of those excitable Americans who felt that the more they hustled and bustled, the better – and to his tennis he added doggedness, so that no matter how off-form he was, sheer toil, he felt, should see him through.

Of course we all went to watch the match and it was one of those days when, from the start, luck was on Krishnan's side. Almost uncannily his shots would hit the tape of the net, hesitate for a moment, then drop over, while Rubinoff's shots fell back. After a while he began a sort of running commentary about this luck – the ball was bewitched; how could this be happening? Had he sinned? God had forsaken him; should he rend his clothes? And so on – and the more voluble he became, the more Fate seemed to have it in for him. Krishnan, meanwhile, regarded the proceedings with a meditative kind of satisfaction, as if everything was going exactly as planned.

We all knew that something had to give. When, finally, yet another of Krishnan's shots hit the tape and dutifully fell over, Rubinoff, instead of more ranting, carefully laid his racket down on the clay, walked up to the smiling Dutch spectators at the side of the court and said in a friendly voice: 'You all saw that. I'm being punished. His fall over, mine come back ...'

And when they smiled he went on: 'It's not funny. It's unfair. I'm a nice person, I should be winning and I'm losing ...' He then moved on round the court, chatting away about his plight until he was almost on Krishnan's side. There he stopped and had a brief meeting with himself. 'Face it, Rubinoff. Jewish people have been taking punishment for centuries and still they suffer ...'

I couldn't hear everything he said, but Krishnan stood waiting patiently, still with his meditative, patient look, and finally the umpire said, 'Mr Rubinoff, play must be continuous,' and Eddie went back to fetch his racket, still discussing his luck with himself ...'

'Oh, we're back on luck, are we?' asked Mark. 'I thought we'd agreed that was an elusive area of discussion ...'

'Some things that happened then could never happen now,' I continued.

Here's another. There was an Australian player called Ken Fletcher, another character, much the same mould as Don Candy. Had his own brand of whimsy. One day, he was playing the Hungarian champion István Gulyás on the Roland Garros centre court. Gulyás was one of those stonewallers, rock-solid, drove opponents crazy by never missing a ball. Fletcher had all the usual Australian skill and determination, but was impatient. The match went on so long you could see Fletcher reaching breaking point.

Finally, after one very long rally, he lost it, as they say these days. On about the thirtieth stroke, he hit what he thought was a clear winner only to see Gulyás run it down and get it back. Faced with a simple shot in the middle of the court, he calmly hit it sideways, clean out of the stadium with a mighty baseball-like stroke – and as he watched it soar over the west stand, he turned to his opponent with a smile and called out in such a friendly way that even Gulyás had to laugh.

'Get that back, you Hungarian bastard!'

Jean would have loved that snippet. In those days men and women shared every event – there were not separate circuits – so we were often together. Mixed doubles was an intriguing event in which all the players took part, and tennis was a 'happy family', uniting women and the men in their triumphs and disasters. Today only the four Grand Slams and a few other select events allow both sexes to compete. It seems to me a great pity.

43

Pray Silence for ...

One tradition that survived the new order is The International Club, known simply as The IC. It was founded in England in 1924 by the famous tennis journalist Wallis Myers, encouraged by the former prime minister Arthur Balfour who saw the many benefits of sport among nations.

The IC colours are white, steel-grey and pink, and its seal contains the four Latin words *Benevolentia* (goodwill), *Aequitas* (sportsmanship), *Virtus* (courage), and *Amicitia* (friendship). If you played for your country you were invited to be a member, and the idea was that after your career was over, you stayed in touch, and continued playing friendly international matches until you could play no more. In 1929 the French IC was formed by Jean Borotra, and this was followed by the USA and the Netherlands in 1931. The IC of South Africa, fifth in the world, began soon afterwards, and there are now thirty-four International Clubs in countries where the love of tennis and sportsmanship still lives.

It used to be a great thrill to be invited to membership of the IC. In England, the annual dinner and ball, held on the Saturday evening

The International Club of Great Britain Tennis Day, at Queen's Club in 1962. In those days, many of the great players used to take part.

Back row: G F, Arthur Ashe, Clark Graebner (5th from left), John Barrett (6th from left), Andres Gimeno (7th from left), Charlie Pasarell (10th from left), Roy Emerson (last man standing). Middle row: Far left, Frank Sedgman (in suit), Fred Stolle, Lew Hoad, Alex Olmedo, and Abe (all in tennis gear).
Front, middle: Roger Taylor, Luis Ayala.

To the others in the photo, my apologies! As the poet said, 'Age makes an autumn in the memory …'

before the Wimbledon fortnight, has endured for over seventy years and, like so many other things about British tennis, it has become a tradition. I will never forget the first IC Ball I attended in 1954, the pomp, ceremony, uniforms, black ties and evening gowns, and the stentorian voice calling out 'Pray silence for Her Majesty the Queen'. The anthem, the grace, the formal dinner courses and the port served in cut-glass goblets! In those days the players never missed an IC Ball – these days I doubt whether many of them know it exists.

PRAY SILENCE FOR ...

In 2005, the president of the International Club of Great Britain asked me to be a guest speaker at the dinner and IC Ball held that year at the Dorchester Hotel. Tradition has it that a member of the British IC introduces an international member, who then thanks the British Club for their hospitality. The Ball had become the opening event of the Wimbledon fortnight, a black-tie affair attended by about four hundred tennis dignitaries from all over the tennis world. When, in January, the email arrived inviting me to speak on behalf of the international guests, I was excited, honoured and alarmed. But as it was January, and the Ball took place only in June, it was distant enough to accept the invitation.

'Suggest you speak for no more than eight minutes', the first email had said, but the British IC committee must have got cold feet, because another one came saying, 'Perhaps you should restrict your talk to five minutes', and a little later, yet another one saying that four might be enough – 'because the members will want to get on with their dancing'. (There was always a big dance band in attendance.) I half expected a fourth saying, 'Suggest you enjoy your dinner and sit quietly without saying a word', but it never came.

By May I'd passed the point of no return, so I began to compile what I thought would be a suitable speech for the international tennis guests who would be there. Conscious of my nerves, I went to an old-world chemist shop in our suburb and asked Dov Cohen, the owner, whether he knew of some kind of anti-crisis pill that I could take in case I felt about to be struck dumb. After some thought he gave me two yellow pills in a small envelope.

'Try one the day before,' he said, 'because you never know how you may react to it ...'

June came sooner than I thought it would, and Frances and I were staying with friends in a house on Clapham Common. As the moment of truth drew nigh, my nerves started to emit warning tremors and so I walked on the Common, reading aloud to myself, and sometimes getting stuck. On the day before the ball, with panic in the offing, I took one of the yellow pills to see what it would do, and to my relief it relaxed me.

The night duly arrived. Frances and I, in our best bibs and tuckers, set off for the Dorchester. On arrival there, the throng of black ties was alarming until John Barrett emerged to welcome us on behalf of the British IC.

'I'll be introducing you,' he said, and I could have hugged him.

If ever there was, for me, a calming presence, it was John. Roughly my age, he had been one of England's best players and one of the first I'd met when, in 1954, Gordon Talbot and I had played our first tournament at Sutton in Surrey. John and I had immediately become friends, in spite of the fact that he'd teased me about my vowels being flat. He was right, of course. His own vowels, buffed up by several years at Cambridge, were smooth, round and lovely.

'They resonated,' I told the Table, who by now had resigned themselves to my stories. 'I've always wanted vowels that resonate like John Barrett's.'

'We'd all like our vowels to resonate,' said Tim. He has a way of putting on wistful looks, and the one that he assumed just then showed that his vowels didn't resonate as much as he would have liked. 'We had an elocution teacher at school who used to wring her hands …'

On the big night we were seated at a table with Tim Phillips, the Chairman of the All England Club, Neale Fraser (previous champion and guest of honour) and his wife, Thea, John and his wife Angela (who, as Angela Mortimer, had won Wimbledon in 1961), Mike Hann, Sally Holdsworth, Barry Weatherill – it was moving to sit with people who had been friends all those years ago, and for a few hours the old days came back, interfered with by the looming speech.

At last the time came, and while John introduced me in his usual calm and polished way, I nibbled at my yellow pill and felt a calmness come over me. By the time he finished and 'gave me the floor', as he said, I was able to walk to the lectern and begin my speech as if I was talking to a roomful of old friends – although there were about four hundred people from all over the tennis world.

It was a simple matter to thank John, and easy to talk about how, when I first met him, he had criticised my vowels. Remarkable how speeches take shape in the first few sentences, and how people seem sometimes to relate to the most trivial of things. That audience took my side in the flat vowel saga and enabled me to tell a few more stories that produced laughter and made it fitting to talk about tennis friendships and how long they lasted. I mentioned that all IC members in South Africa had asked me to convey regards and best wishes. 'All except Abe Segal,' I added, 'and he, too, would have sent warm regards if he'd remembered to …' And they laughed at the news of Abe's paintings with their skies upside down. Funny how many of them knew about Abe.

The speech went on for ten minutes. I told of how the top fifty players in our day all had different styles, whereas the players of today all seemed to play the same way.

'Imagine,' I said, 'if we'd had fifty Ken Rosewalls, or (looking at Neale Fraser) fifty Neale Frasers, with not a backhand among them!'

There was much laughter at this, but I hastened to add that I was teasing Neale and that you couldn't win Wimbledon without a backhand.

When we got home I was able to tell Dov that the yellow pills had worked. He wouldn't tell me what they were, but I think that I have since guessed. I wonder whether one can be banned for drug-enhanced speaking.

⁂

In the realms of tennis, and subjects neighbouring, there can be no truer scholar than John Barrett. One talks about knowing all the facts … Although he never ran the Burmese police force or had a gunshot wound, amongst other things he compiled one of the most magnificent of tennis books – a beautifully presented history called *100 Years of Wimbledon – A Celebration*.

It captures all the richness and tradition of the All England Club, and is divided into eras, from the time tennis rackets cost 5/9p, and the All England Club used a modern horse-drawn roller. The 1956-1965 era, both John Barrett's and my own, was literally taken over by bloody Australians who also happened to be the best, fairest, most valiant sportsmen of any era.

The victory of Virginia Wade in 1977 was surreal in its splendour – her tennis, the timing of her win, and the way she so supremely and absolutely seized the day! The Wimbledon centenary, the rare presence of the Queen, and this slender English girl with blue eyes and a mass of dark hair, so ready to meet the challenge. John captures it all in his book.

I was industriously telling the Table these things, when James cleared his throat.

'A history of Wimbledon is all very well, but like all histories, it needs lubrication to make it palatable. Pass the bottle …'

'Odd sort of word to describe histories,' said Richard. 'Palatable.

Even if you could eat history, it wouldn't be good for you. A succession of wars, revolutions, beheadings, rebellions, and so on. Right, Charles?'

'You're always right, Richard. It's one of your weaknesses. We'd prefer it if you were sometimes wrong. But to answer your question, yes, history is generally inedible.'

※

That IC dinner reminded me of the strong 'family' feeling that existed among the players of those times – Barry trying out a new racket, Carole and Wayne in love, Mimi and Donald teaming up in the mixed doubles, Torben practising his clarinet in the groundsmen's shed, Fletch finding a new restaurant that served *steak frite* with free chips *and* salad ... While playing a match at Roland Garros, Torben Ulrich called on his friend Kurt Nielsen to find a pair of scissors to cut his fringe and Kurt gave him a trim on court three. A singular man, Torben. I once played him in the last sixteens at Roland Garros, quickly led by two sets to love, and began the third set with calm nerves and high expectations. Suddenly he began playing like a long-haired magician, and I lost the last three sets. Later, in the locker room, Torben, with a towel round his waist, came to sit beside me.

'I am sorry, Gordon,' he said in his slow way. 'I thought I was losing, you see, then I suddenly found I was playing very well, so I allowed myself to win.'

What could I say to that? Even in my disappointment, I remember feeling that he genuinely felt sympathy, as perhaps, a brother might feel for a sister who had just lost an important match.

44

The Finest Kind

'Where id is, there shall ego be,' intoned Tim, looking around the Table with the mischievous innocence that only he can achieve. He reached for the butter, spread some on his bread, looked up with a sheepish grin and added, 'Sigmund Freud.' He wasn't showing off. We'd been having a discussion, half serious, half whimsical, about egos in the modern world, and he was simply reminding us that we weren't the first to ponder them. 'What our Table is suggesting is that egos are much bigger than they used to be.'

'Well if Freud is right, ids too must be bigger,' said the Other Peter.

'What *exactly* is an id?' I asked, really wanting to know, for it was a word that had long been lurking in my mind without explaining itself. He was already on his phone summoning the Internet. After a minute or so he gave a satisfied grunt and began reading.

> *Id: Part of the unconscious mind that represents the most basic natural human needs and emotions such as hunger, joy and danger. The id contains the libido, which is the primary source of instinctual force unresponsive to the demands of reality.*

'Good Lord,' exclaimed James. 'I never realised that libido was unresponsive to reality. Hunger, joy and anger, yes. But libido! It just goes to show …'

'Jean told me that the id had something to do with the philosophy of being,' I put in, '*I think therefore I am*. That kind of thing.'

'Descartes,' murmured Charles. 'What never occurred to me was that everyone on earth has one. Seven billion ids! Going by Freud, that would mean seven billion egos. I wonder if egos have mass.'

'Well if they do, Donald Trump has a heavy load.' The One Peter.

'Sports psychologists say that without ego, you can't be a winner,' I said. 'My father used to say, *don't brag, let your deeds speak for you,* while Old Mervyn Thomas Sweet, our school chaplain, used to say: *If the trumpet give an uncertain sound who shall prepare himself to the battle.* I've always been in two minds …'

'These days you need word, deed and trumpet blast,' interrupted the Other Peter. 'What about your tennis stars? Do they have bigger egos than they did in your day?'

'Probably. It's hard to have a Porsche and fifty million in the bank and not have an ego. On the other hand, one can be quite modest with a Harvey and ten dollars a day …'

⁂

All the talk about egos set me thinking about tennis stars again – the way they were then and the way they are now. Strangely, although fame, money and achievement are ideal breeding grounds for egos, on court the modern tennis players don't openly flaunt them. Rather, in a formal sort of way they have about them an aura of superiority. 'They kinda act like they own the game,' was Abe's proclamation over coffee one morning, and as was so often the case his words carried weight – strictly incorrect of course, for no one can own tennis. But the ring of it was enough to set me thinking about how the great players behaved and whether they won graciously, as my mother used to say. Idly, that evening, I found a sheet of paper, wrote the heading 'The Finest Kind', then sat back to see what would happen next.

'The name came via the wife of our doctor in Plettenberg Bay,' I told the Table. 'Joan Berning, her name is, the wife of Peter Berning. He's the only GP that I know of who has walked to both the North and the South poles and planted a flag at each. Comforting in a way. You go to him with torn cartilage and while he examines it you think to yourself, well, if he could get to the poles, he can fix my knee. Anyway, Joan used to make butter, cheeses, yogurt and various other things for the market and named her products *The Finest Kind.* Joan herself, as kinds go, is pretty fine. In her youth a beautiful girl, she is now a handsome, blondish woman with a few silver threads amongst the gold, who walks all over the country conserving things – animals, plants, birds, whole regions, if she can get at them. If anything worthwhile shows signs of becoming extinct, she'll do her best to conserve it.'

'Any chance of her coming to our next lunch?' asked Tim. He glanced around the Table. 'You never know, she could come in handy …'

'The finest kind?' repeated the One Peter, playing the game. 'You will agree that cheese and sports stars are of a different genre …'

'It was a fanciful idea,' I said. 'I thought that while great tennis ability was one thing, I could compile a list of other qualities that players would need to qualify for my Finest Kind category. Only for my own satisfaction, you follow me, not for general consumption – and it's become a habit. When I watch sport, I can't help being aware of how players behave, and if they behave badly I say to myself, "what a pity". Jimmy Connors, for instance. Such a great tennis champion, but for some reason he did some odd things that in those days seemed deliberately disagreeable. Ego, you think? Id? Who knows? Why would a player as good as he need to make rude gestures when his tennis was all he needed?'

'Mind you,' mused the Other Peter. 'Modern viewers love swagger, and players do all manner of things to look famous …'

'Not so much in tennis. In singles, anyway. In doubles the guys go about touching hands, talking in secret, making signs, crouching down, virtually kissing each other at times. Drives us older chaps mad. Abe Segal once actually threw his hat at the TV set. Sorry, where was I? Oh, right, I was making a new list of ten things players had to do in order to behave properly.'

I must have been talking too fast because Charles put his hand on my forehead and told me to take a pill.

'Sorry,' I said sheepishly, 'but as I said, it's become a habit. I watch a lot of sport – tennis, golf, cricket, rugby, and in all of them I find myself watching for the Finest Kind. For example, our cricketers were playing a fifty overs match. Someone went out and A B de Villiers came in to bat. There you are, I said to myself, look no further! Your Finest Kind before your very eyes – and just as I was starting to feel really pleased with myself, he played a bad shot and spat something straight at the TV camera. Damn, I thought, my mother said it was rude to spit.'

'Have a heart, Gordon,' interrupted the Other Peter. 'You have to give the modern guys a bit of slack. Tattoos, beards, sledging, spitting, chewing, colours. It's all part of the modern game. Things have changed. We've agreed that sportsmen have egos so don't let a little spitting worry you.'

'You're absolutely right, I suppose. Let them spit. Perhaps Nike or Adidas should even invent lozenges that players could suck to create spectacular jets of liquid, and not just feeble squirts. Umpires could have expectorometers …'

Richard gave the kind of wave that swept nonsense under carpets. 'Your idea of a new list seemed promising enough before it went down a slippery slope,' he said. 'Never mind. Did you ever make this new list?'

'Absolutely. It might solve another thing that puzzles me. Watching sport, I often wonder why one has instinctive likes and dislikes. For instance, although I don't know them, I like Djokovic better than Murray, or Federer better than Nadal – not strongly, you understand, but distinctly. No real reason, just a feeling. In golf I like Els better than almost anyone, in rugby, the Lions better than the Sharks. I thought my Finest Kind list might throw some light.

'To clarify my idea I brought copies of all the lists,' and I took them out and handed them round. 'The first is the list of players we made in McCormack's tent in Rome. To bring it up to date I've added Sampras, Nadal and Federer. The other lists follow on.'

Greatest Players
Bill Tilden
Don Budge
Pancho Gonzales
Lewis Hoad
Rodney Laver
Bjorn Borg

THE FINEST KIND

John McEnroe
Pete Sampras
Roger Federer
Rafael Nadal

Winning Qualities
Natural talent
Good physique
Perfect eyesight
Courage
Belief
Patience
Love of the game
Love of competition
A big weapon
Playing to win

Finest Kind
Sportsmanship
Grace
Confidence
Modesty
Humour
Appeal
Courtesy
Respect
Magnanimity
Gallantry

There was such a long period of silence while they studied my lists that I knew I hadn't hit the nail on the head. 'So what do you think?' I asked cautiously.

'Old viewers could read their books and young viewers could catch up on some sleep,' said Charles in a gentle voice.

'I thought we'd banned wishful thinking at this Table,' said the Other Peter. 'Now if tennis stars were saints, or Mother Teresa and Serena Williams would team up, your list might have some merit …'

'So your Finest Kind also have to be gallant?' Mark had been looking at the lists with critical eyes.

'Some players were, you know,' I replied defensively. 'In 1954 I played in the mixed doubles at Wimbledon with a Durban girl called Joan Scott. In the second round we played Jean Borotra and an English girl called Jennifer Middleton – lovely, blonde, steady as a rock and with strong British legs. We lost in three sets and were suitably chagrined, for Borotra was by then well over fifty and he muddled us up by wearing a beret and rushing the net peering through the strings of his racket and never missing a volley. At the end of the match, he kissed the back of Joan's hand and took us up to the players' restaurant to give us tea. Later I found a note in my diary saying he was *a gallant man* …'

Mark nodded. The schoolmaster conceding a point.

'An American player named Brad Gilbert wrote a book called *Winning Ugly* which sounded to me like the opposite of winning gallantly – although Brad was in his way a gallant player. He would coach himself during his matches. "Forget about footwork, Gilbert, and watch the ball …" Anyway, winning ugly didn't seem right.'

'Better than losing ugly,' mused the One Peter.

Sandra Reynolds – one of the finest kind. Jean Borotra – a gallant man.

'For the record,' said Richard, 'why are there no women on your list?'

'Because I can hardly cope with the men. In any case, nearly all the women in my day were the Finest Kind, and I can't comment on modern ones. Yelping and grunting wouldn't be allowed, but their legs are the Finest Kind. No. Best leave the women to themselves and get back to the men. Strangely enough, a photograph helped my cause. I have this American friend who, like me, loves tennis the way it used to be and still believes that Lew Hoad produced the best set of tennis ever played. He even sent me some quotes to prove it.'

When Lew Hoad was at his peak, nobody could touch him
– Pancho Gonzales (Hoad's greatest rival)

If Lew Hoad was on form, you may as well just go home or have tea, because you weren't going to beat him
— Don Budge (rated by many as the greatest of all time [with a wood racket])

Lew Hoad could do anything he wanted to with a tennis ball
— Gene Mako (Don Budge's doubles partner)

Lew was my idol both on and off the court, and he once beat me 14 matches in a row, even though he had a bad back
— Rod Laver (also rated by some as the greatest of all time with a wood racket)

If Lew hit the ball any harder it would burst into flames
— Budge Patty (who won the French Open and Wimbledon in 1950)

When Lew felt like playing, man, he was really something. I never saw anybody who could snap the ball back hard off both sides from way behind the baseline for winners the way he did
— Jack Kramer (another 'greatest' contender of the wood men)

Lew's tennis was so great that he thought he was in Heaven
— Pancho Segura (from whom Lew said he learned more about tennis than from anyone else)

He also sent me a photo of Hoad with his singles trophy at Wimbledon in 1957, after he'd beaten Ashley Cooper in less than an

Australia's Lew Hoad poses with the Men's Singles trophy, July 1957.
(© Gallo Images/Getty Images/Popperfoto)

hour. I watched that final from the competitors' stand. After the winning shot Hoad trotted up to the net, shook Cooper's hand as if he'd beaten him in a Saturday afternoon friendly, then sat chatting to him while they waited for the Duke to present the Cup. And, by the way, he had all his belongings inside one of his racket-head covers.

ಊಬಲ

'Allen Fox was another American friend of mine,' I told the Table. 'When I needed someone reliable to test my theories, I thought of him because he is a real tennis scholar and author of the book *If I'm the Better Player, Why Can't I Win?* So I looked him up on the net, and got quite a fright because he obviously knew a lot more facts than I did.'

He's stayed closer to tennis than I have, and his book thoroughly investigates the psychology of winning and losing, so with some trepidation I emailed him for help and sent him my theories, wanting not only his wisdom, but also an American opinion. To my delight I got his reply:

Dear Forbsey,

To a large extent I agree with you. If I didn't have interest in particular players I wouldn't watch much tennis anymore. Yes, everything has changed. Modern players have discovered something that we were taught was wrong. We were taught that power wasn't everything, and that the important part of the game was such things as depth, placement, finesse and strategy. In our day, nobody put balls away from the baseline. In fact, we were taught to come to the net, and I doubt that I ever in my life tried to hit a winner from the back of the court. Now, power is the key. Today's kids practise hitting the ball as hard as they can and they are all taught to hit it in exactly the same way. The two-handed backhand, for instance, that in our day was so rare, is now virtually standard!

And I agree that much of the game is rather dull and repetitious these days – it was less effective in our day, but prettier. Today's game seems more violent and to require more muscle. Better but not as pretty. It was fun, then, because there was less power, more guile and manoeuvring before a winner could be hit. Now, a succession of baseline shots invariably leads to these big, attempted winners that either succeed or fail. Then they start all over again! And, of course, the players are better athletes than we were. And bigger. Guys like Del Potro, 6'7" – Kevin Anderson (6'8"), Raonic (6'6"), etc. – and how would you like returning Isner's serve? Even the regular guys are huge – Murray is 6'3", about the same size as Pancho Gonzalez, who we thought was a

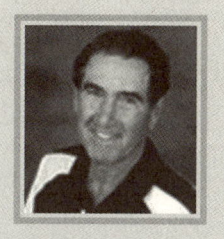

> ### Allen Fox, Ph.D.
>
> **Author, Speaker, Consultant**
>
> Dr. Allen Fox earned a Ph.D. in psychology at UCLA and is a former NCAA champion, Wimbledon quarterfinalist and a three-time member of the U.S. Davis Cup team. Dr. Fox also coached the Pepperdine tennis team to two NCAA finals.
>
> He currently consults with athletes on mental issues, lectures on sports psychology, and is the author of several books on the mental side of competition.

giant. Nadal is 6'2" or 6'1", so they're bigger, and stronger. So, yes, to answer your question, it's not as much fun watching tennis these days, but, then, the tennis they play is much better than ours was.

'So you see? I'm not the only one …'

'Do we qualify?' James wanted to know, and when someone asked what for, he answered, 'the Finest Kind.'

'I can't see why not,' replied Charles. 'We're a gallant bunch …'

'Plato is our only hope,' said Richard.

'In tennis,' I offered, 'they now have every age group, so I'm compiling a Finest Kind list for the over seventies. If James and I don't make it, I'll do another for the over eighties.'

45

The Writers

Thinking back to E M Forster's book on novel writing, I often wondered whether there was one on sports writing and what was it that made some sports writers so good. Knowing all Forster's facts? More and more I have come to admire the writers who so faithfully follow their particular sport, always striving to make their writing as good as the sport they describe.

Of course I didn't have to tell the chaps at the Table. They know. They may not have been at the coalface of sports writing – sitting for hours, analysing every ball – but they know very well how hard it must be to arrange words to satisfy avid sports fans. A thousand words by six o'clock! Day after day, no time to rework, every sentence right the first time. For the writers of my time, deadlines were commonplace, and they seemed relaxed and unhurried – sensitive, brusque, amiable, apparently loving tennis as much as the players. Occasionally I would visit their pub and learn more about a game that I'd just been watching; they picked things up, those fellows. Gleaned things – what an altercation was about or what McEnroe said to the linesman who called a foot

THE WRITERS

fault ... One of them once told me gleefully that he'd asked a player about his game plan for his next match. The player had replied that he was going to lose the first set to find out what his opponent's game plan was.

'At Wimbledon, in the good old days,' I told the Table, 'when there were no seats left in the competitors' stand, the journalists in the adjacent press box would often make room for me and I'd watch them, jotting things down, concentrating like mad, then making jokes, always looking for new angles. Journalism then was a craft, you'll agree, governed, it seemed to me, by some unwritten lore that made writers judge their own work, proud of excellence, spurning mediocrity. And often great passages went to waste, so to speak – forever lost in morning papers that survived only one breakfast.'

Some, of course, wrote books – thus managing to preserve the essence of the sport they loved. A J Liebling's boxing stories for *The New Yorker* were read by people who weren't even boxing aficionados. He often refers to himself as a spectator – a bit of a ham who sits at the ringside and shouts instructions that don't get anywhere near the protagonists. Nonetheless, there's not a paragraph where you don't feel he is inviting you to sit next to him and share his packet of pretzels. His book *The Sweet Science* is worth reading for the names alone: Colonel Stingo, Mush Sallow, Chickie Ferrara, Whitey Bimstein, Tiny Payne, Philadelphia Jack O'Brien, Jimmy Tomato, Bertie Briscoe ... a cigar-chomping, manly America, smoke-filled bar rooms, beer- and mustard-stained menus ...

The British tennis writer and author Rex Bellamy gave me one of my greatest moments. Never was there a man who understood tennis so well, who was able to watch a game and capture so perfectly its

Frances with Fred Perry at the launch of A Handful of Summers.

moments of triumph and dejection. Read his books and you get to know the players and the courts they played on – the spirit of place. They say that each Grand Slam has a soul and, if so, Rex bared it ...

My book *A Handful of Summers* was published in 1978, and released about a month before Wimbledon, and Frances and I went to London for both events. The initial thrill of finding a publisher had quietly turned into apprehension – the same feeling as aroused by the words 'suppose I gave a party and nobody came'. For a week or so after it was released, there was a deathly silence and the usual onset of panic. We watched the tennis at Queen's Club, and searched the morning papers without finding a thing. Then on the Thursday it rained all day. There was no tennis, we had tea in the players' restaurant and made our way back to the little flat we'd rented.

The next morning I went down to the King's Road to buy newspapers – *The Times, The Telegraph, The Guardian, The Daily Mail* – in those days only a few pennies each. Back in the flat, we sat in bed drinking tea and reading, and suddenly, on the back page of *The Times* I came upon one of my own paragraphs. Rex Bellamy had got hold of the book, read it, and was moved to begin a review of it with my own words!

'It's the best review I've ever been able to write,' he said, proudly, as if I was the one who had done him a favour! He told me later that had it not been for the rain, there would never have been room for his review – something that renewed my musing about luck. As it happened, that very afternoon the publishers had arranged a function to launch my book. They, too, had found Rex's review, so there was applause and rejoicing and overnight, thanks to a rainy Thursday, I had apparently become an author!

46

The Spoken Word

In our day there were only the sports writers and radio commentators to tell us about games we were not able to attend, and I came to love the commentators almost as much as the writers. How often, at various tennis parties, social afternoons or stock fairs had I not joined the grown-ups clustered round a car radio listening to Charles Fortune describing how Roy McLean's cover drive raised a cloud of pigeons, Francois Wolfaardt crying out that Sea Cottage had won the Durban July, or that Okey Geffin's place kick had beaten England in a rugby Test series. There was strange magic in the words that emerged from the old-fashioned 'wireless sets'.

In those days, to get a look at your heroes, you had to go to stadiums or find your way to their practice courts or cricket nets, and I grew to love such occasions. There was nothing as exciting as emerging on the North Stand of the Ellis Park tennis stadium and there, in the sun, suddenly finding the player who before had been nothing but a figure in a photograph. Or, as a schoolboy, watching Alec Bedser bowling at the Ramblers Club in Bloemfontein. I was young, of course, and life was new, but never since have I found anything quite as stirring as those first sightings.

Now you get an endless array of live sport, playbacks and highlights, and you can see in slow motion not only A B de Villiers's superb cover drives but also his new beard, and the way he spits when things don't go his way. TV is indeed a wonderful thing for millions of viewers, but the sight of sports heroes is as common as rain …

As an ex-player, I was often asked to commentate on televised tennis tournaments. Kim Shippey was the man in charge. Kim, like Charles Fortune, was one of South Africa's legendary commentators who'd served his time on radio before turning to TV. Commentating, for him, was an art form. Before each TV session he would take me aside and give earnest instructions.

'Never speak once play has begun. Never interrupt the umpire. Always keep an eye on the peripherals. Be brief. Shut up if you have nothing to say, never tell the viewers what they can already see, only what they can't. Don't be afraid of silence and don't give tennis lessons on my broadcasts.' A stern taskmaster, was Kim.

When I think back on commentators such as he and Charles Fortune, what strikes me most was their absolute dedication to the game, to the listeners, and to the players on the field, to the extent that they sometimes became virtual guests in one's living room – I have even heard viewers talking to them: 'Come on, Kim, that wasn't such a bad shot,' or, 'Be fair, Charles. Explain how hard it is to hit a backhand smash …'

One of the first and most famous TV tennis announcers is Cliff Drysdale who in 1979 with Fred Stolle (a famous Australian player and still a doyen amongst commentators) began commentating for the US cable network, ESPN. Bland, urbane and informal, there was (and still is) something about the way Cliff describes tennis in his carefree South African accent that made people like him. Together with Fred's gruff realism, they became a famous combination, and even Rod Laver was heard to remark that while Fred was brief, Cliff was able to talk a lion into becoming a vegetarian. Abe Segal said he could talk the hind leg off a horse and I had to tell him that donkeys, not horses, were the things people talked hind legs off.

Abe, Cliff and I travelled together for years as members of the Davis Cup team, and he and Abe exhausted each other with their constant exchange of insults. At first Abe used to win, but Cliff proved to be a born insulter and, like Abe, became so renowned for insults that important people seemed compelled to come back for more. In fact, the statement 'Cliff Drysdale insulted me' became a badge of honour in some circles. As he and I had once worked together on tennis commentaries, we naturally discussed their merits, finding we agreed that Kim Shippey's golden rules no longer apply. By Kim's credo the new young commentators talk far too much, with the result that when we see Nadal hit a great forehand we are immediately told how great it is – often more than once and in several different ways.

Cliff was also one of South Africa's best tennis players, having one of the best eyes for a ball – any ball – that I have ever known. In the late sixties he joined a famous group of young professionals called *The Handsome Eight*, and for some years professional tennis became his life. Later he took to golf, and he has many stories to tell.

THE SPOKEN WORD

Jack Nicklaus and Cliff Drysdale.

'For instance,' I told the Table, 'about ten years or so ago, his friend Butch Buchholz (also once a member of *The Handsome Eight*) organised a game of tennis at Jack Nicklaus's Florida home, where Jack has three superb grass courts. Nicklaus has grown to love tennis more than golf, says Cliff. He is quite good enough to make a decent game of it with Cliff, Butch, and his landscape gardener, who he calls the Grasscutter. Good hand-eye coordination, says Cliff, but a sore hip doesn't allow him to move as well as he would like to.'

Anyway, the tennis game led to a golf four ball at Jack's club, *The Bear's Club* in Jupiter, Miami, where apparently Cliff's famous ribbing so amused Nicklaus that the same tennis four took to playing a game of golf every month.

'And occasionally, to give us a treat,' says Cliff, 'Jack boots up his jet and flies us to Augusta where we play at the Augusta National Golf Club' – and he produces a photo of the four of them standing on the Hogan Bridge at Amen Corner. Butch, Cliff, Jack and the Grasscutter.

Ever since they first played, Cliff has had a side bet with Jack for $50 a game. Although Cliff's handicap is higher, they play off scratch, and Jack invariably wins.

'He takes my fifty dollar bills and sticks them up on his kitchen wall,' Cliff told me. 'By now nearly half one wall is covered in bills, and when Barbara (Jack's wife) redecorated their kitchen, Jack wanted a special cabinet made for them. When visitors come to Jack's house to see golf trophies, he takes them to the kitchen to show off his sea of $50 bills. Barbara says that all of them together wouldn't buy enough fuel to warm up his jet.'

47

The Challenge

Now living in Florida, Cliff recently emailed to tell me that he was coming to South Africa on a sentimental journey, to show the country to his new wife and to revisit the place. We at once invited him to spend some time with us in Plettenberg Bay and he immediately began issuing all kinds of insulting utterances about my golf and suggesting sedatives and stimulants that I would need if I dared to take him on.

Franny's Project (our son James) is now thirty-three years old and a six handicap golfer with such a natural game that I curse myself for not having given him, aged ten, a set of golf clubs instead of a tennis racket because, while he plays tennis well, I have a sneaking feeling golf might have been his true game.

Anyway, after all Cliff's threatening noises, I thought it wise to summon reinforcements, so I asked James whether he could possibly take enough leave to come to my assistance. To my relief he agreed, and this strategy produced what for me turned out to be an interesting side issue. When I told Cliff about Jamie's golf, Cliff immediately began issuing a different set of warnings, muttering things about key matches and playing for money …

He and DiAnna duly arrived, and for the first two days we did all the things one does in Plett and it was wonderful to get a view of the place through new and different eyes. Both of them seemed enchanted, vowing to make annual visits in future. The golf game was arranged for Saturday afternoon by Don Searle (the arbitrator in the Segal/tortoise incident), who was to be the fourth. As usual, it was Cliff who brought all the good-natured taunting to a head.

'Listen carefully, James,' he said. 'You are a six handicap, and I am a ten. Would you be prepared to play me for a thousand rand, if we both play off scratch?'

'Talk about temperament!' I told the Table. 'Well, I watched James's reaction with great interest, and it suddenly occurred to me that this was a golden opportunity to put it to the test. Now you all know how temperaments intrigue me and, having had a kink in my own, I have often wondered what sort of temperament my son had inherited. To my surprise, after a short silence, James quite cheerfully accepted Cliff's challenge, but suggested they use the South African tradition of playing two-fifty for the first nine, two-fifty for the second, and five hundred for the match.'

Feeling a bit of a heel, I took Cliff aside and told him I would like to see how Jamie handled golf under pressure. 'So don't hold back,' I said. 'Give him your full range of psychological crap!' – of which, I assure you, he has plenty.

So it was. On the very first hole, Cliff mentioned to James that the first stroke in a tight match was always the most important one. To my surprise, Jamie teed up quite calmly, and hit a long drive down the middle.

THE CHALLENGE

'Great shot,' said Cliff. 'Now be careful not to bugger up the second!'

But James's second was on the green, resulting in a comfortable four, while Cliff hit a poor second and made a five. After six holes, Jamie was two up, and on the seventh tee, Cliff said in his most earnest voice: 'Jamie, you have a great swing, and I especially like that short pause at the top of your backswing – do you do that on purpose?' The ultimate con in any sport. Sure enough, James's next tee-shot went among the tortoises, but on the eighth, when he came back with another par, he'd won the first nine. Cliff suggested a 'press' and still James seemed unperturbed.

So it went. Drysdale has an arsenal of 'cons' but Jamie survived most of them and ended up having a ten-foot putt on the eighteenth (for R500) that slid past the hole, as putts have a habit of doing. Still, it was more of a victory than he realised, and for Don and me a quietly fascinating contest. Afterwards, there were the tall glasses of draught beer and the usual ifs and buts ... but Cliff handed over the money, and for me the occasion was touched with sadness, for Cliff is another of the very many great sportsmen that our country has lost.

48

The Otter Trail

'A last trip?' I asked the Table during one of the lulls. 'My book's ending and I haven't walked anywhere. Been on planes, boats, trains, buses, the Underground ...'

'If you must ...'

'In Plettenberg Bay walkers abound,' I said. 'Virtually all Plett Bay folk periodically get the urge to walk, one that can mean anything from a leisurely stroll to robust striding. There are also hikes that take days. Plett is alive with environmentalists who link ecosystems to biospheres, create new habitats for rare creatures and find new regions for growing edible plants, all of which involve walking. One can safely say the coastline is riddled with trails populated by the people who follow them. Go to Plett and you know why.' And I gave Richard's wave.

'We understand ...'

'It was a chap called Desmond came up with the idea. He's in show business. Plett is one of his favourite places and he must have contracted the urge, because one evening at dinner, he put down his wine glass and said 'I think we ought to do the Otter Trail.'

THE OTTER TRAIL

'I didn't realize one *did* trails,' I said. 'I thought one hiked them.'

'Oh, one does. Hiking's how you do them. I've made arrangements for February.'

You have to book well in advance for the Otter Trail, for it traverses forty-two kilometres of the most sublime bit of nature reserve on the southern Cape coast and, as you know, is very popular. We never realised how enthusiastic Desmond and Dawn (his wife) were about the great outdoors. Frances and I made feeble noises about not possessing backpacks and so on, but they had twenty-litre packs to lend us – unsettling news, because I remembered Archibald R Dunne saying that a litre of most things usually weighed about a kilogram, and twenty kilograms was a heavy load.

Anyway, we'd agreed, and Desmond, once a boy scout, took charge and began making a list that got longer by the day. Candles, torches, knives, compasses, water purifiers, containers, underwater goggles (in case one became unexpectedly submerged), string, rope (for precipices), soaps, sunscreen, Band-Aids, aspirin. Then there were what he called survival items (for snakebites, broken bones, palpitations, spider bites, runny tummies, and so on).

For me, the boots alone were testing until I found in my cupboard a pair of grass-court tennis shoes that had once belonged to Jim Courier, whose feet were the same size as mine. He'd been given a dozen pairs for Wimbledon, used only half of them and left the rest to Gavin, who'd given me a pair. They were light, cushioned and comfortable, with pimpled soles that, according to Desmond, would prevent me from going into fatal slides. He, meanwhile, began acquiring things that might be needed. He even discovered a set of pots that nested into each other, ending up in a compact cylinder of metal, small, but heavy, that made Dawn ask if we were going to do a lot of cooking and whether she should take some recipe books along.

The pile grew and grew and Frances and I suggested our old house in Plett as a sort of base camp. As D-Day approached, Desmond and Dawn arrived in a 4x4 crammed with equipment, which when laid out in the spare room silenced even Desmond.

'Is it only the Otter Trail, or are we to venture into the interior?' Dawn wanted to know.

'What's inside the army surplus ammunition boxes?' Frances asked.

'Smaller items,' replied Desmond. 'One of them is full of Dawn's trail mix.'

While he filled his list, Dawn took care of the inner man (and woman), her pièce de résistance being a muesli-like mulch that, she proclaimed, was 'full of goodness' and also dealt with the perils of constipation.

'Plentiful roughage does the trick,' she said, 'and the spaces in the roughage contain vitamins. A single serving will not only give strength, but also clear the pipes.' She paused in her contemplation of blocked pipes to fix her eyes on some hi-tech apparatus that Desmond was unpacking. 'What on earth is that?'

'It's a Swiss Army water-purifying pump,' he said. 'One of the worst things to happen on a hike is to run out of drinking water. You put this tube into any kind of water, turn this handle, and you can get a hundred litres of water in less than an hour.'

'Well, thank goodness for that!' said Dawn. 'If we drink more than a hundred litres in the first hour, we simply turn the handle again.'

Desmond ignored the interruption. 'I also have water-purifying tablets and a collapsible bucket.'

'The word Tsitsikamma,' Dawn said, 'means "the place of running water". The Otter Trail traverses the Tsitsikamma.'

'With global warming, water can go green,' explained Desmond. 'The last thing we want are runny tummies.' He'd produced a large Leatherman and opened it so that all its tools protruded in a remarkable fanlike display of usefulness.

'Perfect,' said Dawn. 'A hacksaw, a shifting spanner and a screwdriver. All we'll need is something to unscrew.' One of the tools was the customary spike to remove stones from horse's hoofs. 'And a lame horse …' She was busy with an array of sun lotions, creams, oils, shampoos, atomisers and the like. Her browsings had unearthed a multi-pocketed toilet bag which, when unrolled and equipped, looked like a portable pharmacy.

It was Desmond's turn: 'You realise of course that you've only got one body?'

'I'm much more likely to get sunburn than a runny tummy!'

'And if your tummy does run, you can simply run after it,' I mentioned.

Finally the equipment was divided into four heaps: (1) Essential (2) Nice to have (3) Useful but heavy (4) Better left behind. 'We need a trial run,' said Desmond, eyeing his 'must have' heap. He unfurled his backpack and began filling it, being expert at finding spaces in which to tuck things. When he'd finished, it had a solid look to it.

'Right,' he said. 'That should do.'

He hung on to the door, while Frances, Dawn and I hoisted the pack, attached it to his back, helped him put his arms through the shoulder straps, and fastened the straps around his waist.

'Right,' said Dawn. 'Send it!'

Letting go of the door, he stood erect for a few seconds and then, with his arms making circles, he staggered back across the room and collapsed into a couch with his legs in the air.

'You'll be needing more forward motion,' I noted. 'Unless of course you do the trail going backwards.'

'Too heavy,' muttered Desmond to himself, still pinned to the couch. Then, with a smile, 'Too much muesli.'

'Oh,' said Dawn. 'I see. Pots, knives, hatchets, trenching tools have no mass? It's the nuts and raisins. What a relief! We can do without food, but if we need to dig a well …'

The lightening process began. 'I simply don't see how we can last four days on twenty kilos,' said Desmond.

'In the olden days explorers used to take fish hooks,' I mentioned. 'Much lighter. Instead of digging for roots, they fished …'

Finally, Desmond could manage his backpack, and with his staff, battered straw hat, slight stoop and the long-suffering gleam in his eye, his whole being had a biblical aspect.

'What we really need is a desert,' said Frances.

***

'Without the use of a hatchet or a screwdriver,' I told the Table, 'we walked that 42-kilometre footpath.'

'Did you see any otters?' asked the One Peter.

'Only dolphins, seagulls, birds and a whale. At the end of each day, you come to one of the four lodges: Ngubu Hut, Scott's Hut, Oakhurst Hut, Andre Hut. The guidebook says they're lodges, but they remain huts – musty, sparse, with grubby floors and walls, and bunk beds. At one of the huts the latrines had become iffy and had to be given a wide berth. Dawn took immediate charge. Men in bushes to the west, women to the east, and sandy soil would do the rest.'

'I knew we'd need the trenching tool!' cried Desmond.

'You can't dig a long drop in one afternoon with a trenching tool.'

'A short drop is enough for one night,' he said and for a while they debated the ideal depth of a one-night drop. But sandy soil proved the answer.

'I still miss the trenching tool,' said Desmond. He was subdued because the Swiss Army pump had let him down. In one of the camps the drinking water had been suspect and he triumphantly went to the river with his Swiss pump. Finding a suitable pool, he inserted the intake hose, vigorously turned the handle, and to his delight, for a while clear water came out of the landward spout. Then, suddenly, the pump gave a hiccup and the water turned muddy.

'So much for the Swiss,' he said scornfully, then suddenly brightened. 'Do you know what the difference is between a good vacuum cleaner and a sailor in the Swiss Navy?' he asked me.

'No,' I replied.

'Well, a good vacuum cleaner sucks and sucks and never fails! And the Swiss don't have a navy ...' and he walked back to the hut, hugging his spoonerism to his chest.

On the fourth morning, we shouldered our packs for the last time and presently the magnificence of Nature's Valley came into view. After a last steep descent, we walked along the lovely beach and finally got to the little café-cum-general store that is the Nature's Valley shopping centre. Laying down our much lighter packs, we grouped ourselves around a little table and discovered a last feature of the Otter Trail. At the end of it, to eat bacon and egg with toast and coffee is one of life's great experiences.

Dawn and Frances on the Otter Trail.

49

The Light at the End of the Day

In late December 2015, the whole family again gathered in Plett and for three weeks the Old Farmhouse reverberated with fun and laughter. With the weather so fine and the house so full it was hard to imagine it any other way – peals of laughter, the tap and thud of table tennis, click of boule, shouts from the pool and aromas from the barbecue. The grapes are ripening and there is often an American football flying about, for both Gavin's boys are good players. How we love these beginnings, when the days are long and time lies gently stretched out. Later, of course, it will betray us by slipping away ever faster as the days pass, but in the beginning …

Each year Gavin brings with him a litre of Glenfiddich that he buys in the duty-free. And in the evenings he, Ashley, James, Frances and I sit on the deck of the Old Farmhouse and drink it the Scottish way. Frances, James and I had made a journey to Scotland to visit the seat of the Forbes clan, and at the Glenfiddich distillery in Dufftown they'd shown us how to drink single-malt whisky, so we know. At the Old Farmhouse it's always at its best on the first evening, remaining so all through the first week. Then it gradually changes as the days slip away, until in the last few days, with the bottle nearly empty, we add a little Famous Grouse. True Scots wouldn't like that, but for us the purity doesn't matter provided the evenings last a little longer.

Last year the holiday ended in one of those sublime Plett evenings, simultaneously warm and cool, with a faint breeze and the reflected colours of sunset on the mountains in the north. When it happens it's a display that slowly fades from glowing orange, through a hundred shades of red, grey, violet and pink, to a dense and brooding purple. Then, very occasionally, by some strange quirk of nature, a last beam of sunlight breaks through the western clouds, and you get a straw-coloured shaft of light that floods a part of the lagoon with, well, a … a flame, I suppose you can say, although it sounds far-fetched – but, yes, a flame! And although it quickly dies, for that minute or two it's quite surreal.

Anyway, on the last evening of that holiday, it happened. The sunset colours faded away and as they were about to die, our lagoon was suddenly alive again, the water gleaming, the sand on the far beaches aglow. For a minute we all stood in a row, transfixed, then Gavin raided the fridge where there remained a bottle or two of the Christmas champagne. There was a popping of corks and presently, although the light had already faded, we all stood by expectantly, with glasses in hand.

It was a poignant moment, I can tell you – a gentle sort of nudge from something out in that immense purple gloom. For quite some time we stood in silence, holding our glasses of champagne, and then, thank heavens, Jamie's cheerful voice enabled us to relax.

'There you are, everyone! That was a sign – telling us that there's more light to come. It calls for a toast, so will everyone please raise their glasses. To the twenty-one great Christmases we've had in this old house!'

He lifted his glass, and when he caught my eye, I realised again how lucky I'd been. Finally, one of those rare occasions when past, present and future really did seem one moment.

❧

The next morning everyone left. The house was quiet, and outside the boule still lay on the grass, the table tennis bats on the table, the towels in the sun, the swimming pool quiet. In every corner there were signs – the football on the lawn and even the drinks tray still in place. That evening I poured the last of the Glenfiddich into a glass and sat looking out over the lagoon. The Keurbooms lights were starting to show, there was a long bank of cloud out to sea, and the last of the sunset colours bathed the mountains. No sign of a last-minute flame. More breezy, the serenity not as profound, yet somehow the whole scene presented me with a comfortable sort of sadness …

❧

'There can be hints of joy in certain kinds of sorrow,' I said to the Table – to my own surprise because the thought had only just struck me.

Friday, 29 January 2016, our first lunch of the year, all eight of us were there, and I had returned from Plett for the occasion – the Rainbow Room again, a summer's day, sun shining, light breeze blowing, clouds billowing, and a table near the windows with a pair of Egyptian geese nibbling the lawn outside.

We'd arrived earlier than usual, I remember, hale and hearty, with even James fairly certain he wasn't someone else, and while Richard poured the wine a silence fell around the Table as if everyone suddenly felt a slight touch of melancholy.

'Kindly explain,' said Charles, referring to my remark about joy and sorrow. Typical of the man – hundreds of thousands of perfect words in books, but few in conversation.

'Not so easy,' I said. 'These feelings fade away the moment I try to define them. A new year, something to do with the winding road we've travelled since our last lunch and the fact that we're all here again …'

Richard had finished pouring the wine, so I raised my glass.

'Here's to the beginning of our sixth year – borne out by one of my old diaries. *Friday, 15 July 2011. Senior Lunch, Rainbow Room.*'

'Lord love us! It just goes to show –' James glanced at Mark and added quickly '– how time passes!'

The Other Peter looked up with a grin. 'Six years. Let's say an average of eight lunches a year, ten oysters per lunch, that's nearly five hundred oysters.'

'Ten breakfasts for Casanova.' Tim, of course, deadpan as always. He looked very well that day.

50

All Things Begin and End

Left alone with the rest of the year stretched out before us, Frances and I stayed on in the quiet house, doing our best to fill the days with words and music, hours in the garden, walks on the beaches, and in the evenings a drink or two while the sun set. January is the warmest month and that year (2016) it slipped past in a welter of summer days abetted by the knowledge that in February Abe Segal and his friend Deborah would be staying with Tony and Gisela for a week or two. To be together with Abe at Tony's house was tradition, but first we had to make the trip back to Johannesburg, Frances to see her mother, soon to be ninety-nine years old and me for the first lunch of the year.

But February arrived on time and there we were, back again, Abe and I sitting on Tony Bloom's patio in the cool of the evening each with the glass of whisky and soda he'd brought us.

'I know it's February,' I remember saying to Abe, 'because my birthday's in February, and I always get a dozen handkerchiefs to last me until the next February comes along. I use one a month and there're none left so it must be February again.'

He'd laughed at that and told me that in the women's coat-making business he'd once run, February was the worst month because it was too hot for women to buy coats. We'd been chatting away as usual – used to go at it hammer and tongs, but now our conversations had pools of silence in them, comfortable ones, we found, especially as our hearing wasn't as good as it used to be.

A night or two ago we'd sat for a full five minutes, listening to the waves break and suddenly he said to me, 'One thing's for sure, Forbsey. You got to know someone really well before you can sit that long without sayin' a word.'

But as always the days went past in a flash and on the last evening there was a particular kind of stillness that made our silences seem even longer. Being such different people, we've always been, well, surprised you could say, to be such good friends, and I suppose because it was our last evening Abe seemed to think it needed confirmation. Towards the end of it he actually mentioned the fact, finishing up by saying, 'Otherwise, Forbsey, why would we have kept talking to each other for over sixty years?'

At about eight thirty, when the sun had finally set and a gloom fell over the sea, Abe made another of his observations.

'The world sure looks different when the sun goes down. But I'll tell you one thing, Forbsey, we've still got a bit of light left,' and he held up his glass and gave it a twirl as if to prove it.

But, as it turned out, not much.

He hadn't been feeling well for a few months, had lost weight and although he had more pains than usual, I wasn't worried because as I've said somewhere before, he wasn't the dying type. Come to think of it, I'd really never imagined life without him. Granted, he was eighty-five

G F, Tony and Abe at the Old Farmhouse, doing away with evil.

and I was eighty-two, and on our walks around the cricket field we'd sometimes talked about our lives coming to an end, but always agreed that we'd both led good ones – and as I've said, dying never occurred to us, although one of Abe's latter-day sayings was, 'Listen, Forbsey, we got to make sure we stay out of those wooden boxes.' For a long time we'd steered clear of them, and there'd always been another round of coffee and sandwiches, a whisky or two and more tennis to grumble about.

That last night Tony must have been aware of our pensive mood, because just then he appeared, holding his own glass of whisky, apparently determined to cheer us up. To do so, he recalled incidents we'd often laughed about in the golf games we used to play, Abe and me against Tony Bloom and Tony Behrmann at the famous old Plett

Country Club. Tony Behrmann was one of the finest lawyers who ever practised in South Africa.

'Pure poetry, he called the agreements he wrote,' said Tony Bloom. 'He never failed to tell me Shakespeare would have been envious.'

The Plett Country Club golf course is tucked into a beautiful valley with a stream, giant yellowwoods, Knysna loeries and sometimes, on the twelfth fairway, baboons that pick up golf balls and run away with them (players are allowed a mulligan).

Throughout our games, both Tonys either looked for ways to put each other off, or to see who could deliver the keenest insults. For instance, one of the fairways ran parallel to the stream, and Bloom discovered that if he sang *Old Man River* just as Behrmann began his swing, he invariably hit his ball into the water.

Hiding his smile, Tony reminded us of the river, Behrmann's repeated folly and his determination to prove Bloom wrong.

'And on the short hole,' he said to Abe, 'if I sang *Abide With Me* you always hit your ball into the cemetery.' (There was an ancient little graveyard near the eighth green.)

We laughed together of course, but it turned out to be for the last time. Abe went to see doctors in Cape Town, and the tests they carried out didn't bode well. So it was that his goodbye to me that evening in Plett turned out to be the last one. I can still hear his voice, just before he got up to go to bed. Although our glasses were empty, he still touched his to mine.

'Thanks for everything, Forbsey, we had a lot of good times over the years,' he said, and out of the blue he spoke of our first night in Paris, 'when we stuck on ties and those green blazers they gave us and we walked out on the Champs-Elysees, with lights shinin', people walkin' up and down and that black guy playin' the saxophone in the doorway.'

To me too that Paris evening was clear as day. Abe had dropped a coin in the black guy's hat and I still remember the tune he was playing. It was called *Take the A Train* – Abe was always singing bits of it – he'd call it his Frank Sinatra act and in good moods he'd add a soft shoe shuffle to go with it. Then he'd take his hat off, hold it against his chest and sing *The Nearness of You*. He had a good voice …

❧

I wrote this tribute for the *Jewish Times*:

> Abe Segal died in Cape Town on the night of 4th April 2016. I'd met him 61 years ago in the locker-room of the Ellis Park tennis courts, when he came over to my corner and told me I was being too quiet. 'Don't they make noise on that farm of yours, Kid?' I was 19 and he 22, and we have been friends ever since. There'll never be another Abe. They talk of breaking moulds, well, his mould was well and truly broken! Such a good man. Generous, forthright, strong, big-hearted, loyal, compassionate – a rough diamond, with the diamond part flawless, and the rough part filled with a unique kind of humour that made his friends laugh in amazement, while shaking their heads at the same time!
>
> Only a few weeks ago, on a still evening in Plettenberg Bay, we sat together, looking at the sea, yakking away, and sipping the whiskies that Tony Bloom had poured for us. Lately, we've talked nearly every week, being able to say the

same things more than once, because we would both forget what we'd said the week before. Suddenly, though, this time, towards the end of the evening, he touched his glass to mine and said, 'Cheers, Forbsey. We've had a great time, but the game's over. Thanks for everything.' Maybe he had some kind of premonition, for I know he wasn't feeling well … But he never complained. In all the time I have known Abe, I have never, ever, heard him complain (except once or twice when I missed very easy volleys). And he thanking me! I ask you! It was I who should have …

He was a great tennis player, was Abe, much better than most people realise. Look up his results over the years, and one is full amazed! For a start, he had one of the best left-hand serves of all time – fine volleys, safe backhand, and a huge forehand, that sometimes went off at a tangent and ran amok. I still remember the time at Roland Garros when he hit a forehand into the President's Box without a bounce. It hit one of the officials in the chest, while the base-linesman triumphantly called 'Out'! Or the time, on the Wimbledon Centre Court, playing Rex Hartwig, when Rex tried to run around his serve to hit a forehand. The ball simply followed him, until he had to catch it with his left hand, in front of his chest. Abe's serve used to swerve like mad, especially the second one. And what about the lineswoman at Wimbledon who had too much wine for lunch and was asleep when Abe, playing Clark Graebner, won the match-point? 'Clark's game is kinda boring, Forbsey,' he told me. 'So I guess she's entitled to take a nap.' He got to the quarter-finals of the

Wimbledon singles, and together we won a lot of doubles matches ...

I could go on and on, and I am sure that I speak also for his daughters, Nancy and Susie, his wonderful wife and soul-mate, Heather, who died some years ago. I can't believe I'll never hear his voice again. Never again have him walk across the court to me, cup his hand and say, 'For God's sake, Forbsey, can you please stop bein' nervous, grip your racket and watch the friggin' ball!' A part of my life, and, I am sure, a good many other lives, will go with Abe. We wish him a good rest, and salute him for a game well played, and a life well lived.

※

As if losing Abe wasn't bad enough, in about September of that year at one of our lunches, Tim's hand shook a bit when he sipped his wine, and he didn't look well. I had just about finished this book and I'd brought a final draft for him, hoping for more of his red-ink comments, but I never gave it to him. The next week Charles emailed us to say that Tim had had a bad fall, that he was in a coma and needed brain surgery. Well, Charles and Tim had been friends for as long as Abe and I, and you could somehow tell from the few words Charles wrote that a precious piece of his world was in peril. Tim had the surgery and every day Charles reported to us in the same sparse words that gave no hope.

We'll have other lunches, of course. Tim wanted his friends to be happy, because if they were happy, so was he.

51

The Top of the Pass

'You and your winding road,' said James. 'You've got us all wondering where it ends.'

'Only when we get to the top of the pass and it's too misty to look forward,' I said. 'We can only look back.'

Richard, as he often did, had brought a new book for inspection by the Table. It was called *The Greatest – The Quest for Sporting Perfection* by a man named Matthew Syed.

He laid it down, looked at me and said, 'You once told me that the first lines of books always intrigued you. Have a look at this one.'

I duly opened the book and read it out loud. '*What does it take to reach the top?*'

'There you are, you see. We're not the only ones who've wondered.'

'If he knew what we know about Plato and Socrates, he wouldn't have to ask,' said Charles wryly.

'Oddly enough, he mentions them,' said Richard, 'although not in the same context as Mark. Matthew Syed writes of such people as Muhammad Ali and Jack Nicklaus, Federer, Sampras, Don Bradman,

THE TOP OF THE PASS

etc. and of course he's right. They have all reached the top.' He gave a short chuckle. 'And as for Edmund Hillary, the first man to climb Everest, well, he got two for the price of one, didn't he?' and he gave his wave.

'Matthew Syed,' James mused, frowning at his own pronunciation. 'I don't suppose he mentions us?'

'I haven't read the whole book,' Richard replied, 'but I don't think he deals with Small Folk.'

It wasn't the most philosophical of conversations, but I had the feeling it was deliberate – kept going to counter winding roads, lunches past, the passage of time.

When it finally ebbed I decided it was time for me to risk my new theory. 'Talking of Small Folk,' I said, 'Jenny's questioning of our father still sometimes crops up in my mind. "What is this Top you're always on about?" she'd asked, then told him that everyone had their own Tops ...'

'I thought we'd agreed we'd all reached *that* Top,' said Charles. 'Even Gordon's barber, as far as I remember. What was his name?'

'Giuseppe Rossi. Odd that you remembered him because he was the one who set me thinking. Ever since my McCormack days, if you recall, I've been preoccupied with lists. I've even tried listing ten particular kinds of Top one could reach, but I couldn't do it. Too many kinds, too many levels, too many things to be top of, if you get what I mean – sport, music, business, writing, science, history ... ad infinitum. I've toyed with it for years, and then just the other day – I'm wrong, it was the middle of the night – it suddenly struck me.'

'We're eagerly awaiting details of this nocturnal strike,' said Charles.

'I found the common denominator! The key, equaliser, catalyst – call it what you like. There it was, is, has been, all my life, lording it over everything with a smile on its face!'

'All right, all right, we give up,' said James after a silence. 'Everyone agree? Right. Out with it. What is this Holy Grail of yours?'

'Happiness!' I cried triumphantly. 'Don't you see? It covers whatever you undertake, whatever level you reach, whatever you achieve. If, after whatever you do in life, you can say with complete honesty, "I'm happy", then you've reached the Top – the very one Jenny was talking about when she said "everyone has their own Top". Giuseppe Rossi is happy cutting hair – and who's to say that he doesn't cut hair just as well as Federer plays tennis?'

'That may be going too far,' said Charles. He was inspecting my haircut. 'Never mind, you may have a point …'

Everyone was quiet for a while, thinking, and it was the Other Peter who broke the silence.

'Let's sum up,' he said. 'We've already agreed we've all reached the Top.'

Cautious murmurs of accord.

'Then surely, by Gordon's thesis we must all be happy?'

'No doubt about it,' said James. 'Especially if they keep serving oysters …'

THE TOP OF THE PASS

All things begin and end.
In every life a line of time
with past explicit, present
an elusive instant
turning future into past.
Tomorrow? Let it be,
for it belongs to Destiny.

Tranquillity descends
on those who love the morning glow,
enjoy the silences at dusk
and understand the quiet flow
of passing time – accepting that
no matter what fine messages it sends
Fate has its way;
All things begin and end.

Postscript

2017. We still have lunches, and in March they virtually ordered me to go to Wimbledon, the instruction triggered by an old newspaper cutting emailed to Richard by a tennis-playing friend. He'd brought it to one of the lunches and handed it round – a story I'd once written about Wimbledon that began as follows:

> My sister Jean so loved English that she had lines of poetry for many of the things she did. On a June day in 1956 when she and I arrived at Wimbledon for our first practice game she stood on our court, took a long look at the perfection of the lawns and the grave old Centre Court, then she nudged me in the ribs and murmured:
>
> *'Breathless we flung us on the windy hill.*
> *Laughed in the sun and kissed the lovely grass.*
>
> Rupert Brooke. Now, let you and me fling ourselves on to the grass and hit some balls!'

POSTSCRIPT

The consensus around the Table was that if *they'd* played at Wimbledon as many times as I had, they would return, so I went – left at the end of June, got back on 18 July, and when we had our next lunch on the first Friday of August, they wanted to know how I'd got on.

'Quite well,' I said, 'although getting there at my age was hard, especially as Frances was not able to accompany me. She keeps watch when we travel – tickets, passports, phones, hearing aids, that kind of thing – but her mother was not well, so I had to go alone. British Airways. Damn big things, those A380s. You get to Heathrow Terminal 5 and walk for miles. Visas, crowds, security, fingerprints, lines of people.'

Anyway, I continued, I got through unharmed and was met by my son James and his friend Sarah. They've taken a flat in London for a year to try out the English way of things, in East Acton it is – Hammersmith, Shepherd's Bush, Wormwood Scrubs, that sort of area. Typical London suburb, terrace houses, little gardens, Pennywhistle Road, the Askew Arms with its draught ales and pub grub. London Underground, Tescos round the corner. Big relief to get there, I can tell you. Threw myself on the bed for half an hour ... But I was telling you about Wimbledon ...

'Thank goodness,' said Charles. 'I thought we were stuck in East Acton ...'

James and I went to Wimbledon on the first day, I said, ignoring the interruption. We got there long before the matches began, collected our passes and went straight to the Last Eight Club for a cup of tea. It's a little lounge near Gate 5, very simple, but for me a godsend. Once you've played at Wimbledon, you feel you belong and if you don't have a place to go, life's not worth living. Margaret Beim and Tony Gathercole have looked after the Club for over twelve years and they make me feel like I've arrived home ...

'But what about the tennis ...?'

What struck me harder this time, I continued, harder than ever before was the place itself. Wimbledon. Very occasionally in life you get phenomena that are impossible to describe. It's easy enough to use extravagant words – Wimbledon is magnificent, stunning, etc., which of course it is. But that's not it at all – there is something else about it, which is why Jean turned to Rupert Brooke for help. It's not so much the visual impact, but rather a feeling you get. For all its splendour, it's only a small tennis club with a few hundred members. The fact that it also happens to be the purest and richest tennis club on earth, staging the most distinguished sporting event that it, itself, invented, is the true miracle. An exaggeration, you say? Well, you're wrong. If anything, it's an understatement because Wimbledon has gone far beyond being a miracle.

Picture a little croquet club in the eighteen sixties – tucked away in the country near London, a few dozen members in flannels and top hats, meagre little clubhouse, chalk lines, hoops and mallets, lawns cut with scythes. Then one of the members, a Major Walter Wingfield, experimented with a lawn version of tennis developed from the indoor game of Real Tennis, a game he first called Sphairistike, or Lawn Tennis. I picked up this information at the museum, together with an old poster ...

In 1877 the members held the first tournament and a chap called Spencer Gore won it in straight sets. All right, I agree, so far it's not so extraordinary – small sports clubs must have been coming to life all around London about then.

But somehow the members of this one little club were able not only

THE GAME OF
SPHAIRISTIKE
OR
LAWN TENNIS

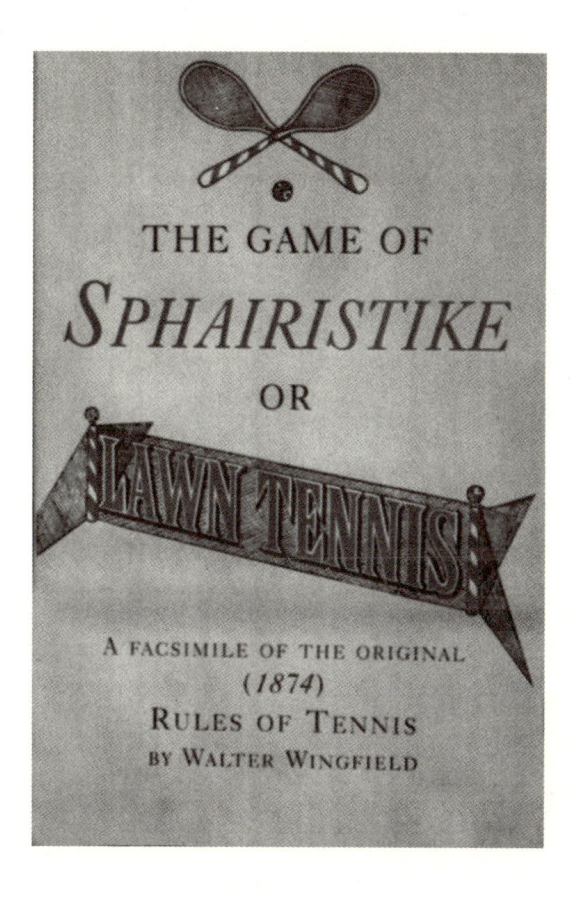

A FACSIMILE OF THE ORIGINAL
(1874)
RULES OF TENNIS
BY WALTER WINGFIELD

to conceive a path of pure excellence but to follow its every turn for a hundred and forty years, stick to their dream and end up with this extraordinary place: distinction; quality; wealth; style – grandeur even, yet with a simple sort of nobility. It's everywhere, this excellence. Go to the museum and you can actually see its progress, step by step through the years, each step adding to what must have been an abiding obsession that only the best will do. One of the exhibits, for instance, is a mock-up of a section of the old locker room and there it is, fine fittings, woodwork, lockers, bathroom ... Perfection, always perfection. Sitting on the Centre Court watching Federer play that day it didn't matter how good he was, because it suddenly occurred to me that the real winner was Wimbledon itself …

The Table chaps must have been listening to my outpourings because, for a while, no one said a word. Then Richard stirred himself. 'Well, now that you put it that way …' His wave was more reflective than usual. 'But what about the tennis …?'

'I saw all my old friends at the Last Eight Club. Neale Fraser, Ken Rosewall, Fred Stolle, John Newcombe, Frew McMillan, Manuel Santana, Roger Taylor, Billie Jean King. I even had a cup of tea with Rod Laver and asked him whether he remembered me asking him how carefully he watched the ball. Vaguely, he said, but not as well as he remembered me scaring him in the night. We'd roomed together during a tournament in Boston and I'd had one of my dreams. We've all aged at the same speed and it's amazing how age strengthens friendships.'

John Newcombe won Wimbledon in 1967, and Tennis Australia gave a party to honour his fiftieth anniversary. How I envied the Australians, their freedom and their sporting achievements. Imagine a country with a Grand Slam tournament, at least ten Wimbledon singles champions, and the whole population united! Compare what they have achieved in tennis with our own pitiful efforts. Ironically, Craig Tiley, who virtually runs tennis in Australia, is a South African. He could have worked for us instead of them …!

As for the tennis, I said finally, James and I watched Alexander Zverev playing Evgeny Donskoy of Russia. Zverev: German, aged twenty, 6-feet 6-inches tall, fair, good-looking, huge serve, fearless, hits every ball as hard as he can. He's touted as the next Boris Becker, and he might well be. He beat Donskoy. All these new names! Bublik, Džumhur, Fucsovics, Kuznetsov, Gojowczyk – if you try to say them,

POSTSCRIPT

At the 50th anniversary of John Newcombe's first Wimbledon victory. Left to right: Ken Rosewall, Geoff Masters, G F, Rod Laver, Neale Fraser, John Newcombe, Fred Stolle. All of them (except me) used to be young Australian players who got to the top. Ted Tinling said it was something they put in the food ...

you get tongue fatigue. Imagine being an umpire and having to call out 'game, Gojowczyk!' Hat falling off, false teeth flying out ... But then you'd suddenly get a Jack Sock (USA) and your faith would be restored ...

'Oh, and I visited the Wimbledon library. Alan Little, now ninety, has nurtured it for forty years, and knows every book in the place. I asked him about Archie Halliday's two little books, Peile and Wilberforce, you recall, and he walked straight to a shelf and pulled them out, easy as you like ...'

'But what about the tennis?'

Oh yes, of course, I said. Tennis. Trying to describe it over one lunch is like trying to move a mountain with a shovel. There it was before me, my passion and my tribulation – smiling, frowning, beckoning, loving,

339

mean, noble – and yet of course it is none of those things because it is only a game! They belong only to those who play it, who pant to compete and who elect to use its soul to test their own skills and ambitions …

'For God's sake, Gordon, we don't need a metaphysical probe. All we want is your view of the tennis you saw.'

'Well', I responded, 'this year Federer towered over Wimbledon as never before. But then he's not a player so much as a sorcerer who moves about the court casting spells over his opponents. No fuss, effortless ease, everything looks easy … but I'm tired of trying to explain how good he is. Nineteen Grand Slams, eight Wimbledons, thirty-five years old, never put a foot wrong, made a fortune! I ask you. As an ex-tennis player you can't help feeling that he has had far more than his share … Anyway, he's starting to lose a bit of hair in front …'

There were some wonderful matches. Nadal playing Gilles Müller was as good as any I have ever seen – but generally the tennis was a little disappointing, and plagued by injuries. Both finals ended in whimpers rather than bangs. If you'd asked McCormack to define the tennis in ten words he'd probably have said 'situation normal, weather good, tennis the same as always'.

We watched England play New Zealand at rugby in the Wimbledon Village pub, saw flowers at Kew Gardens, had tea at Fortnum & Mason, went to Churchill's war rooms, saw a show called *Forty-Second Street*, had ale at the Drawn and Quarter, didn't go on the London Eye, had two dinners with Gavin and his tennis friends, got insulted by Cliff Drysdale, nearly went to two museums, had tea with Leslie McCormack (Mark's daughter), saw the two Wimbledon finals, and watched with disdain as the men's doubles chaps touched hands after every point, and then

POSTSCRIPT

talked behind their hands as if they were agents for MI6 ...

I suddenly realised that I'd talked far too much and still hadn't had a plate of caramel custard.

'That's the best I can do, chaps,' I concluded. 'It's a big world out there. I left Wimbledon that final Sunday evening with a strange feeling, I tell you. Sudden waves of emotion that knocked the wind out of me. Fortunately Gavin and James were with me and we walked up to the IMG house and had a last whisky and soda. The next day it was flight BA 056 and the big A380 again, and in twelve hours it was back to reality. Chilly morning, stuck in traffic ...'

'It just goes to show,' said James. 'Pass the bottle.'

Acknowledgements

Many people helped and encouraged me in this writing and my thanks go to them all. Richard Steyn suggested I write the book, and found time for many discussions, Frances Forbes put up with me while this happened, and the chaps at that table all read excerpts and made remarks sufficiently encouraging to keep me going. My sons and daughter, Gavin, James and Ashley gave constant encouragement and had faith in the book's completion; Simon Kuper, Tony Bloom, Jacques Sellschop and Alison Lowry burdened themselves with reading drafts. Then there were so many tennis and other friends who put in good words – important for me, because without fairly regular egging on, I tend to fade.

There are lines of poetry and lyrics, and a few photographs of unknown provenance. For these I am most grateful, and should any copyright be claimed I would be pleased to correspond with the claimant and make any arrangements which may prove appropriate.

My thanks also go to Basil van Rooyen, Louise Grantham, Russell Clarke and the Bookstorm team of editors, designers and proofreaders who produced the book with such cheerful thoroughness.